Lin Bothwell

The Art of
LEADERSHIP

Skill-Building Techniques
That Produce Results

PRENTICE HALL PRESS
New York   London   Toronto   Sydney   Tokyo

This book is dedicated to five great leaders
who showed me most of what I know
about leadership that is good and true:
Jae Ballif, Reed Bradford, John Covey, Steve Covey, Bill Dyer.

This book is available at a special discount when ordered in
large quantities. Contact Prentice Hall Press, Special Sales
Department, 13th floor, 1 Gulf + Western Plaza, New York, NY 10023.

Copyright © 1983 by Lin Bothwell
All rights reserved, including the right of reproduction
in whole or in part in any form.

Published in 1988 by Prentice Hall Press
A Division of Simon & Schuster, Inc.
Gulf + Western Building
One Gulf + Western Plaza
New York, NY 10023

Originally published by Prentice-Hall, Inc.

PRENTICE HALL PRESS is a trademark of Simon & Schuster, Inc.

Library of Congress Cataloging-in-Publication Data

Bothwell, Lin.
The art of leadership.
Bibliography: p.
Includes index.
1. Executive ability.   2. Leadership.   I. Title.
HF5500.B686   1983   658.4   82-12222
ISBN 0-13-047092-9 (pbk.)

Manufactured in the United States of America

5 6 7 8 9 10 11 12 13 14

First Prentice Hall Press Edition

Contents

3

Whom: The Leader's Followers   82

4

Who: The Leader   131

Preface

The purpose of this book is to help you apply current theories of leadership. If you are in a position in which you influence others, give directives, or have people follow you, then you are a leader. There is a shortage of good leadership books, and those that do exist are written for the student and academician. If you read them as a practicing leader called on to produce results, you find yourself left with the question, "But what am I supposed to *do*?"

This book features fourteen leadership-technique sections. The sections are designed to show you how to apply specific leadership actions where you live and work. Properly applied, these techniques will create a desire in those with whom you associate to follow you and help you achieve success as a leader.

For the first time under one cover, information is presented in a "how to use" format on such essential topics as leadership by objectives and results, interpersonal communication, problem solving, decision making, time management, career planning, and organizational development. You will also gain some unconventional insights, such as how to overcome another person's mystery-mastery approach, how to resolve the Baskin-Robbins dilemma, how to engage in double-loop learning, how you function as a guided missile, and how to change every single person you know.

The six chapters of this book present the latest in leadership theory. Chapters 1 through 4 present the four independent variables in any leadership situation: (1) *What* the leadership is meant to accomplish, (2) *where* the leadership is taking place, (3) who the followers are for *whom* the leadership is provided, and (4) *who* the leader is. Chapter 5 explains how a consideration of these four variables in the leadership situation can give you an understanding of *how* best to lead to produce results and ensure success. The figure showing how each element of the theory will be linked is shown on the Introduction opening page. It will be reintroduced at the beginning of each chapter as a road map to guide your understanding of the leadership theory. Chapter 6 looks to the future and the role that you can play in a world short on skilled leaders and long on serious problems.

The book features a major section of assessment exercises on personal leadership that will allow you to pinpoint your strengths and weaknesses as a leader. Several case studies on leadership are presented and analyzed in the chapters. The book concludes with an extensive annotated bibliography of some great sources for additional personal improvement.

ACKNOWLEDGMENTS

There are two kinds of people in this world: those who divide the world into two kinds of people and those who do not. My two kinds of people consist of those who have given me moral support and those who helped me directly. Without the former, I would have given up on this book and gone back to contemplating my navel. Without the latter, this dream would never have moved inch by tortured inch into reality.

The greatest measure of moral support and encouragement has come from the members of the B'Hive: Julie, Jeremy, Bonnie, Amy, Jonathan, and Joseph. Without their willingness to sacrifice a husband and father for several lonely months, this book would still be an outline. Sam and Dora Black constantly reminded me that I had been given a nose that could withstand the grindstone. Tom Mills and Ronda Lee Wanberg also provided a needed push.

Over the years many have provided indirect help to me, often unaware of their contribution. Without them the content and richness of this work would be lacking. As explained in Leadership Technique Section #11, my Air Force Academy experience was in many ways the beginning of this journey. I am grateful to my classmates in the USAFA class of 1964, of which I will always be a part. I would also like to acknowledge the contribution of the Academy administrators, so many of whom provided wonderful examples of what leadership is not.

I am grateful to the dedicated dozen of Resource Systems Development Corporation who started me down the yellow brick road of leadership training. I wish to thank the thousands of participants in management development programs on whom I have tried and refined these principles and stories over the last ten years, especially those at the University of Colorado, U.S. Civil Service Commission (now Office of Personnel Management), the University of New Hampshire, Dartmouth College, the University of Southern California, and the staff at Stonebridge Institute. Special thanks go to my M.B.A. students in two Whittier College "Leadership in the Work Environment" classes for bearing with and contributing to my "Whats, Whos, and Hows"!

I am grateful to the faculty and staff of the Harvard Graduate School of Education for their leadership, inspiration, and example, especially: Chris Argyris, Lee Bolman, Nathan Glazer, Sara Lawrence Lightfoot, Barry Stein, Rosabeth Kanter, Fritz Steele, Bill Torbert, and George Weathersby. Jackie Roy and Maureen Mahoney have been good friends and endured me since the first day of orientation. Don Schön and Dick Beckhard of the M.I.T. Sloan School taught me much that has aided in the production of this book.

Those who provided direct help to this project are the ones who helped me take all the indirect contributions just mentioned and turn them into the book you are now holding. Without their direct assistance you would be looking into empty hands. Phil Beukema of Whittier College's Department of Business and Economics has been for the past three years an example of the best in higher-education administration. He helped with the production of the manuscript above and beyond the call of duty. Bruce Bothwell, a talented writer in his own right, assisted with reading and editing of several drafts, and he helped me to laugh at myself whenever I took any of this too seriously. I would like to thank those who have read and commented on drafts of the manuscript, including Dean Hughes, Lyn Greene, and Marla Webster.

I am especially grateful to the human "word processors" who made this book possible: Valentine Lyn Houle, Barbara Ensley, Janine Gadd, Gina DiGiorgio, Cheryl Penny-Kasper, Terri Matheson, Myrtle Allen, Lynette Daley, and Juanita Withers. I thank Doug Himes for his work on the illustrations. I especially want to thank John Hunger and Marlys Lehmann and others of the Prentice-Hall staff for the professional manner in which they moved this manuscript through production.

Last but first, I would like to thank my mother for working in a motel cleaning toilets and making beds to put me through school. She always believed that my leadership ability would go beyond leading the Grant Avenue gang in setting fire to vacant lots.

Introduction

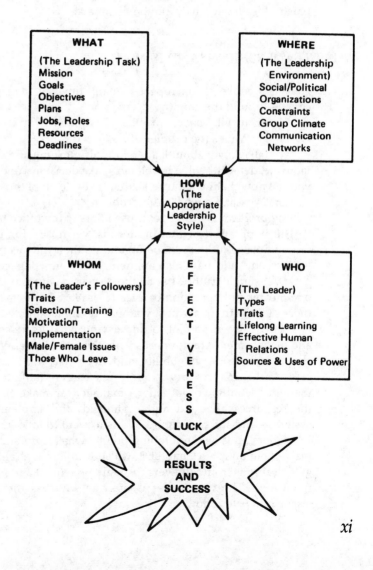

WHAT

(The Leadership Task)
Mission
Goals
Objectives
Plans
Jobs, Roles
Resources
Deadlines

WHERE

(The Leadership
Environment)
Social/Political
Organizations
Constraints
Group Climate
Communication
Networks

HOW
(The
Appropriate
Leadership
Style)

WHOM

(The Leader's Followers)
Traits
Selection/Training
Motivation
Implementation
Male/Female Issues
Those Who Leave

E
F
F
E
C
T
I
V
E
N
E
S
S

LUCK

WHO

(The Leader)
Types
Traits
Lifelong Learning
Effective Human
Relations
Sources & Uses of Power

**RESULTS
AND
SUCCESS**

A president of a small, rapidly growing firm has the disquieting feeling of losing control. A supervisor faces a seemingly unresolvable conflict between a male subordinate and a female subordinate. The head of a voluntary organization finds the workers lacking motivation and direction. A coach cannot get any team effort from the team. Parents agonize over a model child who suddenly is no longer interested in work or school.

Do you recognize any of these people? Are any of them you—or frighteningly close? What's wrong here? All of these people are in leadership positions, but their attempts to lead are leading nowhere. Goals and plans are not working; situations are disintegrating; followers are increasingly unhappy; and the leaders are beginning to wonder if they will ever do anything right.

Can these people be helped? Yes. In fact, you will see them again in the chapters of this books and see specific solutions to their problems. For you, the quest begins by understanding what leadership is and is not, and where practical leadership help can be obtained.

WHAT LEADERSHIP IS (AND IS NOT)

Here is a conversation repeated many times at management development courses around the country.

"Mr. Bothwell, I have a problem; I wonder if you could help me."

"I'll try. What's the problem?"

"We talked a lot about leadership this morning and discussed how leaders motivate, delegate, solve problems, make decisions, and give direction. I want you to know that I am a true leader, that I do all of those things."

"That's great. So what's the problem?"

"My problem is I can't get those idiots in my office to follow me."

The implication of this humorous, yet not-so-funny comment is that if those idiots would just shape up and do their duty as followers, what a great leader you could be. This comment, while amusing, contains the seeds of a great yet simple truth. After all the discussion of what leaders are and do, the one meaningful definition of a leader is *one who has followers*. If you can't get those "idiots" to follow you, you may be something, but you are *not* a leader.

It is equally important to understand what leadership is not. Leadership and management are not necessarily the same thing. While managers ideally should have leadership ability, and vice versa, this is in reality often not the case. And managers are certainly not leaders (able to get others to follow them) by definition or job title. A manager can make excellent plans, get all of the resources allocated and organized, and implement effective control systems—and still not inspire others to want to follow.

Leadership is also not telling people what to do and having the power to make them do it. As Chapter 3 will show, there is a great difference between getting results from followers through movement and getting results through motivation. The true leader is the one who has the ability to *influence* or *inspire* others to follow.

How to Succeed in Business Without Really Trying* showed the hero, J. Pierrepont Finch, climbing up the organizational ladder from window washer to corporate president. His secret was a small book he had found that told him what to do in every challenging situation. Every leader has dreamed of possessing such a book and has been waiting to see which social scientist would write it. If you are such a leader, your wait is over! Oh, don't misunderstand, this is not that book. In fact, such a book will never be written. Considering the number of variables in any leadership situation and their possible combinations, it would take a computer that could analyze 1 million items a minute 31.5 years just to scan the index for the appropriate section. By then the situation is rather likely to have changed.

Does that mean that you as a leader are left helpless, that you have to search for the appropriate action through trial and error? Not at all. But you're not likely to find the answer by looking for leadership in the place that you work. Leaders in most bureaucratic organizations are mummified in regulations and red tape. Leadership in bureaucracies seems to be on the road to becoming a lost art. The person whose actions consist of following someone else's policies and staying one step ahead of the mob can hardly feel like much of a leader.

The answer is also not likely to appear among the current leadership literature. A study of this "scientific approach" to leadership will provide an exhaustive scholarly presentation of the latest research studies, complete with hypotheses and graphs. The practical questions you have, based on the leadership problems you encounter every day, will remain unanswered.

Many leaders pass their level of frustration toleration and decide to desert the zoo they are working in for another where things are done right. They inevitably discover that while there are some differences between donkeys and laughing hyenas, the new zoo looks and functions remarkably the same as the old one.

The answer, then, is not to be found in the blind leading the blind, or in texts full of sound and fury signifying nothing, or in escape from the zoo. This book is written to provide you with sufficient survival skills to avoid permanent commitment to a padded cage. The answer lies in understanding *How who* leads *whom where* to do *what*, and in knowing how to apply key leadership techniques. This book may also reinforce your faint hope that there just might be a better way.

If you wish to expand your knowledge and understanding of leadership principles, if you want to really get excited again about being at the head of a group, if you want hands-on leadership techniques that work, then *The Art of Leadership* was written for you. Read . . . enjoy . . . and do!

---

*Abram S. Burrows, Jack Weinstock, Willie Gilbert, *How to Succeed in Business Without Really Trying.* Musical based on a book by Shepard Mead.

Note to Instructors
and Trainers

This book can be used as a text or supplemental reader in college courses and management development programs. A guide has been developed describing use of the book with courses of various semester hours and training programs of various lengths. To obtain a *free* copy of this instructor's guide, send a stamped, self-addressed envelope to:

> Instructor's Guide
> c/o Dr. Lin Bothwell
> P. O. Box 1874
> Provo, Utah 84601

SHOULD I BUY THIS BOOK?
(A Self-Scoring Test)

	YES	NO
1. Do I know the four major concerns in a leadership situation?	☐	☐
2. Do I know the difference between goals and objectives and how to write objectives that increase my chances of success?	☐	☐
3. Do I know the process of short- and long-range planning?	☐	☐
4. Could I enrich the job of a subordinate if I had to?	☐	☐
5. Do I know why large bureaucratic organizations, such as the federal government, are in serious trouble today?	☐	☐
6. Can I employ the best method for resolving conflicts and frustration?	☐	☐
7. Can I speak effectively to groups, remember important facts, think clearly and creatively, and give effective feedback?	☐	☐
8. Do I employ the key approaches that guarantee my meetings will be successful?	☐	☐
9. Does my organization orient and train new employes in a way that increases their productivity and reduces their anxiety?	☐	☐
10. Do I know when being helpful is not helpful?	☐	☐
11. Have I sorted out how I should act in terms of the new male/female relations?	☐	☐
12. Do I consider people's four different learning styles when teaching my subordinates or my children?	☐	☐
13. Can I overcome the barriers to "multiplying my hands" through delegation?	☐	☐
14. Does my team of followers have unity and esprit de corps?	☐	☐
15. Do I continually grow through "double-loop learning"?	☐	☐
16. Can I overcome another person's mystery/mastery approach?	☐	☐
17. Do I know how to get power and how to use it?	☐	☐
18. Do I creatively solve problems rather than avoid them?	☐	☐
19. Can I successfully deal with the Baskin-Robbins dilemma?	☐	☐
20. Do I know how to manage myself in dealing with my time and stress?	☐	☐
21. Do I have a clear plan for my career and life?	☐	☐
22. Do I know and can I employ the ten leadership styles that best fit various situations?	☐	☐
23. Do I know how to constructively change every single person I know?	☐	☐
24. Is the world still producing great leaders like it used to?	☐	☐
25. Is this the only book where I can learn all of these things under one cover?	☐	☐
Should I buy and use this book?*	☐	

*This could be the most important decision of your life! (Would you believe third most important?)

1
What:
The Leadership Task

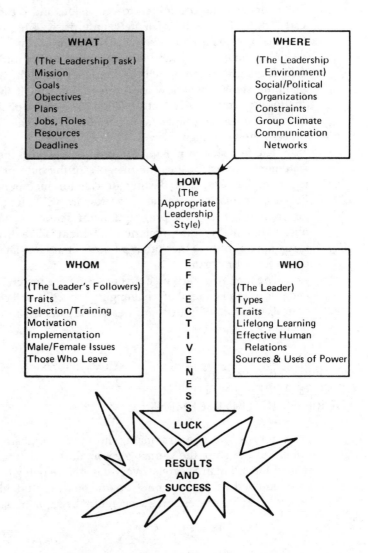

WHAT

(The Leadership Task)
Mission
Goals
Objectives
Plans
Jobs, Roles
Resources
Deadlines

WHERE

(The Leadership
   Environment)
Social/Political
Organizations
Constraints
Group Climate
Communication
   Networks

HOW
(The
Appropriate
Leadership
Style)

WHOM

(The Leader's Followers)
Traits
Selection/Training
Motivation
Implementation
Male/Female Issues
Those Who Leave

E
F
F
E
C
T
I
V
E
N
E
S
S

LUCK

WHO

(The Leader)
Types
Traits
Lifelong Learning
Effective Human
   Relations
Sources & Uses of Power

**RESULTS
AND
SUCCESS**

IN THE BEGINNING . . .
THE CREATION

It begins with a dream! You want an ideal family. You want to create the world's most profitable business. You want to discover a new land, a new planet, a new galaxy. You have a vision—a vision of something new. It is this spark that is the catalyst driving creators and discoverers through the ensuing adversity toward the goal they envision. Without the dream, the vision, there is not sufficient energy to carry on in the face of seemingly insurmountable obstacles. It is the vision that creates the spark to start the motor, but it is the practical act of planning that actually gets things running.

MAKING THE VISION TANGIBLE

Followers become committed to the vision, and it carries them through the early, difficult months of a new enterprise. But political supporters and financial backers are not likely to lend support on the basis of a dream. The vision must be transformed into a tangible reality if it is to be promoted and sold. If the dream can be achieved independently by the creator, some of the planning steps that follow are unnecessary. But if the creator's vision of a "better way" requires collective action to be accomplished, the dreamer must become a planner, manager, and leader. He or she will have to follow the process shown in Figure 1.

The first step in making the vision tangible is the creation of a mission statement that establishes the purpose of the enterprise. The mission statement implies a special destiny or call for members of the organization. Because the mission statement is written in "warm fuzzies"—positively stated generalities—it is not a prescription for action or evaluation. I'm sure the observation that reading a mission statement is like drowning in warm maple syrup applies only to the "other person's" mission statement, not the one that describes your dream.

The next two steps essential to action are the creation of inspiring goals and the establishment of challenging, specific objectives. These steps are critical, which is why they are described in detail in Leadership Technique Section #1.

MAKING THE TANGIBLE
CONCRETE: REALLY PUTTING
YOUR FEET INTO THE CEMENT

The story is told of a first mate who upon the death of his famous captain inherited the ship, the captain's cabin, and a box that all hands knew contained the old man's secrets. Every day before going to the bridge the captain had removed a sheet of paper from the box and studied it carefully. At last the mate had in his possession the secret to the captain's success. With trembling

FIGURE 1. What is to be done when the leadership takes place

PURPOSE/MISSION

What is to be accomplished . . .
our reason for being, the vision, the dream

⬇

GOALS

Positive statements of what needs to be accomplished over the long
haul to achieve our purpose.

OBJECTIVES

Short range, specific, measurable, accountability statements, the com-
pletion of which will lead to achieving our goals.

⬇

PLANNING PROCESS

This is an organized approach to accomplishing the objectives that
breaks them down into (1–5)

(1) TASKS

Generic functions to be performed that will lead to completing the
objectives.

(2) JOBS	(3) ROLES
A specific function to be per-formed by an individual. The scope of the mission will determine whether there is to be one job or many.	The behavior and performance of individuals related to the various positions they occupy. One person performs many roles.

(4) RESOURCES

The plan should specify the quantity and quality of these necessary to
accomplish the mission.

(5) DEADLINES

One of the most important resources is time. Deadlines specify the
time for the task to be performed, the objective completed, the goal
achieved.

⬇

Once you're clear about WHAT . . .
on to
Leadership

hands he unfolded the sheet and read, "Port is to the left, starboard is to the
right." (I'm told the same story exists in accounting circles using "debits and
credits.")

The moral is obvious: If you are going to be the leader it is essential that
you know which way you're going. Establishing the direction and surveying

the terrain that is going to lead to the accomplishment of the mission and objectives are part of the planning process. The following steps outline the basic planning process that you, as a leader, will want to follow in charting your journey to success.

1. Determine what is to be done—the mission and purpose.
2. Define the goals to be accomplished in successfully completing the mission.
3. Develop specific objectives to be accomplished.
4. Analyze the environment for threats and opportunities.
5. Determine your organization's comparative advantage against its competition.
6. Consider alternative approaches to achieving the goal.
7. Develop a strategy for accomplishing the objectives.
8. Develop an organizational structure and climate that will support the strategy.
9. Determine short-range plans and programs as part of the overall strategy.
10. Develop an evaluation and feedback (control) system.
11. Implement the plan and modify as needed.

Some form of planning and vision is essential to success as a leader. If the leader is not constantly surveying the terrain ahead, the leader and the followers can often find themselves in the type of situation envisioned by the following cartoon.

FIGURE 2. The leadership dilemma (By permission of Tribune Co. Syndicate, Inc.)

The problem for any leader, however, is the difficulty of being able to foresee the future. As the Chinese have wisely stated it: "To prophesy is very difficult ... especially concerning the future." It's important when an enterprise is being established that initial planning sessions be held. It's probably even more important in ongoing operations that someone consistently survey the organization for the attitudes and feelings of the members. The survey must identify the places where the system has gotten off track, and some device must be developed to make sure that the data obtained is fed back into the organization so that changes and adaptations can be made. The important point to be noted here is that planning is a somewhat unnatural process, and that we Americans especially tend to be obsessed with "doing."

Chris Argyris of Harvard University once pointed out to me that in his twenty-five years of research in management and leadership he had discovered that the single biggest weakness of most corporate managers and leaders was that they "spend too much time doing and not enough time thinking about what they are doing." Many times the "remedy" for having lost sight of the vision of the enterprise is to increase the efforts and drive the herd forward. This inevitably leads to disaster, as the cartoon of the caribou points out. It is important that any leadership enterprise, if it is to be successful, establish early a strategic planning process that monitors the environment, considers the strengths of the members of the organizations, devises plans to be accomplished, and creates a structure and a climate that will support the achievement of those plans.

A final point to remember is the importance of contingency plans that can be put into operation should something unexpected go wrong. The leader who is truly on top of things comes to expect the unexpected, to realize that nothing is going to work out exactly according to plan.

Obviously, a certain number of little emergencies can be handled with fancy footwork. I always remember one fellow in an organization I was with who tap-danced his way out of a difficult situation. We had ordered some very expensive binders for the training materials for a seminar. Then we realized that there was no place for the participants to write their names on the binders. We thought we solved the problem by attaching an adhesive strip, but about three days into the seminar the strips started to peel off. Some of the people complained, since the materials were becoming hard to keep track of, what with all the moving about everyone was doing. But our instructor merely assumed a serious tone and said, "But don't you see the symbolic implications of having name labels that peel off and fall away on the third day?" People all over the room began to shake their heads and nod approval, apparently seeing some significance in such careful planning.

Well, the "emperor's new clothes" trick may work once in a while, but for the most part, such quick adjustments are not a substitute for planning and leadership. Inevitably, in any enterprise, things are going to go wrong—things that are totally unexpected. Staff members are not going to show up at the proper time; money is not going to appear when needed; contracts will not always turn into contracts; people quit; accidents happen. The wise planner will have contingency plans for all such situations. This gives the leader not only the appearance but the fact of being in control, no matter what happens.

In developing the corporate structure, a number of items have to be included: tasks and jobs to be performed, roles to be played, and resources to be available. The resources must be organized and a time frame must be set for the accomplishment of the objectives.

Tasks are generic functions to be performed that will lead to the accomplishment of objectives. In a small business, the task and jobs may be synonymous, but as the enterprise grows, general tasks such as inventory, storage, and purchasing, are often broken down into very specific jobs. In a giant corporation such as General Motors, there may be three dozen tasks to be performed, but these might sort themselves out into tens of thousands of different jobs.

Jobs then become specific functions that will be performed by an individual. The scope of the mission and the size of the enterprise will determine quantitatively how many jobs there are to be done. When the jobs are looked at qualitatively, the concern is with the job design. Jobs can vary in several ways. For example:

Job Elements	Examples
Location	Indoors, outdoors, office, shop
Environment	Temperature, light, noise, odors
Schedule	Nine to five, shifts, flextime
Stability	Established, fluctuates, high risk
Contacts	Work alone, few people, general public
Variety	Routine, number of operations performed
Size of the task	Whole work, piecework
Pace of the work	Slow, variable, fast, machine-paced
Amount of freedom	Self-control, control of others
Responsibility	None, varies, great amount
Exertion required	Little; physical, mental, emotional
Power source and amount	Formal, informal; small, great
Hierarchical level	Executive, management, supervisory, labor
Job traditions	Related to: sex, age, race, nationality
Preparation required	None, education, experience, training
Form of compensation	Wage, salary, commission, equity

Compare your job to some others along each of these sixteen dimensions and notice the way jobs can vary. It's important for you as a leader to be in tune with your own interest, values, and abilities as they pertain to these various job elements; it's even more important for you to be in tune with the needs, wishes, interests, and abilities of those that you're leading if their talents are to successfully mesh with their jobs.

Employees may occupy many different jobs or positions within an organization. For each position that they occupy there is an associated set of role behaviors. Here are examples of positions you might occupy and the associated roles:

Leader	Have a vision of what to do.
	Speak eloquently of this vision.
	Point out the direction and set the pace for the followers.
Principal	Handle administrative planning and control.
	Supervise faculty and staff.
	Discipline students.
	Communicate with parents.
Minister	Counsel members of the congregation.
	Deliver sermons or perform services.
	Collect and disperse moneys of the church.
Father	Earn a living for the family (?)
	Discipline the children (?)
	Put out the garbage (?)
	Wash the dishes (?)

The last set of roles demonstrates some of the problems you can run into in this area. In a rapidly changing society many roles are in transition. There are often real gaps between role expectations and role performance. Where is the universal operating manual that defines what a man is "supposed to do," what a Republican is "supposed to do," what a supervisor is "supposed to do"? These changes and ambiguities can lead to confusion, frustration, and conflict. It is important that as far as possible the expectations and standards of performance related to any role are clearly spelled out and agreed to by the members of the organization. There is no universal right or wrong, only that which is agreed upon by the group.

The roles of members of an organizational hierarchy are going to vary depending on the position they are in. For example, the president of an organization should be concerned with the big picture, with the vision, with planning and policy making. Those at the middle-management level should be concerned with translating those policies into plans and setting up programs that can be accomplished. The first-line supervisor is concerned with nuts-and-bolts details that have to be accomplished in order to make the programs successful.

To be successful as a leader, you need to be clear about the types of resources essential to the accomplishment of your mission. You must also have the sense of whether your supply is under your own control or someone else's. It can be stated absolutely that many, perhaps most, new ventures fail within the first two years of their inception because they are never able to solve the problems related to demand. One of the things you have to do as a leader is to expand your view of the resources you have available to do a job. These resources can include people, money, ideas, plans, facilities, equipment, supplies, energy, communication systems, contacts, vendors, legal assistance, and time. They are the keys to your success as a leader. One of the responsibilities you have is to take these resources and organize them in such a way that they will help the organization accomplish its mission. You can organize resources in several different ways. It can be done by:

- Number (twelve here, three there, and two in the back)
- Function (cook, waiter, receptionist, dishwasher)
- Process (sales, operations, research, marketing)
- Location (Midwest, region, garage area, storage)
- Product/Service (Insurance: auto, health, life)
- Time (day shift, swing shift, graveyard shift)
- Project (education design project, P.T.A. bazaar project)

The problem that plagues individuals generally and leaders specifically is that they are often looking for money, fame, and power initially and assume that many of these other things will flow out of that. They of course have the equation reversed. It's the establishment of goals and objectives, the development of a clear plan, the assignment of roles, the organization of resources, and the implementation of the task from which the money, the fame, and the power will flow.

One of the most valuable resources available to a leader and to an enterprise is time. Time must be effectively utilized if the organization is to accomplish its goals and objectives. One of the key tools in managing this organizational time is the establishment of deadlines. Deadlines are not just arbitrary limits imposed from above or outside. The leader should consider very carefully the use of deadlines because they serve several useful purposes:

1. Deadlines will determine the time the project will take to complete. The operating law is, "Work expands to fill the time allotted to it." If you set aside one day for completing the task, it will probably be done in one day. If you give it a week, it will take a week.

2. Deadlines provide incentive and motivation. This is true as long as the deadlines are reasonably set. Deadlines will motivate if they are challenging but attainable. If the leader errs in one direction or the other, the deadlines will have just the opposite effect. If they are not challenging, the followers will get bored and turn their creative juices to other things. If they are so challenging as to be unreachable, the followers will get frustrated and give up.

3. Deadlines provide the leader and the group with something against which to measure progress. Records are broken by runners who are trying to beat a deadline over a given distance, not by runners who say, "I think I'll go out and run the best I can." Just as the distance runner is given lap times, the leader should establish benchmarks against which ongoing progress can be measured and things speeded up or slowed down as needed.

4. Deadlines, when met, provide all involved with a sense of achievement and success. This provides additional motivation, enriches the job, and provides a control system in determining whether goals and objectives are being achieved in a timely way.

5. Deadlines, whether met or not, should now provide the guidelines for establishing new deadlines that are again challenging and attainable. This process is known as the cycle of management, but it applies to virtually every form of human activity, from moon shots to housework.

HOW TO FAIL
IN A NEW BUSINESS
WITHOUT REALLY TRYING

In 1970 I had a vision of "the better way." I set out with six former faculty colleagues to create the world's greatest service organization. In the process, we violated most of the principles discussed in this chapter; within eighteen months the company had folded. This experience provided some valuable lessons for me, but there is no reason why you should have to learn the same hard way. Listed below are ten guidelines that can lead you on the way to business success or a good tax write-off.

The Ten Commandments of Business Failure

1. Thou shalt spend more time thinking up lofty names than in concerning yourself with what you're really doing. We spent hours considering various names. The parent company became Resource Systems Development Corporation, with a subsidiary named The Center for the Development of Human Potential. Needless to say, we were very serious about our lofty aims.

2. Thou shalt spend large amounts of time concerning yourself with nonprofitable details such as a corporate logo, the design and quality of business cards, finding an

attorney, considering stock, developing a sign for the business, and so on. This is not to say that each of these actions does not have a place, but are they mainstream or peripheral?

3. Thou shalt run up your overhead as quickly as possible. Rent an expensive office in a central location. Lease large amounts of office furniture. Buy large quantities of office supplies. Hire a decorator to do your offices. Retain the services of large legal and accounting firms. Advertise widely and frequently. Buy company cars for all of the executives. You get the point.

4. Thou shalt avoid planning and goal setting whenever possible. These require meeting and thinking, obvious time wasters. Better to rush ahead and do something.

5. Thou shalt avoid following the management cycle of planning, organizing, leading, and controlling. This will lead to a crisis management approach, and you can spend a lot of time running around playing Smokey the Bear and stamping out forest fires.

6. Thou shalt hire large numbers of people, anticipating those you will eventually need before you actually need them. Proceed to put them to work prior to establishing any coherent personnel policy. Don't worry about frills like grievance systems or suggestion systems.

7. Thou shalt keep functional work roles ambiguous, overlapping, and consistently changing. I was brought up short one day by my secretary following me into my office and slamming the door. The lesson she taught me went something like this: "I don't know if you're intending to make me look stupid, but you're doing a very good job of it. You're the corporate president and you're supposed to be managing and making decisions. I, as the corporate secretary, am supposed to do the typing. Everyone sees you take the work off my desk, and anyone who listens knows that you type faster than I do. If you don't stop embarrassing me and let me do my job, I'm going to quit." I learned something not only about clearly defined roles, but also how it's not always helpful to help.

8. Thou shalt assume naively that if you have a better mousetrap, the world *will* beat a path to your door. That way you can avoid putting a lot of energy into letting the world know where your door is.

9. Thou shalt reorganize and diversify whenever what you're currently doing is not working out as you would like. Trying new things, acquiring new firms, starting new lines of products and services is always more exciting than redoubling your efforts on the course to which you were originally committed.

10. Thou shalt seek the assistance of those who *know*, when all else fails. When our floundering had reached the point of desperation, we went to the S.B.A. (Small Business Administration), who sent in a man from the Service Corps of Retired Executives (SCORE). After a careful examination of our operation he: 1) said you're doing everything extremely well; 2) suggested we begin a phone solicitation campaign—which resulted in the hiring of several new people, the installation of new phone lines, a sharply increased overhead, and *no* new clients; and 3) had the bank at which he worked (he turned out not to be retired) repossess my car when I told him I was behind on my loan payments.

There you have it—ten steps to guaranteed failure or success, depending on which points you learn and how you apply them. Starting your own business is exciting. Becoming part of the 85 percent who fail is not.

Summary

In conclusion, there are several points I would highlight as part of this beginning process on the road to leadership success.

1. As the leader, you are the individual who has to see the distant point, provide guidance and direction for the followers, and set the pace. If you do not have prophetic vision, the process you're going to have to use to accomplish this important leadership role is the process of planning, whether using the model outlined in this chapter or some other.

2. Planning is not exciting, but producing results can be very exciting. If you want to turn your work from the mundane into the interesting, plan—and execute that plan in such a way that you successfully achieve your objectives, produce the results, make the product, provide the service that is part of your motivation for doing the things you are doing as a leader.

3. If you as the leader of an organization, operation, or enterprise don't know where you're going, who in the group is going to know? And if that direction is not clearly established and continually checked, how do you expect to accomplish the things that you set out to accomplish?

4. The process of goal and objective setting and the process of planning and resource allocation of management should not be something that are simply carried off on lofty levels in the organization. The resource allocation of management should be pushed down as far as possible in the organization.

5. Lead your people from thinking to planning to action to results to new plans, new actions, and new efforts toward success. You do not want to find yourself as a leader in the embarrassing situation of the football coach who gave his team a rousing send-off at the conclusion of halftime, accidentally opened the wrong door of the visitors' dressing room, yelled "Follow me," and ran full speed out the door into the indoor swimming pool, to be followed by forty-eight fully uniformed football players. If you do not want to be part of the six out of every seven enterprises that are established and fail each year, the processes that have been described in this section are essential. It is the beginning of the road to leadership success.

Leadership Technique #1
LEADERSHIP BY OBJECTIVES AND RESULTS

Establishing objectives and accomplishing results are what managers and leaders are supposed to be doing. "Management by objectives" (MBO) is what this process has been called for the past twenty years. Management by objectives has been known for good and ill throughout the breadth of the land. Those leaders and managers who have been establishing objectives and using them to monitor their progress finally have a buzzword that they could use to apply to the process they were already using. Those who had not been following this process because they were ineffective, autocratic, insecure, or unable to handle paperwork, only used this new system to heighten their ineffectiveness, to punish employees, to formalize confusion, or to multiply paperwork. The point is that management by objectives does not cause good leadership or bad. It is a tool that can be very helpful in assisting a leader in being effective if it is understood and used properly. The purpose of this leadership-technique section is to outline the basic approach to be used and suggest some of the ways that management by objectives can be helpful.

How Leadership by Objectives and Results Works

The first thing that needs to be accomplished if leadership by objectives is going to be used, whether it's in an organization, a church group, or in the home, is to make sure that the people who are involved, both the participants and the leaders, have been properly prepared. It would be helpful to test the members of the organization to find out if they are responsive to using this type of an approach. Often a new system creates fears. People who do not understand what the new system is or how it's going to work will often assume that it's going to mean more work on their part. The group needs to be very clear about what its goals are, and individuals need to know their personal career and developmental goals. If this is an organization that is about to adapt this approach, those involved may wish to sponsor orientation training programs. They may wish to provide training in techniques of interviewing, giving effective feedback, and writing clear objectives.

It is important that the leader also prepare himself or herself for the task of leadership by objectives. A first step would be to clarify what good goals and objectives consist of. A goal is a long-range statement of what is to be accomplished, usually worded in positive terms. Because goals are purposely stated in generalities, it is impossible to use them as guides to action or in a meaningful control system to determine what really has been accomplished. For example, if you say that your goal is to become a better manager this year, how can you determine if this has been accomplished? Is it a feeling you get or do you ask one of your subordinates? Asking the subordinate if you are a better manager may give you some information, but it is not the answer. If your subordinate had needed more discipline and you provided it, you could have indeed been a better manager without the subordinate really agreeing. It's also possible for your subordinate to report you as a better manager when in fact you are not.

The same problem is encountered with goal statements such as "I want to improve as a manager," or "Our organization will provide better service this year," or "If I am elected I will be the finest public servant this city (county, state, nation) has ever seen." Since this type of statement cannot be used as a guide for action or as an aid in meaningful evaluation, think of the implications. For goal setting to be helpful, the broad, long-range goals need to be translated into more fine-tuned objectives. An objective is a short-range, specific, measurable, challenging but realistic accountability statement. Objectives deal with immediate accomplishments. If they are tied directly to the stated goals, then as objectives are accomplished hourly, daily, or weekly, the goals are being achieved. An objective, to be useful, must be specific and measurable. To be measurable it must be tangible. You have to base it on something that can be seen, heard, touched, tasted, or smelled. It is true that "Not everything that counts can be counted, and not everything that is counted really counts." But with effort, the purposes of most any enterprise can be stated in measurable terms that approximate the goal to be achieved.

The objective needs to be challenging to make members stretch and exercise their need for achievement, but it must also be realistic so that it does not lead to frustration, disappointment, and failure. Finally, an effective objective should be an accountability statement, indicating whose lower back will be in a sling if the objective is not achieved.

The leaders should put effort into prioritizing goals and objectives and seeing how the tasks of the different subordinates integrate in helping the leader accomplish his or her goal. The leader should be clear about responsibilities and about the results that are expected by the organization. The leader should also review areas of accountability, both those that reflect upon the leader and those that are assigned to the personnel.

Prior to the first objectives-setting meeting, it is helpful to send your subordinates a list of the ground rules for the session and a form that will get them thinking about what their objectives are and what the strengths and weaknesses of the organization are. Many of the management-by-objectives books will provide sample forms that can be used as guidelines, but I would suggest that you design your own forms to fit your own situation. Once people understand the kinds of questions to be asked and the rules that will govern the interaction, a great many fears will be alleviated.

The meeting itself is usually held annually, although it can be held more frequently, and probably should be when it's being introduced for the first time. Sufficient time should be allocated for this session to allow for thorough discussion of the objectives and the plans to be accomplished. Experience has shown that usually two to four hours will be needed for the initial session. This meeting should occur somewhere in a comfortable setting, one that is free from interruptions. Your initial objective as the leader should be to put the other person at ease. You may wish to do this by reviewing with him or her the ground rules that you have provided them.

The process is one of working with subordinates, whether team members, students, or family members, in establishing the prioritized objectives that they will be expected to accomplish during the coming year and for which they will be held accountable. The process is one of reaching agreement on what should be done, obtaining commitments from the individual, and then forming a contract between the two of you.

There are four areas that are used for objective setting; each of these is discussed here in turn. One of the laudable aspects of this approach to work life is the recognition that a person can and should be involved in doing more than just his routine duties. It is this aspect of getting each person involved in his or her regular duties, plus problem-solving projects, innovative projects, and projects that will further personal growth, that produces job satisfaction and motivation.

Regular Duties

The first thing you will do in meeting with your followers is to help them establish a list of their regular duties. The first time you ask them to list the normal things they are expected to do, they will provide you with a list of 112 separate responsibilities, from planning their budget to sharpening pencils. This gives you an opportunity to train the person in becoming more effective by teaching the 20–80 principle and helping them to identify the six to eight core tasks that they are to perform that produce 80 percent of the results. These six to eight core tasks are the ones that the two of you will want to approach jointly in establishing objectives. You will talk together to try to decide what standards will be used to measure the results produced. The results will normally be tied to quantity, quality, timeliness, or cost of the task. You will want to establish a plan for accomplishing the objectives and agree on deadlines. If the objective involves a shared accountability with someone else, this also needs to be stated. Obviously, the focus on achievement of regular duties will be the primary concern and should take up the bulk of the planning time.

Problem-Solving Projects

Many leaders jealously guard the problem-solving and decision-making tasks for themselves because it is this work that is most challenging and rewarding and perhaps makes them feel indispensable. It is for these very reasons that the opportunities for problem solving should be shared with subordinates. It provides them with involvement, incentive, and a sense of accomplishment.

Planning in this area might include: 1) a statement of the problem as seen by the employee; 2) a description of the present situation; 3) a description of the desired or improved situation; and 4) some steps that might lead to a solution to the problem. It may not be possible to see these four areas clearly at the time of the planning session, but they could be sketched out for filling in as the process progresses. If a form is created for the second area, it should include a space to list the person's contributions and the possible results.

Innovative Projects

Innovative projects differ from problem-solving projects in that the objective is not to make a bad situation good, but to make a good situation better. The effort is to work together to increase productivity, achievement, and growth through new ideas, new programs, improved technology, or increased personnel skills.

The challenge for the subordinate is to conceive a better way of doing things and develop a plan for how this might be achieved. Your subordinates will sometimes need help in weighing costs versus benefits and in considering the various ways in which an improvement might be measured. You will also want to consider with this person the ripple effects of any change efforts, as discussed in the two leadership-technique sections on organizational and individual change.

If significant improvement comes about as a result of the person's efforts, you should implement appropriate rewards, which might include recognition, an award, a bonus, a raise, and/or a promotion. One important reward is the chance to try again next year regardless of whether the project succeeds or fails.

Personal Development

The fourth area of objective setting that you will pursue with your subordinates is their personal growth and development. The inclusion of this fourth area in objective setting is one of the most important contributions of the MBO system as conceived by Peter Drucker, George Odiorne, George Morrissey, and others. When you meet with subordinates and suggest that they are going to be setting objectives for their personal growth and development, their expressions will range from disbelief to absolute amazement and joy. I remember one employee who couldn't believe that I was actually going to be paying her to read a certain book that we had both agreed would be valuable for her own personal development. I would often find her sneaking peeks at the book at her desk, and she would loudly protest that she was not taking work time to read the book. It took me some time to convince her that this was exactly what I wanted her to do. Efforts at personal development might include any of the following:

1. Reading self-improvement books.
2. Programmed instruction.
3. Correspondence courses.
4. Management development programs.
5. Skills-training programs.
6. New assignments and responsibilities.
7. Membership in a new professional association.
8. Visits to customers, vendors, or new sites.
9. Coaching or counseling by you, the leader.
10. Involvement in meetings not currently attended.
11. Opportunities to help or train others.
12. Involvement in problem-solving and innovative projects, as mentioned above.

Don't make the mistake of seeing the personal development work as inherently rewarding and stop there. It is an agreed-upon project to be completed by the person, and if it is accomplished successfully it should be appropriately rewarded. Is this a double reward? You bet it is. That's the whole idea. No one has ever broken down from finding her work overly rewarding and satisfying. (Has your boss read this book?)

At the conclusion of the interview, commit the person to achieving agreed-upon objectives. Put the objective and maybe the plans you have discussed in writing. Make a copy for the other person, for yourself, and for your boss.

The Follow-up and the Next Cycle

During the following period, continue to monitor progress against the objectives set (not busy work, remember). You may wish to meet for more formalized reviews, but these will not be anywhere near the length of the annual meeting.

The final phase of this cycle and the beginning of the next cycle consists of establishing the results-oriented performance appraisal. This is to be used for the evaluation of the results achieved and the development of the person involved. Remember, you are not only evaluating the person, you are evaluating the objectives and standards you established. If these are inadequate, the person may not necessarily be held responsible if they were not accomplished. Some of the very objectives you set may have been laughers and very easy to do. Others might have been unreasonably difficult. This should be taken into account as you go into the next year's planning cycle. Agree on the rewards earned, and don't be stingy with the praise for the results produced. Then . . . you start all over again.

FIGURE 3. The cycle of leadership by objectives and results

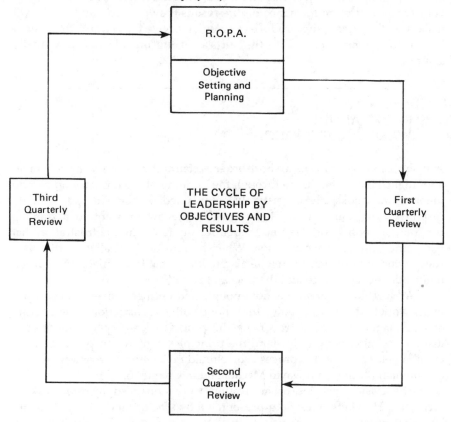

Advantages of Leading by Objectives and Results

Leadership by objectives and results can accomplish a number of things for you as a leader and for the organization for whom you work:

1. It can provide a systematic approach to your success and the success of your subordinates.
2. If used properly, it can help to improve communication and the interpersonal relationships you have with those who follow you.
3. It provides for improved planning and organization.
4. The focus of the things that you do and that your subordinates do is on results, not on busy work.
5. It will consistently answer for your employees two of the most important

questions asked by any members of an organization: first, "How am I doing?" and second, "Where do I go from here?"

6. It provides motivation and development for members of the organization.
7. The appraisal procedure assists in the tough judgment decisions that have to be made on who is going to be terminated, who is going to be transferred, and who is going to receive raises and promotions.

If you as a leader will focus all your energies and those of your subordinates on establishing clear objectives, and if you will concentrate your appraisal of your subordinates' performance on the results they produce, and if you will make sure that those who produce the results receive the rewards the system has to offer, your success and the success of the organization is virtually assured.

Leadership Technique #2
JOB ENRICHMENT: ADDING THE SILVERWARE IS NOT ENOUGH

A dishwasher working in a short-order restaurant had the same job night after night. He ran the dishes through the machine, stacked them, and carried them to the cooks. He consistently complained of being bored, with no response from the owner. Then one day the owner went to a training program on motivation. He understood for the first time the frustration that had come from job specialization. When he returned he called in the dishwasher and announced, "You'll be glad to know that I am enlarging your job to include the silverware and the pots and pans."

Adding the silverware is not enough, and until employees have meaningful work to do, they are going to respond with dissatisfaction, absenteeism, and sabotage. The key to reversing the process of overspecialization and make-work tasks is to understand the principles behind and practice of job enrichment. To begin this process you should review the motivation theories of Abraham Maslow and David McClelland in Chapter 3.

The classic theories of motivation were enhanced by the work of Fredrick J. Herzberg. Herzberg presented a two-factor theory of motivation. His basic premise was that people have two types of needs, which he calls "dissatisfiers" and "motivators." The two types of needs are different and lead to different types of behavior on the part of the employee. Understanding this theory should also lead to more effective behavior on the part of the leader.

The dissatisfiers have the following qualities. First, because they are closely related to the physical needs of the body, they will be cyclical. With effort, the person can be brought to a zero point or point of satisfaction, but he or she will return to being dissatisfied again. Second, the zero point, or point required to satisfy the person, will escalate over time. Third, the person's satisfaction or dissatisfaction is not an absolute, but is relative to what others have.

Herzberg listed five basic dissatisfiers. The first is the organization's policies. With bad policies there will be dissatisfaction. Good policies will not

16

create motivated employees. They will just lead to an absence of dissatisfaction.

The second set of dissatisfiers has to do with the work group and their interpersonal relations. There is no satisfaction in having unpleasant people to work with. On the other hand, having a lot of nice people to work with not only does not lead to motivation and productivity, it can distract people into spending a whole lot of nonproductive time enjoying each other.

The third set of dissatisfiers are related to the work environment. No matter how nice the facilities you provide, the level required to maintain satisfaction will continue to rise. Linoleum is sufficient until they've seen a carpeted office; the fan is okay until they experience air conditioning. No matter what you provide, more will be desired. It's in the nature of the person.

The fourth dissatisfier, somewhat of a surprise, is the supervisor or leader. Conventional thought has pointed to this person as a *source* of motivation. Herzberg showed that this is not true, since the locus of motivation is in the employee. The best the supervisor can do is to provide a climate in which the person has a desire to motivate himself or herself.

The fifth and final dissatisfier presented by Herzberg has stirred quite a controversy. It flies in the face of two hundred years of thinking about how you get people to work. This dissatisfier is money. The classic idea was that you paid people to work, and if you paid them more they worked harder. Herzberg showed that compensation has all the features of a dissatisfier. No matter how much money you give, dissatisfaction with the amount inevitably returns. The amount required to satisfy an employee continues to escalate each year. (This is a psychological function, not one of inflation, although inflation accelerates the process.) Finally, how satisfied people are with what they are getting is relative to what others in comparable positions are getting. Not only that, it is possible to give a person a raise and have this act *increase* the amount of dissatisfaction. This occurs when what employees get is less than what they expected. (I know, because I've had it happen to me. Have you?)

These five dissatisfiers can be looked for in all nonmotivating work (look at housework and the assembly line as classic examples). As a leader, you must attend to each of these five areas. You have no choice if you don't want bad attitudes and the resulting problems. But no matter what you do about the quality of policies, interpersonal relations, working conditions, supervision, and compensation, you will not get motivated followers.

What's left, then, with which to motivate? The dissatisfiers have to do with factors external to the work. The motivators have to do with the quality of the work itself.

The first motivational approach is to give your people interesting work to do. All work is not equally interesting. (Think of the jobs in our society that are inherently distasteful, but have to be done. That's why they pay so well. The message is, "Take the pay and go meet your needs someplace else.") But if you want motivation on the job, the first task is to make the job interesting.

People want to be more than just entertained with their work. As McClelland demonstrated, they have a built-in "need for achievement." They want the work to be challenging, which is the second basic requirement for motivation. The challenge, however, must be realistic, or the people will get discouraged by their failures and quit.

The third motivating factor is that people experience a sense of achievement and accomplishment when they complete a task. The sense of satisfaction is internal and personal, regardless of how others react to the accomplishment.

The fourth motivator is recognition for a job well done. People want to do more than just feel good about themselves. They like to know that what they do is recognized and appreciated. The strength of the person's motivation will be increased if the recognition is both informal (thank you's, praise) and formal (raises, bonuses, publicity).

The fifth motivational factor is providing people with an opportunity to advance and/or increase their responsibility. Note the relationships to Maslow's highest level of need, that of actualizing oneself.

In relation to this last motivating quality there is an additional insight. The opportunity to increase one's responsibility is motivational only insofar as the work the person is doing is inherently interesting. If I go to one of my managers and say, "If you do a good job in running this division I will give you three divisions to run," I'm likely to get a highly motivated employee. But if I go to the custodian and say, "If you do a really good job of cleaning this rest room I will give you three rest rooms to clean," that will not lead to motivation. There is an inverse relationship here. If a person's work is inherently uninteresting, you would motivate him by giving him an opportunity to decrease that type of work. "If you do a really good job of cleaning these three rest rooms, I'll see that you only get one rest room to clean." Then you'll get motivation.

A final note on the Herzberg theory. While all that he says about money as a dissatisfier is correct, there is a truth that goes beyond those points. There are at least two broad social groups for whom the acquisition of more money acts as a major motivator. The first group in America's 20 million poor and the tens of millions more in the middle class squeezed by taxflation. For these people, the energy expended in acquiring more income represents survival. The other group is the very rich, those who "play Monopoly for real." These people view wealth not as a means to an end, but an end in and of itself. Money represents visibility, conspicuous consumption, status, and power, and they are very motivated toward its acquisition. Money should be on both sides of Herzberg's zero point.

Refer to Figure 4 for a graphic illustration of what has just been presented on Herzberg's two-factor theory. Understanding these ideas is essential to enriching someone's job and life.

The second set of principles to consider is based on ideas advanced by Scott Myers. Myers, in his article "One More Time—How Do You Motivate Employees?" (*Harvard Business Review*, Jan./Feb. 1968, pp. 53–62), breaks the work to be done in an organization, into four parts: planning, organizing, leading and doing (the same step), and controlling. Myers points out that in

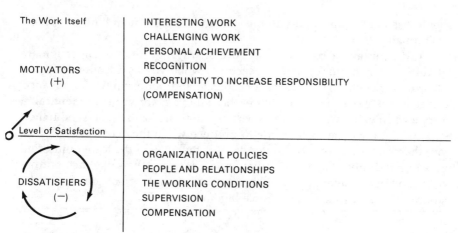

The Work Itself

MOTIVATORS
(+)

INTERESTING WORK
CHALLENGING WORK
PERSONAL ACHIEVEMENT
RECOGNITION
OPPORTUNITY TO INCREASE RESPONSIBILITY
(COMPENSATION)

Level of Satisfaction

DISSATISFIERS
(−)

ORGANIZATIONAL POLICIES
PEOPLE AND RELATIONSHIPS
THE WORKING CONDITIONS
SUPERVISION
COMPENSATION

The Work Environment

FIGURE 4. Herzberg's two-factor theory of motivation

this age of specialization employees are doing the doing and their leaders and managers are performing the other, more interesting functions.

Putting the two theories together, the process of enriching a job consists of the following steps:

1. Pick a job to be analyzed and enriched.

2. Look at all the factors in the job environment to make sure they are being taken care of. This will minimize any associated dissatisfaction.

3. Can the job be enriched by the Herzberg factors, that is, by making it more interesting or challenging, by giving more recognition and compensation, and by providing opportunities for enlarging responsibility? (This does not necessarily mean that they have to advance vertically in the organization. It is possible to expand the scope of their job and increase their influence horizontally.)

4. Can the job be enriched by the Myers factors, that is, getting the employee more involved in planning and organizing the work to be done, allowing leadership within the work group, having the employee co-establish standards and administer a self-control system?

5. Work with the employee(s) involved in analyzing and enriching the job(s). Continue to monitor results as the changes are occurring. Don't expect instant improvement; change takes time. Don't try to force the process; remember, motivation must come from inside the person.

Research has shown that where job enrichment is used there is not only an increase in work quality and productivity, but also the changes of increased morale and cooperation and lowered rates of tardiness, absenteeism, and sabotage.

One of the questions consistently asked is, "Is it possible to enrich every job?" The answer is, "Probably not." Thought and effort on your part, however, can usually produce ways to make work more challenging and allow employees to participate more in the planning and controlling. Jobs can always be expanded for those who are doing good work. As leaders, you should use every opportunity to recognize accomplishment both informally and formally.

It is a mistake to assume that those below you in the organization are interested only in money and job security, while you as a leader are interested in "higher things" such as a challenge and opportunities to advance. Research has shown that the factors that motivate are virtually identical at every level. If you want employees who are motivated and excited about their work, who are willing to continue to produce when they could be off, who pour themselves into the challenges of a job, then you as the leader must find ways to build those factors into the work. These are the same factors from which you as a leader derive the motivation to do a great job. Share the opportunities and watch your people bloom.

Preface to the Cases

Scattered throughout the pages of this book are eight short cases for your thoughtful consideration. The position of the main character in the case is meant to represent a number of similar positions that leaders might occupy. The beginning of each case analysis will describe the type of leadership positions that particular case might represent.

The content of each case represents a problem tied to certain of the leadership principles and techniques discussed in this book. If you read and understand the chapters and sections, the solutions to these problems should be obvious. Therefore, the analysis of what each of these leaders might do to solve the problem they face will be kept brief. The approach to the solution offered does not preclude other approaches that could be used. You should also keep in mind that knowing what to do and being able to actually do it in your leadership position are two different things. The challenge is in effective implementation.

ILLUSTRATIVE CASE A

The Case of Terry and Dee Erdmann

Terry and Dee Erdmann stared into the crackling fire. Outside, the midwestern wind whipped snow against the frosted windows. It was the third night in a row that Dave had not returned from his paper route. During his first thirteen years Dave had been a model child, always setting a good example for the other children. But lately all of that had changed. Dave complained about having to help around the house and complained about homework. He would frequently go over to a friend's house after completing the route, often missing dinner. This had led to several angry exchanges between Dave and Dee that had Terry very upset. Terry had tried the reasoning approach, which now led with predictable regularity to the sullen, "You just don't understand me." Terry felt like giving up. But you can't give up on needed income; you can't give up on school grades; you can't give up on family unity; and you can't give up on a son. Every attempt to pull him back into the family circle only seemed to drive him further away. The only thing Terry and Dee agreed on was that parenting was the hardest thing they would ever do.

FUNCTIONAL TYPE   *The Erdmanns as parents are in one of the most demanding, challenging, and important leadership roles. There might be similarities between this situation and those faced by school teachers, counselors, and social workers.*

LEADERSHIP FACTORS   *The principles involved in this case include* human relations, communication, *and* job enrichment.

QUESTIONS TO CONSIDER

1. *Does Dave's behavior have something to do with his stage of development? Since he has changed his behavior from the positive of the past to its current negative form, might it not change to positive again in the future?*
2. *What part does communication play in this situation?*
3. *What factors of job enrichment are involved here?*
4. *What factors of motivation are involved here?*
5. *Why is parenthood such a demanding leadership role?*

ANALYSIS   *Terry and Dee should first understand that there are no simple solutions to this type of situation. Several principles need to be understood. The first has to do with the stages of growth that all human beings go through. These changes can often be rapid and bewildering in adolescents. A good boy, from a good home environment, may experiment with rebellion, but he is not necessarily going off the deep end. A reversal of the well-known Mark Twain quote might observe how "the child who was so rebellious at the age of fifteen has become so 'establishment' by the age of twenty-five."*

Therefore, the parents need to be patient; they also need to be empathetic, clear communicators. They need to talk to Dave repeatedly, but they also need to listen to the situation from his point of view. Love, patience, and understanding will win the day, though at times there will seem to be little sign of results.

In regard to the paper route and the homework, an understanding of the job enrichment principles based on the theories of Herzberg and Myers could be very useful in this type of case. To the extent possible, the work should be made interesting, challenging, and achievement- and reward-oriented. The son should be involved in planning, organizing, and assessing the quality of the work done, not just in the doing. If the work cannot be made to include these qualities, maybe it's time for Dave and his parents to find other work that is more motivational. If none is available on the outside, could they start a family business that could involve Dave in these ways? Whether the work is selling worms for fishing, neighborhood yard work, furniture repair, or washing cars, the "business" could be designed to get the son involved in more meaningful ways. If none of these options is pursued, the parents could at least empathize with the boredom and dislike that accompany nonmotivational work.

2

Where: The Leadership Environment

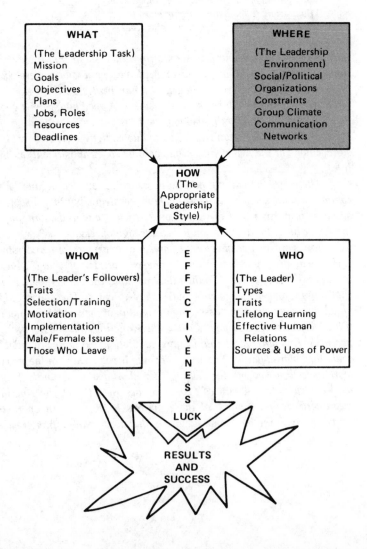

WHAT

(The Leadership Task)
Mission
Goals
Objectives
Plans
Jobs, Roles
Resources
Deadlines

WHERE

(The Leadership
  Environment)
Social/Political
Organizations
Constraints
Group Climate
Communication
  Networks

HOW
(The
Appropriate
Leadership
Style)

WHOM

(The Leader's Followers)
Traits
Selection/Training
Motivation
Implementation
Male/Female Issues
Those Who Leave

E
F
F
E
C
T
I
V
E
N
E
S
S

LUCK

WHO

(The Leader)
Types
Traits
Lifelong Learning
Effective Human
  Relations
Sources & Uses of Power

**RESULTS
AND
SUCCESS**

Chapter 1 begins at the beginning ... by examining what is to be done if leadership is to take place. Chapter 2 is concerned with the environment in which the leadership occurs. Action does not occur in a vacuum. Most major leadership and management theories today have a situational or contingency focus. If the leadership effort is failing, the reason may be that the leader and the group are insensitive to critical realities in the larger environment.

It is helpful first, however, to have some sense of the work environment of the past and how that climate has been changing. The leader who understands the past is in a better position to influence the future.

UP THE DOWN ORGANIZATION CHART: THE THEORY OF ORGANIZATIONS AND SOCIAL SYSTEMS

This complex area will be made as simple as possible and will point out some important truths that should enhance your bureaucratic survival skills. The first important insights come from gaining a historical perspective on our organizational problems.

A Mini, Pseudo-Historical History of the World of Work

Through most of the history of civilization—really until very recently—the world of work was largely agrarian, with people working individually or in small groups. If the time line in my chart (Figure 5) were drawn to scale, the first period would actually extend fifteen feet to the left of the page. Such a scale drawing would demonstrate more dramatically how very little things changed for thousands of years. Early workers made things by hand, and they did the whole job, following a project through to the end. Such a system, of course, took a great deal of time, but workers felt pride in their craft. This pride was often expressed by their stamping their names on the final product.

The concept of career didn't exist in those days. A lad or lass turning seventeen didn't go to the high school vocational counselor and ask, "Which of the jobs in the *Handbook of Occupational Titles* should I pursue?" If grandfather was a baker, father was a baker and you, by heck, would be a baker too! When surnames were adopted, your family surname would become, for example, Baker, Smith, Plowman, Archer, or Gardener—well, you get the point; it was a rigid, caste-type system.

In this way of life, the advantages of stability and predictability were offset by many disadvantages, as noted in Figure 5. Those who want to go back nostalgically should take a hard look at that list of related problems.

The Revolution and Its Aftermath

The industrial revolution, which took place around the end of the eighteenth century, changed the world forever. The revolution was not an event, but an

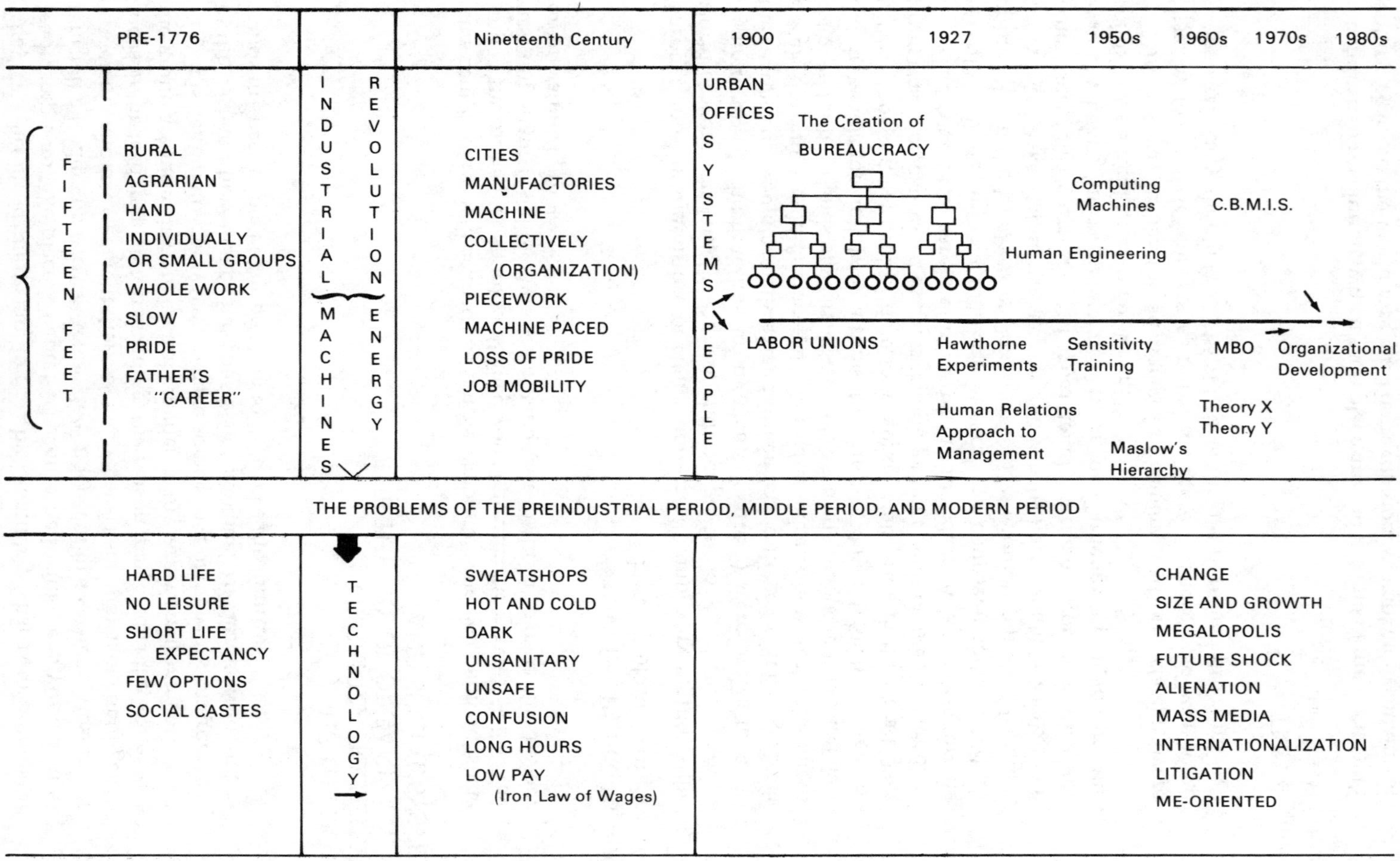

FIGURE 5. A mini, pseudo-historical history of the world of work.

PRE-1776

RURAL
AGRARIAN
HAND
INDIVIDUALLY OR SMALL GROUPS
WHOLE WORK
SLOW
PRIDE
FATHER'S "CAREER"

Nineteenth Century

INDUSTRIAL REVOLUTION — MANAGEMENT

CITIES
MANUFACTORIES
MACHINE
COLLECTIVELY (ORGANIZATION)
PIECEWORK
MACHINE PACED
LOSS OF PRIDE
JOB MOBILITY

1900 · 1927 · 1950s · 1960s · 1970s · 1980s

SYSTEMS PEOPLE

URBAN
OFFICES   The Creation of BUREAUCRACY
Human Engineering
Computing Machines
C.B.M.I.S.

LABOR UNIONS

Hawthorne Experiments
Human Relations Approach to Management
Sensitivity Training
Maslow's Hierarchy
Theory X
Theory Y
MBO
Organizational Development

CHANGE
SIZE AND GROWTH
MEGALOPOLIS
FUTURE SHOCK
ALIENATION
MASS MEDIA
INTERNATIONALIZATION
LITIGATION
ME-ORIENTED

THE PROBLEMS OF THE PREINDUSTRIAL PERIOD, MIDDLE PERIOD, AND MODERN PERIOD

PRE-1776:
HARD LIFE
NO LEISURE
SHORT LIFE EXPECTANCY
FEW OPTIONS
SOCIAL CASTES

Nineteenth Century:
SWEATSHOPS
HOT AND COLD
DARK
UNSANITARY
UNSAFE
CONFUSION
LONG HOURS
LOW PAY (Iron Law of Wages)

24

ongoing process of new ideas, discoveries, and inventions. New machines and new sources of power combined to produce what we now know as technology. And technology continues with us in ever-increasing complexity to the present day.

With the advent of machines, no longer was there a need to have twelve carriage makers in a town. One machine would be brought in, a roof was put over it, and a "manu-factory" came about. Men and machines literally began to work together under one roof. People who wished to make carriages came to the manufactory, and organization was born.

Follow the plight of our proud friend Fisher, the carriage maker, as he appears, hat in hand, at the wagon-factory door to apply for a job. "Fisher, come in, we know your work well. You are a skilled craftsman, and we are happy to have you as part of the team. Here at the carriage works we don't need you to make whole wagons anymore. Our machine stamps out the carriage bodies, but we would like you to make the wagon wheels."

Fisher starts on wheels. Time passes, the organization grows, and specialization is increased. Fisher is shifted successively to the right rear wheel, to the spokes, and finally ends up making the thirteenth spoke of the right rear wheel—2,124 times a day. Because the work is machine-paced, it goes faster and faster. Fisher is now caught up in a large organization, where he does a piece of a job at increasingly pressured rates, working with inanimate objects. He feels alienated and unappreciated. He has no pride in the final product, the carriages he used to make so well. With this loss of pride comes a whole series of modern concerns:

- How do you motivate people to want to do work that is inherently uninteresting?
- How do you reduce tardiness and absenteeism?
- What can be done about employee sabotage?
- And how do you cope with turnover?

That's right, turnover. For the first time, people begin to have choices about what they will do with their work life. John Baker XIII comes to his dad one day and says, "I quit! I'm eighteen years old, and I want to get out of this stinkin' bakery. I've been putting in fourteen hours a day here since I was five, and I'm fed up. Besides, all you ever pay me with is doughnuts, and I'm sick of doughnuts. I'm going to work down at the carriage factory where there's the excitement of those big machines, and they pay in real pence." Exit son. What does John Baker XII do, fold up the tent and retire? Not at all; he hires the carriage maker's son. And the merry-go-round begins: recruiting, selecting, hiring, orienting, training, motivating, rewarding, and on and on. But that's not the end of the bad news.

Because this form of collective work was a new experience, a whole new set of problems appeared. The factories were often called sweatshops, referring both to the hard labor involved in the work and the lack of central heating, which made them freezing in the winter and sweltering in the summer. The places were dark, operating for decades without electric lights. With people bringing their collective germ fields together, for the first time they were also unhealthy. It was not uncommon for smallpox or diphtheria to sweep through the plant, leaving a number of the employees dead. The work was often unsafe, particularly around the new machines, with which most workers were unfamiliar.

Picture our friend Fisher sticking his head in the wagon-making machine to see how it works. Zip! Off goes the right ear! Now what is he to do? Does he go to the personnel office and apply for disability benefits? No, because not only are there no such benefits, there is no personnel office. If he goes to the owner and tells him he's lost an ear in the machine, the response is likely to be, "Keep your head out of the machines, you're slowing the work down!"

Confusion was the order of the day. With no organized management, the scene was often one of utter chaos, with people shouting through the dim lantern light, "Is this wagon done? Where's the other wheel? Who are you?"

Under these harsh conditions, people worked twelve- to sixteen-hour days. You would assume that for such sacrifices they would be well paid, but such was not the case. Up to this time there had been a barter economy, trading a wagon for a year's supply of bakery goods, for example. Paying people to do work was a new experiment. Following an oft-repeated pattern, the leaders turned to the social scientists for the answer.

An economic philosopher by the name of Ricardo developed what became known as the Iron Law of Wages. He looked at the hard labor performed amidst confusion and squalor and said, "It seems to me that no one would work here if they had the choice." (Note the keen mind!) "Therefore, I conclude, if you pay your people more than a bare subsistence wage, they will run off with visiting sailors and never return to work." So, at the end of fourteen hours of drudgery, Fisher, the carriage-wheel-spoke maker, would take his work chit to the cashier and be paid his "thr'pence." At the local grog shop the thr'pence brought a tankard of ale and a loaf of French bread (no peanut butter). Fisher would take the bread and ale back to his cold-water flat, consume it, watch the news, and retire. Surprise—next day he'd be back in the factory again.

The Bureaucratic Revolution

After a century the industrial revolution had not created Utopia. In fact, as shown, it *had* created a whole set of perplexing problems. Once again, business leaders turned to the social scientists and said, "Help us bring order to this chaos." The social scientists were more than happy to oblige.

The great social scientists at this time were European, and they gave a French name to the system they developed to organize the world of work. They called it *bureaucracy*. Not only was *bureaucracy* not a dirty word in those days, but these social scientists were firmly convinced that bureaucracy would finally bring Utopia.

There are two things that should surprise you about this: first, that bureaucracy was an idea developed fairly recently as an experiment in collective work life; second, that bureaucracy is a system made by man to serve man. Bureaucracy is not the inherent nature of the universe. The world was not created to resemble General Motors. Bureaucracy was created by man to serve his collective needs. It is hard for us to grasp this important truth in the 1980s because we live in a world that is totally bureaucratized. There is nowhere to escape. Somewhere during the past decade the creator and the servant have changed roles.

Numerous management "scientists" came forward to present their principles of organized work life. Any good management text presents these in exhaustive detail. The objective here will be only to give highlights of some of the major perspectives, and to show that they are not working and stand as major impediments to leaders in today's bureaucratized world. Specifically, this section examines eight aspects of the system called bureaucracy: 1) departmentation, 2) hierarchy, 3) job descriptions, 4) lines of authority and communication, 5) line and staff, 6) span of control, 7) unity of command, and 8) functional positions.

The term *bureaucracy* encompassed two organizational concepts contained in the root words *bureau* and *cracy*. The French word *bureau* is rendered "department" in English. This principle was based on the idea of organizing employees into functional areas of similar type work. For example:

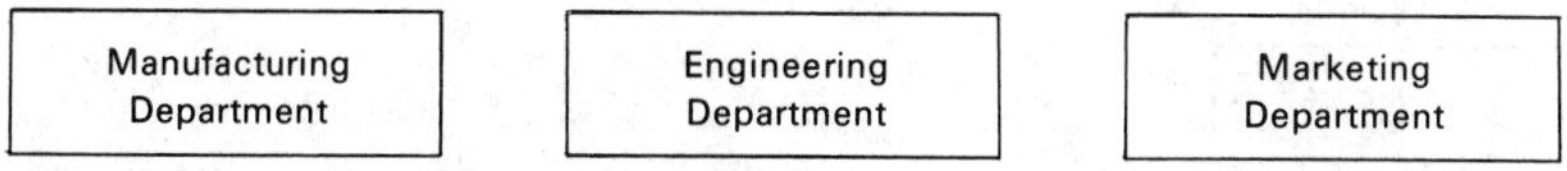

| Manufacturing Department | Engineering Department | Marketing Department |

FIGURE 6. Organizational departments

Each of these larger boxes on the organization chart was to show where all those involved in marketing, for example, were to work.

The *cracy* part of the word *bureaucracy* is a derivation of the word *hierarchy*. To arrange objects (in this case the boxes on the chart) in a hierarchy is to place them in layers above and below each other. A hierarchical arrangement shows the relative rank or grade of persons and things. (See Figure 7.)

At the lower levels on the chart the boxes represent jobs or functions to be performed. The boxes *do not represent people*. After a hundred years it had become clear that machines were reliable, dependable, and compliant; it was the people that caused all the problems. So the business leaders asked the social scientists, "Can you get people to function as efficiently as the machines?" The social scientist took this charge so seriously that for decades this work was known as "human engineering." (Shades of Dr. Frankenstein.)

The idea was to take the humanness (unpredictability, irrationality) out of the functions in the organization. Look at the next chart and picture two human beings serving as sales director of Region 1 and sales director of Region 2. Clyde with Region 1 is a solid, dependable type. The problem is, he's a plodder. His salespeople lumber along at the same rate of productivity month after month. Sylvia, in Region 2, is, by contrast, a roller coaster kind of person. When she is in her high stage, her crew can outproduce Clyde's four to one. But when she gets into her down phase, she shows up late for work or not at all, tends to sip at her brown lunch bag a great deal, and once hit a salesman with a flip chart.

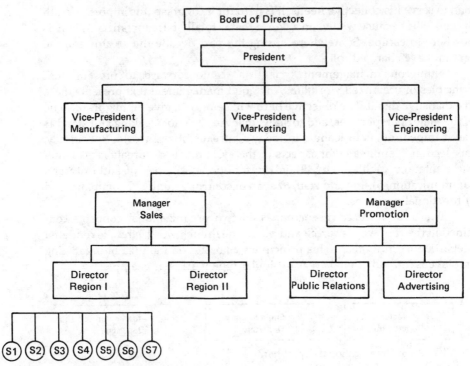

FIGURE 7. An organization chart hierarchy

How do you get sameness from these two? Simple—put them in a box. Develop a job description telling them what they will do (high productivity, show up for work) and won't do (fall asleep on the job, hit employees with flip charts). Then, to insure conformity, you explicitly link the job description to the salary (the jelly beans for compliance) and implicitly to the "or elses" (the cattle prod). Now Clyde and Sylvia, regional directors, will function (look) the same. If one of them doesn't work out, you get rid of that person and find a replacement. The players in the box are interchangeable.

The boxes are connected by lines that represent the flow of power (lines of authority) and information (lines of communication) through the organization. (See Figure 8.)

Notice that the organization chart looks like a waterfall. It shows where the power originates (at the top) and which way it flows (down), and where the "word" originates (at the top) and which way it flows (down). Let's face it, Harry Truman never fooled anyone with his "buck stops here" sign. Everyone has known for two hundred years that the buck stopped in the lap of the employee until the union created a dam, and now the buck stops squarely with the first line supervisor.

Positions in the organization were classified as to line or staff. Line positions were in the direct flow of authority and possessed the power to

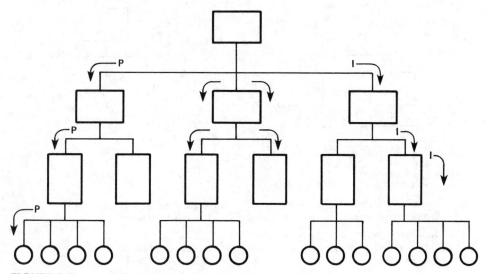

FIGURE 8. Power and information flow through the hierarchy

make decisions and take action. Staff positions were more advisory and provided information, counsel, and assistance, but had no direct influence on
operations. (See Figure 9.)

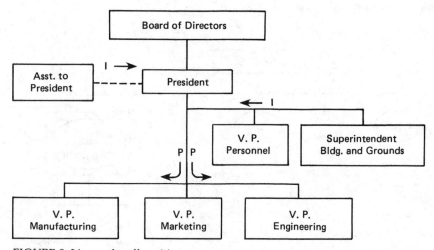

FIGURE 9. Line and staff positions

Span of control is a concept that creates a norm for how many subordinates a supervisor can reasonably and effectively handle on a face-to-face
basis.

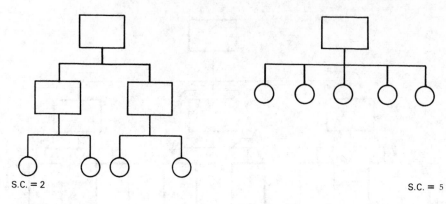

S.C. = 2   S.C. = 5

Narrow Span of Control   Broad Span of Control
Centralized/tall structure   Decentralized/flat structure

Advantages: Close Control Communication   Advantages:
Communication conformity   Autonomy for subordinates
Employee develops by training   Employee develops by doing

Disadvantages: Disadvantages:
Little innovation   Loss of control
Communication loss down through layers   Communication lacks conformity

FIGURE 10. Narrow and broad spans of control

Unity of command is the principle that each set of boxes is connected only to one box above.

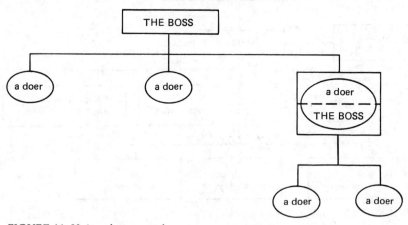

FIGURE 11. Unity of command

It is clear to everyone who is in charge and who is responsible for what to whom.

The functional positions in the hierarchy of a bureaucracy are each labeled, and most everyone knows exactly what title goes with each.

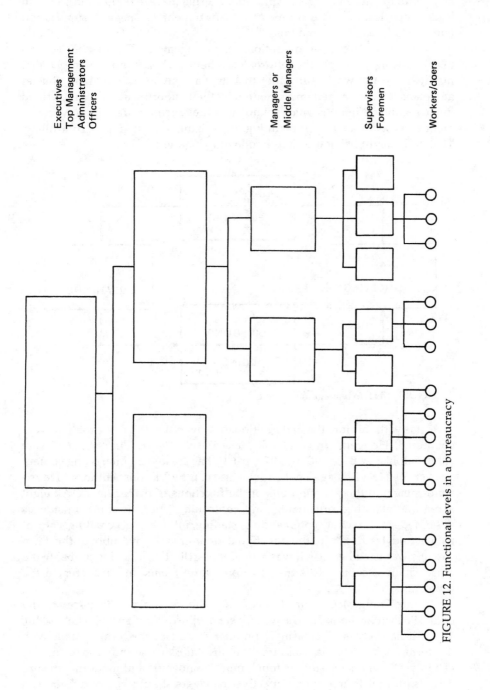

Executives
Top Management
Administrators
Officers

Managers or
Middle Managers

Supervisors
Foremen

Workers/doers

FIGURE 12. Functional levels in a bureaucracy

Before returning to the chart and the history of bureaucratic work, it will be helpful to pause here and explore four terms that are often confused with leadership (leader). The terms are: management (manager), supervision (supervisor), executive, and boss.

There are two basic definitions of management. The first is "accomplishing work through the efforts of others." This is not to imply that managers do not work, but rather that they are involved in making policies and plans which are then implemented by their subordinates. This is clarified in the second definition, which is known as the functional definition. Management consists of a cycle of planning, organizing, directing, and controlling. That cycle might be viewed in the following manner:

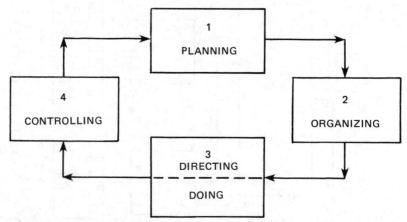

FIGURE 13. The management cycle

It is with this functional definition, however, that the first problem is encountered. Hodgetts, in his book *Management: Theory, Process and Practice* (Philadelphia: W.B. Saunders, 1979, p. 64), has created an interesting content analysis of "The Management Process as seen by Various Authors." He examines eight authors' definitions of the functions of management. All eight agree on "planning, organizing, and controlling," but the third function is described as: "directing, commanding, staffing, influencing, actuating, coordinating and leading." In the functional definition I gave above, the term *directing* was used because it was one of the earliest used and is probably the most widely accepted. It is the functional term *leading* that has created the problem.

Since Doug McGregor's "Theory X—Theory Y" was introduced in the early 1960s in his book *The Human Side of Enterprise* (New York: McGraw-Hill, 1960), it has become increasingly popular to replace the term *directing* with the term *leading*. This is, I assume, because *directing* sounds too autocratic (Theory X) and *leading* sounds much more democratic and modern. I'm sure it is also meant to imply that effective managers should be good leaders, a principle with which I fully agree.

However, if management is defined as "planning, organizing, leading, and controlling," the definition does two things with which I strongly disagree. First, this definition gives the impression that leadership is a subset of management, a subordinate function or process. This is not true. If anything, leadership is a broader concept and process than management. Secondly, it implies that managers are leaders by definition. This is also not true. I have known many competent managers who could not lead a thirsty horse to a trough. I have also known many leaders who could not manage anything, including their own lives. To imply that management and leadership are part and parcel of the same ability is misleading and confusing. The term *directing* can adequately describe the third function in the definition of management, and does not have to imply a Theory X approach to managing.

Supervision is a specialized form of management. Going back to the previous functional definition, high-level managers may spend a great deal of time planning and/or organizing and/or controlling, but have little or no contact with those who actually do the work. Supervisors, on the other hand, may have limited opportunities for planning or organizing, but have a primary responsibility for directing (and usually controlling) the activities of the workers. Based on the reasoning in the previous discussion, it would be even more important for a successful supervisor also to be an effective leader than it would be for many upper-level managers.

Leaders are often seen as executives or bosses, and yet these terms do not necessarily mean the same thing either.

Executive implies one who executes. The word *execute* has two distinct connotations. First, to execute is to make things happen, to set them in motion. Executives are usually high-level managers who make things happen by creating policies and plans for their organizations and by delegating to subordinate managers the authority to see that they are implemented. A second implication of the word *execute* is the Marie Antoinette definition. Executives have the power to fire, transfer, promote, and alter the careers and lives of subordinate employees in several ways. Neither of these executive processes necessarily implies the exercising of leadership.

Boss is a very interesting word *for two reasons*. First, when you ask managers what bosses do, they will respond by saying that bosses give orders, reprimand, criticize, control and fire incompetents—always very negative terms. Having asked this question of hundreds of managers and employees, I can't think of a half dozen times that someone has responded, "Bosses are people who love you, support you, compliment you, reward you, and promote you." So the term clearly has a negative connotation. Second, people use the term *boss* to refer to the person they work for. Rarely do managers remember that to their subordinates they are the boss, with all of the aforementioned negative references.

Does the word *boss* serve any useful purpose then? A few years ago I embarked on a crusade to eliminate the word from my vocabulary, since it was such a negative term. When I would speak to someone about how my career had been helped, they would ask, "By whom?" and I would answer,

"Oh, by the person I work for, the one just above me in the organization."
And they would say, "You mean your boss?" I decided after repeated
experiences such as this to go back to using the one word that says it best:
boss. However, of the four terms examined here, if the negative baggage is
brought along, I would have to say that the word *boss* has the least in common
with the term *leadership*.

Meanwhile, Back at the Chart

You've noticed that this history of the world of work divides into two parallel
stories at the beginning of this final century. We have just examined the
beginning of the story on the system side, and will turn our attention now to
an analysis of the people side of this continuing drama. (Be patient, dear
reader. Remember, in the standard text this little history would take up at
least three chapters!)

By the twentieth century, business had begun to clean up its act. Not
that leaders had suddenly become benevolent and caring, but workers had
slowly grasped the power in numbers. When Fisher, the carriage maker,
threatened to quit over his lost ear, he had no leverage (not to mention
balance). But if all the workers in the plant had threatened to quit if something were not done about Fisher's ear, that would have gotten the owner's
attention. This is not to say that owners just rolled over and played dead:
Strikes often led to violence and deaths. It was a bloody period in work
history. As in the case of the industrial revolution and bureaucracy, however,
workers assumed that unions would create Utopia.

On the people side, years passed, and while union pressures resulting in
new legislation humanized the business environment, Utopia did not come.
The year was 1927. Social scientists from a "small college in New England"
(Harvard) were engaged in doing some human engineering work at the
Hawthorne plant of Western Electric. The idea was to see if productivity
could be increased by improving the work environment (lighting, room
temperature, comfort of one's chair). The studies indicated that when these
things were improved the productivity went up. The scientists were ecstatic.
Give workers better lighting and work becomes more profitable.

Then one junior-deputy-assistant social scientist suggested that to be
truly scientific they ought to run a control experiment and make the environment worse. If the theory was correct, productivity would go down. So they
turned the lights down, turned the heat up, gave the hard chairs back, and
waited, and measured . . . and the productivity went up again. What did it
mean? This question has been asked and answered for over fifty years now,
and every year a new article comes out entitled "What We Really, Really,
Really, Really Learned From the Hawthorne Experiments." What they
thought they had learned at the time is that the increase in productivity had
nothing to do with the environment, but occurred because, for the first time,
someone paid attention to the employees. Voilà! If you pay attention to

34

workers, productivity and profitability increase, and you get Utopia. The Human Relations Approach to Management was born.

For the next twenty years managers tried caring about their employees, but Utopia did not appear. The business leaders went back to the social scientists. "What's wrong?" they asked. The social scientists thought about it for thirty seconds and said, "It's simple: The supervisors are not really sensitive to the employees and themselves. They're not really clear about what makes people tick." And sensitivity training was born.

For the next twenty years the T-groups (training groups) were in. Managers marched dutifully off to a secluded retreat in the mountains and sat around for a week in unstructured sessions, contemplating their navels and asking, "What do people really want and need to get from their jobs?" During this era all the motivational theories were developed and passed on to management.

The arrival of 1970 had not brought Utopia, and managers were fed up. They said, "I liked the good old days when I could yell at people and they jumped. Now I have to come in smiling every morning and say, 'Hello, Clyde. Hello, Sylvia. Would you like to do a little work today? I don't want to push you, now—don't file a grievance or anything. I just thought you might want to come to bat for the old corporate team!' Well, phooey on that. I'm going back to yelling—at least that's a release for my tension headaches!" This was the era when articles appeared in business publications on "hard versus soft management" and "the people approach versus the push approach." And still no Utopia.

Meanwhile, Back on
the System Side of the Chart

During the twenties, thirties, and forties corporate bureaucracies grew in size and complexity. This created a serious problem. The chief executive officer (CEO) sat at the apex of the pyramid, paid, supposedly, for being an effective decision maker. This person sat in the large executive office (with the rubber tree plant in the corner, the broad, uncluttered desk, the push-button phone with unblinking lights) and asked, "I wonder what they're doing out there?" This problem existed because the organization had been created to have the word flow from the top down. There was no mechanism for getting the word up through the system.

Once again scientists came to the rescue, but this time it was the natural scientists. At an international fair a group of mathematicians exhibited a large machine they had developed called a mathematical computing machine. The machine was fed the question, "What is $1+1$?" Whirrr . . . hiss. After a long wait came the ticker tape answer "$1+1=2$." Polite applause.

Today computers can still add only two numbers, but over the ensuing three decades several things have changed. The computer got smaller (currently wristwatch size), the memory core got bigger, and the speed increased dramatically. Now when the computer is asked "What is $1{,}367{,}421^3$?" it spits out the answer and says, "I'm bored, mostly resting." The ability to handle large numbers was disturbing to people who took solace in saying, "At least computers can't think." The computer scientist responded and said, "You give us an operational definition of thinking, and we'll program a computer to do it." More scary. "Well, at least we build them." Wrong again: Computers design and build themselves. Fourth generation computers are conceived by third generation computers. Scarier. Finally, "At least we can pull the plug." Wrong! Robotized computers not only plug themselves in, but solve the problem of *how* to plug themselves in.

FIGURE 14. "I hate to tell you, but that wasn't here when we left yesterday"

As the technology improves, two subtle and disturbing changes occur. One is that the line between what a machine is and what a person is becomes increasingly fuzzy (per Toffler's *Future Shock* and Sagan's *The Dragons of Eden*). Secondly, we wake up one morning to discover that the computers have taken over and we are working for them (per the movies *Colossus II: The Forbin Project* and *2001: Space Odyssey*).

Returning to the problem of the CEO who previously couldn't make a decision because of a lack of information, a major change has now occurred with the introduction of the computer into corporate decision making. The leader now arrives in the morning only to be confronted by a six-inch pile of computer printout. Whereas no decision was possible before because of inadequate data, now no decision is possible because of a data overload. How does the leader decide what is the most relevant data? You guessed it—he turns the problem over to another computer. The Computer Based Management Information System (CBMIS) becomes the ideal scapegoat for every bad decision and communication failure. How often have you heard, "The computer gave us that answer," ignoring the reality of "Garbage in, garbage out," or "We can't answer that for you; the computer is down," implying there are *no* answers without a functioning computer. Computer-based information/ decision systems notwithstanding, the era of clear, effective organizational communication is not in sight.

Systems Theory:
An Attempt at Integration

The effort over the last decade has been to develop people-oriented systems. Two of the best known are management by objectives (MBO) and organizational development (OD), both presented in the leadership-technique sections of this book. Systems theory in general has been popular since its introduction by Kenneth Boulding in 1956. Boulding's General System Theory attempted to show the interconnection of all phenomena. The phrase *a systems approach* has become one of the most popular buzzwords of the day.

A system is composed of parts that are connected and interdependent in a way that presents an identifiable whole. A closed-system perspective consists of looking at a phenomenon without regard to its external

FIGURE 15. The management process as a closed system

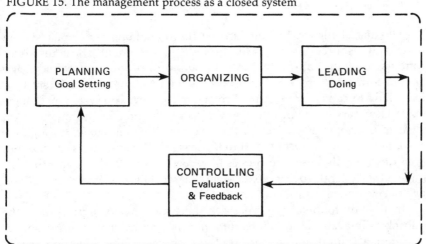

environment. This approach can be used to look at anything from marriage to a basketball team to a corporation to a country. It is concerned only with what happens within the system. How wide or narrow the boundary is drawn is purely arbitrary.

An open-system perspective consists of looking not only at a given system, but also at the relationship between the system and its larger environment.

FIGURE 16. An organization as an open system

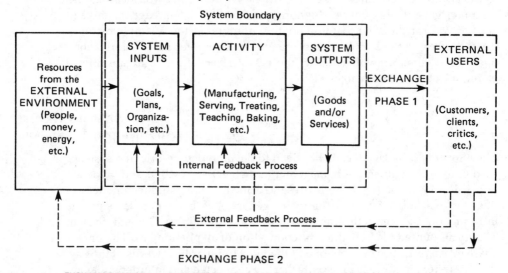

EXCHANGE PHASE 1 = The goods or services the organization provides to the world.

EXCHANGE PHASE 2= The money, materials, energy or people that the world returns to the organization.

RESULTS OF EXCHANGE:

    If Exchange Phase 2 > Exchange Phase 1—Profit, Growth, Vitality

    If Exchange Phase 1 > Exchange Phase 2—Loss, Entropy, Death

Looking at Figure 16 you can see the operation of an open system. Energy and resources are imported from the environment. These resources, or inputs, are then transformed into an output of products or services. It is this transformation process that makes General Motors look different from McDonald's or the Environmental Protection Agency. The system exchanges its goods or services with other systems in the larger environment. If the exchange is favorable (profitable) the system will be energized through the flow of new money or resources into the system. The system has a tendency to run down or die unless resources *in* exceed resources *out* (a fact that has escaped the federal government, several large cities, major corporations, small businesses, and a million marriages).

In addition to the above processes, there must be some process for the feedback of relevant information from internal and external sources so that the planning (input) and activity (output) phases of the operation can be adapted to changing conditions (a fact that escaped the dinosaurs, several organized religions, and a number of major businesses). Over time the system has a tendency to grow in size and complexity and develop new subsystems to aid in survival.

Open-systems theory can be extremely useful in teaching, counseling, and consulting. The discussion of double-loop learning in Chapter 4 is based on an open-system analysis. While systems theory will not solve the problems of bureaucracy presented in this section and the next, it is a useful tool for diagnosis and planning which you can apply to your business, your social club, and your marriage. If you wish to develop a more sophisticated familiarity with systems theory, its uses and abuses, refer to the Boulding, Hardin, Gall, and Katz and Kahn books in the bibliography.

ORGANIZATIONAL CONSTRAINTS, OR WHO PUT THE GLUE ON THE SLIPPERY SLIDE?

The first section has examined the historical development of a bureaucratic approach to collective work activities. Bureaucracy has become a way of life for virtually everyone today. A leader has to cope with the realities of bureaucratic constraints. These constraints that are often imperceptible are one reason why the text book theories do not work in real world fact. There are other obstacles such as group dynamics, interpersonal problems and individuals themselves. But in this section the obstacles based in the culture of the organization itself will be established. Their existence and some sense of their nature is required before a problem solving approach or change strategy is employed.

Norms and Sanctions

Why do people do what they do? It may seem the intuitively right thing to do, it may seem reasonable, it might accomplish some end, it may be a part of human nature, it may satisfy some human need, or it may have been requested or required by others (by the state or the church, for example). Whatever the original motivating force, behavior repeated over time becomes the norm or accepted way of doing things. To be normal, you simply act as others are acting, regardless of the rightness or wrongness of their acts.

These accepted patterns of behavior, adopted over time, provide stability in society and predictability in human relations. To insure normal behavior, an elaborate system of rewards and punishments, called sanctions, are employed. Figure 17 shows some of the more common sanctions and how they might be grouped for understanding.

Customs

Customs are traditions that have evolved over time. Some of them served a functional purpose originally, others have served no purpose other than superstition. For example, the tie worn by many men in formal work situa-

FIGURE 17. Types of sanctions employed to insure normative, predictable behavior

	POSITIVE	NEGATIVE
	(*Rewards* for accepted normal behavior)	(*Punishment* or deprivation for unacceptable, abnormal behavior)
INFORMAL (Based on customs and mores, employed by individuals)	Smile Pat on the back Compliment Inclusion of person Applause Recognition	Frown Gossiping about Ridicule Sarcasm Excluding the person Boos, hisses Reprimand
FORMAL (Based on organizational policy or what society allows)	Bonus Raise Promotion Privilege Medal Picture in paper	Fine Dismissal Demotion Removing privileges Dishonorable discharge Imprisonment (Temporary, formal exclusion) Capital punishment (The ultimate negative sanction, permanent exclusion from the system)

tions today is derived from the shawl worn by Bedouin tribesmen. This long, flowing scarf was wrapped around the face to protect the wearer from sandstorms. This use made a lot of sense for those men then. Few businessmen use their ties in windstorms today. The tie serves no other useful purpose, yet men are negatively sanctioned if they do not wear one. (Women have their own problems, but they will never appreciate the torture of the tie, relieved in that one blissful moment at the end of the day when the restrained Adam's apple is exposed and the man is able to breathe without constraint.)

An example of the superstitious type of custom is the blessing given to persons when they sneeze. The practice originated when it was believed that during the sneeze evil spirits might enter the body of the person sneezing. Today that is not a common concern, but people are nevertheless blessed whenever they sneeze.

One might assume naively that customs are not enforced as strongly as, say, policies or laws. This is not the case. In fact, it is often harder to change a customary way of doing things than it is to amend a policy or remove a law. Many women will remember the battle (not won yet in some places) to allow women to wear pants to work. Wind chill factors of −30°F notwithstanding, the infallible logic was that if God had wanted women to wear pants he would have made them men.

Customs and traditions serve the purpose of providing people with stability, meaning, and predictability. A most delightful and understandable presentation of this function is presented in *Fiddler on the Roof*. The disadvantage of customs and traditions is that they stand in the way of progress, improvement, and positive changes.

This does not imply that all changes are positive. But you should examine the "culture" of your organization, office, team, or family for existing customs. Are they serving a purpose, intangible though it may be (such as esprit de corps), or should they be changed for new ways? For example, are there in your office routinized procedures, such as the number of forms required and who they go to, that have no functional purpose now? When new employees or outsiders point out a different (better?) way that things might be done, do you respond, "Yes, but we've always done it this way"? Take a hard look around at the dysfunctions you have built in that are now becoming fossilized.

Mores or Morass?

Where customs and traditions have no connotation of right or wrong, mores imply definite judgments about the quality of an act. If I come into work with no tie on, I violate a custom. No one is terribly upset and only mild negative sanctions are applied. If I come into work with no pants on, I violate mores. I will certainly empty the room and probably be locked up (excluded from the company of those who wear pants).

Why is it okay to uncover one part of the body but not another? Mores serve to protect that which society judges to be essential to society, usually things related to procreation, health, and defense. That explains the differential covering of women's tops versus women's legs in various cultures. Our culture views the female breast as a sexual object; other cultures do not. Other cultures view the legs as sexual objects; our culture does not.

Our word *moral* is derived from the word *mores*. A person who behaves according to the mores is thought of as moral; one who does not is immoral. Referring again to the bell-shaped curve, there are approved and disapproved violations of the mores.

It is difficult to identify mores in American society and see the informal negative sanctions applied to their violation because we are such a legalistic culture. We have laws forbidding nudity and spitting, and we inevitably punish by fine and imprisonment. This is not true in "less developed" cultures.

Business leaders today are facing a reemphasis of organizational values and managerial ethics. As the person out front, you should set the example and lead the way in examining and acting on notions of right and wrong.

Policies, Rules, and Regulations

The policies and rules created by the executive, administrator, coach, or director fall somewhere in the area between customs and laws. In which of these two categories they tend to be viewed depends on how many there are, how clearly they are communicated, whether or not they are written down, whether the sanctions for violations are informal or formal, and how consistently they are reinforced.

There are two implications here. One is that if you are the leader you can determine whether you want a legalistic, heavily enforced organizational environment, or one that is informal and inflexible. The other implication is that if people are going to operate according to an effective set of bureaucratic survival skills, they need to quickly size up which type of policy operation they are going to be working within and determine which are the critical, enforced policies. Violation of these core policies can unfortunately mean the end of a career.

The leader of the organization sets the tone for whether or not the policy will be followed. If the example of the leader is one of consistently violating the established policy with impunity, there should be no surprise if the followers follow suit. Preaching one policy and enforcing it, while practicing another, will only lead to organizational schizophrenia.

Laws

Currently, the United States is the ultimate example on this globe of a legalistic society. We have laws for everything from corporate mergers to closing curtains, to abortion, to sports violence, to seat belts, to making love. It's almost impossible to think of any human product or act that is not government regulated. For example, the fast-food hamburger has over a thousand regulations governing its manufacture. The federal regulations on beets alone contain over fourteen thousand words. The legal and judicial system in this country, set up to codify and enforce this plethora of laws, is enormous and works less than well.

As a leader working within this society, you need to be aware of how the law affects the direction of your business, church, team, or family. In most cases, ignorance of laws is no excuse, and violations can be costly. Truly, the attorneys (many now judges and politicians) shall inherit this earth.

Summary

This section raises some important issues for leaders. If your organization or group is to survive, you must strike the fine balance between change and stability. If you go too far in creating changes, you run two risks. First, you can go so far outside of normal environmental constraints as to elicit severe societal sanctions. On the other hand, if your policies and customs are cast in concrete, you will fail to adapt to a changing world and be the lone manufacturer of hula hoops. You as the leader walk the tight rope and, as I'll show in the next section, someone is shaking the rope.

The first two sections of this chapter have examined the structure of the leadership environment. This section is concerned with the climate of that environment—specifically, the management of problematic elements in that environment.

A group's climate consists of the collective feelings that exist in the place where people work or live. Every group has a climate, and most people can sense it the first time they walk into the room. There is an immediate sense of friendliness, hostility, business-above-all, or confusion. This climate may be perceived based on observation of interaction and/or nonverbal behavior, and it may even be felt through charged particles in the room. If that strikes you as an odd statement, you may wish to examine the hardening of your own categories.

The leader more than any other group member influences and controls this climate. Sometimes this is done intentionally, and sometimes it simply results from the followers taking their cues from the leader's behavior. The leader's objective should be to promote the most positive climate to foster effective achievement of the group's goals. Despite the best intentions, however, frustrations and conflicts will arise. They are an unavoidable and sometimes desirable aspect of people living and working together. It is really remarkable that two or more completely different human beings can get along at all. But to say that frustration and conflict can and do exist is not to say that they should be ignored or accepted in whatever form or magnitude they come. They can be managed, altered, and resolved. These processes are the object of discussion in the following sections.

Frustration: Fruitful or Frantic?

As discussed in the section on motivation, human beings are moved by pursuing goals, the attainment of which will satisfy their needs. When a person is in pursuit of a goal and something blocks its attainment, the feeling that the person experiences is called frustration. Frustration, then, is goal-directed behavior that is blocked.

One of the best-established theories of human behavior is called the frustration/aggression theory. This theory presents the two most common reactions to the feeling of frustration that the psychologist calls "fight or flight." In other words, when your goal-directed behavior encounters a barrier, you usually attack or give up.

These two responses to frustration are functional in a jungle setting. The thirsty tribesman who encounters a nine-hundred-pound tiger sunning in

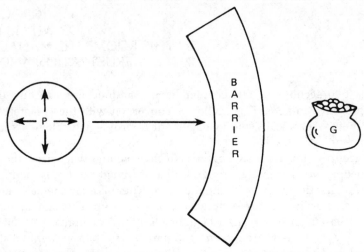

FIGURE 18. Simplified frustration situation

front of the water hole may say, "No one ever explained it to me that clearly before," and give up. On the other hand, he may really be thirsty, pull out his bone knife, yell "Kawa bonga!" and charge.

Attacking or giving up may be functional in the jungle, but they are rarely acceptable, productive responses in the modern bureaucratic jungle. Throwing your boss through the window may make you feel better, but it will do little to further your career. Attacks from frustrated employees come in the form of sarcasm, gossiping, scapegoating, back stabbing and interpersonal politics. Giving up takes the form of the employees' physical presence but psychological absence, as evidenced by apathy, tardiness, absenteeism, drug use, turnover, and stress-related breakdowns.

The most common response by extremely frustrated workers is called employee sabotage. Overtly or covertly, the leader's attempt to produce results is thwarted by those who have had enough. Over the past decade I have put on several hundred leadership training courses across the United States. At every program leaders share interesting and disturbing stories of employee sabotage.

Some of the stories are humorous (to all but the eventual victim), such as the assembly line worker who was welding pop bottles in the door frame of very expensive cars. Each bottle contained a note with the question, "How do you like that, you rich S.O.B.?" Some are very ingenious, like the frustrated teller who went up and down the line each day putting forty-two cents into one drawer and seventy-one cents into another. When he was finally caught, he ignored the hundreds of dollars the bank spent to apprehend him and pointed out the seventy-five dollars he had "contributed" to the bank.

Some of the sabotage is not so much overt action as neglect. An old railroad worker had asked repeatedly without success for a venetian blind to cover one window in his tower. One day a co-worker noticed a very dangerous condition in the switching yard which, if neglected, could cost the railroad a hundred-thousand-dollar accident. When the switchman was asked if he had reported it to management, his response was, "I told 'em about the venetian blind. When they deal with that, then we'll talk about the rail yard." The sabotage stories from airline employees and hospital supervisors are more than you would want to know about.

It's unfortunate that attacks and absenteeism are often the responses to frustration, because there are more productive ways for your people to deal with frustration; but before explaining those, let's reexamine the frustration model in its true complexity.

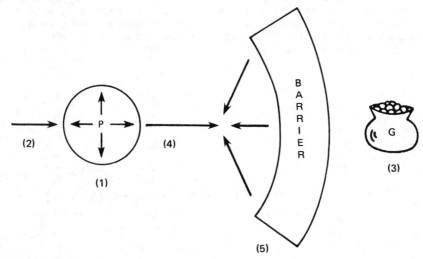

FIGURE 19. Detailed frustration situation

Referring to the numbers in the diagram, (1) represents the striving person, but it is obvious that the person is striving in many directions, for many goals, not just the one originally identified. This often causes internal tension and frustration. The environment is represented by (2), indicating that there are often pressures outside of the person pushing toward achievement of the goal. The goal being sought after is (3). The person's movement toward the goal is (4). The barrier blocking goal achievement is (5). By now it is evident that the barrier is not just a passive brick wall blocking the person's path, but may be a very dynamic force, such as another person, capable of counterattack.

The uselessness of attacking the barrier, in most instances, can readily be seen. Attacking a nonexistent scapegoat, such as the system, might be temporarily satisfying, but it will produce no change and is not likely to lead to goal achievement. Attacking or pushing another person or group will only produce an equal and opposite force pushing back. This may succeed if your power is greater than theirs, but if the reverse is true, you could be pushed even farther from the goal. Many times it is not possible to identify the barrier, so it is not clear where or what to attack. Finally, you may discover that you yourself are the barrier to goal achievement. It is hard to see any value in attacking yourself.

Alternatives to Fight and Flight

There are several constructive alternatives to attacking the barrier or giving up. As the leader, it may be your responsibility to teach those to your followers.

1. Use a problem-solving approach to remove the barrier. Using the problem-solving technique presented in Leadership Technique Section 8 can be an effective approach to identifying, diminishing, or removing the barrier. There is a subtle but important distinction between attacking the barrier and removing the barrier (the stunt driver's approach versus the magician's approach).

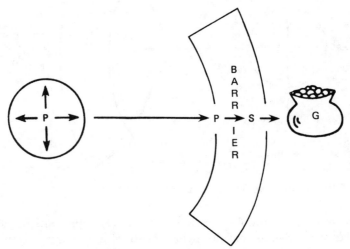

FIGURE 20. Problem solving to remove the barrier to achieve the goal.

2. Find an alternative path around the barrier. There are usually many paths to achieving a goal, and one of these may avoid the barrier completely while leading to the same place. A problem-solving approach will often identify this different path. This is known as the "old end-around play" or "many roads lead to Rome."

3. Change the goal. Once you have done a cost/benefit analysis of the situation, you may decide that it's not worth the cost of dealing with that barrier to achieve that goal. An alternative goal might be just as satisfying and involve less cost or risk. This is known as the "Aw, who wanted her anyway?" or "Nobody ever explained it to me that clearly before" approach.

4. Sometimes none of the previous options can be exercised, and the person is left to cope with the feeling of frustration and stress. It is helpful to realize that *nobody or nothing stresses you: You stress you*. People sometimes eat themselves up with anger or envy or guilt over some situation or opportunity long past. What they have done to themselves has been far worse than anything done to them by the situation. It is not

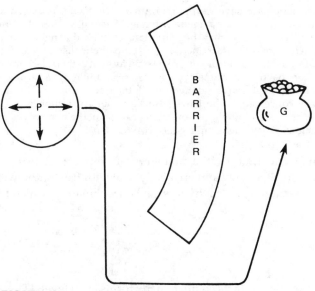

FIGURE 21. Finding an alternative path to the goal

what is done to you, but how you react to what is done to you that determines your character and your health.

5. Finally, it helps to have some way of releasing the emotions and internal

FIGURE 22. Obtaining an alternative goal

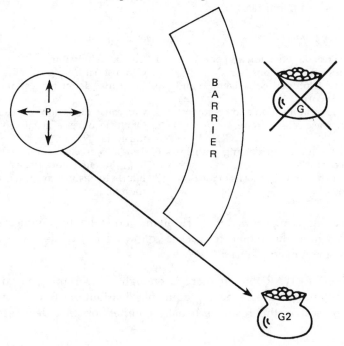

pressures. First, it helps to have a support group of at least one. You need somebody in your life who can provide empathetic listening. Second, if the situation and your reaction is very complex, it may be important to seek the help of a professional counselor. Such a person is trained as an empathetic listener and professional problem solver. Finally, it helps if you have some form of catharsis—emotional release. Ideally, you can tie this to some type of exercise, building a strong body while releasing emotions that can be dangerous if they accumulate. The most creative solution I have conceived, if the barrier causing your frustration is another person (your boss, let's say), is to purchase a punching bag, paint the person's face on it, and at the end of each workday engage in a good workout. *Bam!*

Teaching and training the members of your office, team, church, or family in how to effectively and creatively deal with frustration will go a long way toward developing a healthy interpersonal climate in which to work and live.

Conflict:
Constructive or Chaotic?

Disagreements and conflicts come in many forms at all levels. There are international conflicts, organizational conflicts, conflicts between interest groups, between work groups, and between individuals. There are also internal conflicts, which are discussed elsewhere in this book. The type of conflict confronted often varies within the organizational hierarchy.

Conflicts are often thought of as being reacted to in purely negative terms, but conflict can also make a positive contribution. Compare the advantages and liabilities:

Advantages of Conflict

1. Can increase motivation and energy.
2. Clarifies issues and positions.
3. Can build internal cohesiveness and esprit de corps.
4. Can lead to innovation and creativity.
5. Can increase self-awareness.

6. May be a means of dealing with internal conflicts.
7. Can lead to a new synthesis of ideas or methods.

Liabilities of Conflict

1. Can be debilitating.
2. Can distract from goal achievement.
3. Can cause defensiveness and rigidity.
4. Can cause distortions of reality.
5. Often becomes a negatively reinforcing cycle.
6. Tends to escalate (more serious) and to proliferate (more issues).
7. Efforts to resolve are often not reciprocated.

The beginning of wisdom in resolving and managing conflicts is understanding where they come from. The following list, while not exhaustive, presents seven major *sources:*

1. LIMITED REWARDS: If there is enough of everything to go around, the main concerns are regarding equitable distribution. But if rewards are limited or scarce, the result is usually competition that degenerates into

conflict. The difference between competition and conflict is discussed in Chapter 4.

There are many types of rewards that people seek, including material rewards, psychic rewards, and emotional rewards. These rewards form a hierarchy very similar to Maslow's hierarchy of needs, which is discussed in detail in Chapter 3. If you take the students in a class and tell them that everyone can get A's, recognition, and respect, there is great incentive to cooperate so that all are successful. If you tell them, "I'm grading on a curve, and only three of thirty will be able to get A's," then competition and cheating are likely to result. However, if you seal off the room and tell them the air is being pumped out and there will only be enough air left for three to breathe, then conflict resulting in death is a likely result. You can see the implications for international relations, your place of work, and your home. Operating principle: *Whenever possible, see that every member can gain the most important rewards.*

2. UNCLEAR ROLE DEFINITIONS: The first section in this chapter talked about the dramatic changes that have occurred over the last two hundred years in developed nations. One significant result has been confused role expectations and performance. As an example, I tell my single students that the first great challenge they will face in marriage is the garbage crisis. As they move into their little honeymoon cottage and start life together, the garbage will begin to pile up under the sink. She'll think, "Why doesn't he do *his job* and take it out?" He'll think, "She was always such a clean person before we got married." Neither one will want to confront the accumulating crisis until the garbage is about waist deep. Finally, the shouting will start, and one or the other will commit the major sin. (I'll pick on him.) He shouts at the new bride, "Putting out garbage is women's work! Any man who handles garbage is a fairy!" Who has he just insulted? Her father! Where did she get the idea that men handle the garbage? Where did he get the idea that women handle the garbage? Who is right? There is no absolute answer to this question. It just needs to be negotiated and clear. Operating principle: *For every position there is an associated role behavior. Discuss these with all concerned and make sure the expectations are clear, the performance is appropriate, and the rewards related.*

3. TERRITORIALITY: It is in our nature to be concerned about turf. "That's my toy," "She's my girl," "Sharks' territory—stay out," "Your people are meddling in my department again" are all expressions of territorial concern. Ownership provides material and emotional maturity, and kingdom building brings psychic satisfaction. It also inevitably leads to conflict (especially as in point 1, if there is not enough territory to go around). Ironically, in big bureaucratic organizations, this leads to two paradoxical problems: "That's our responsibility; mind your own business" and "No, we don't do that anymore—try checking over there." In other words, everyone squabbles over

the bones, or things fall through the cracks. Operating principle: *Clarify boundaries, remember that they are arbitrary, and then respect them.*

4. ETHNOCENTRISM: An *ethos* is a person's life-style or world view; *centrism* implies centrality. To be ethnocentric is to assume your way is the right way, the best way, or the only way. Everyone is ethnocentric. There is nothing wrong with favoring your own view as long as you are open to the possibility that someone else might have a better way. Bigotry is the real problem.

The best way to confront your own ethnocentrism is to be submerged in a different culture (or subculture). I remember many shocks on my first trip to Europe, at the age of twenty. I spent much energy trying to convince European women of the hygienic value of shaving their legs, and the importance of holding their utensils correctly when eating. It was disturbing to consider their rebuffs and admit that maybe their way worked just as well. As the Chinese philosophers and William Shakespeare both reminded us, "There are more ways than our poor philosophy has ever dreamed of." Operating principle: *Do it your way until you find a better way. Then adopt that way and press on.*

5. FEAR: The barriers caused by fear are discussed elsewhere. The point here is that people who are pushed until their fear level is great enough often respond by fighting back. This is the instinctive survival response of anyone who is concerned. This fear can be based on ignorance or actual threat. Operating principle: *Remove the anxiety or fear-producing source, and you will remove people's need to counterattack.*

6. FRUSTRATION: One reaction to frustration is attack. In the path of someone else's goal achievement, you (or your group) may be the barrier. Operating principle: *Use the techniques for resolving frustration presented in the previous section.*

7. INCREASED DIVISION OF LABOR, SPECIALIZATION, AND INTER-DEPENDENCE: Do you know how to bake a loaf of bread? Make a pair of shoes? Repair a car? Landscape a yard? Fix a broken tooth? The complexity of our modern society forces us to rely on others for the accomplishment of many tasks vital to our own lives. When you feel you are cheated, disappointed, ripped off, the response is often conflict. The majority of murders in this country are perpetrated not by gangsters or crooks, but by those engaged in domestic or business arguments. The violated trust is a major source of conflict. Operating principle: *Become totally self-sufficient* or form all of*

*Being one of the last living generalists, I cannot resist sharing one of my favorite quotes:
A HUMAN BEING SHOULD BE ABLE TO:
change a diaper, plan an invasion, butcher a hog, conn a ship, design a building, write a sonnet, balance accounts, build a wall, set a bone, comfort the dying, take orders, give orders, cooperate, act alone, pitch manure, solve equations, analyze a new problem, program a computer, cook a tasty meal, fight efficiently, die gallantly.
Specialization is for insects!
Robert A. Heinlein, science fiction writer

your working relationships on clearly understood (often written) agreements. Get a good attorney and/or assume good faith, and trust the person you must rely on. Remember the principle of the self-fulfilling prophecy.

An Approach to Conflict Resolution*

In any social interaction, three levels of relationships can be identified. Each level has certain preconditions as outlined in Figure 23. The approach to resolving conflicts then consists of the following steps:

1. Begin with two basic assumptions: A) Every conflict can be resolved or diminished, and B) collaboration is better than bargaining is better than power tactics.
2. Diagnose the situation. Become clear about problem definitions, symptoms, and causes.
3. Attempt resolution at the highest level possible.
4. Fall back if necessary, but advance as soon as possible.
5. Evaluate results and repeat, until a desirable level and working relationship is achieved.

Figure 23. Approaches to conflict

LEVEL	PRECONDITIONS
COLLABORATION	Superficial differences
WIN/WIN	Mutual gains
	Power parity (balance)
	Both parties mutually committed
	Problem-solving approach
	Organizational support
	Climate open and trusting
	Assumes all can win
BARGAINING/NEGOTIATION	Substantive differences
WIN/WIN OR WIN/LOSE	Differential gains
	Gaining power parity
	Written agreements with sanctions
	Task orientation
	Limited organizational support
	Climate suspicious, manipulative
	Assumes someone must lose
POWER TACTICS	Critical differences
WIN/LOSE OR LOSE/LOSE	Unilateral actions
	Major power differences
	Neither commitment nor enforceable sanctions
	Hoarding, sabotage, coalitions
	Threat, force, withdrawal
	Organizational support nonexistent
	No perceived alternatives
	Climate hostile and secretive
	Based on self-interest and winning at all costs

ILLUSTRATIVE CASE B

The Case of Adrian Kim

Adrian Kim stared across the desk at the two police officers seated sullenly at angles to one another. In the five years since making sergeant, "Kimbo" (the only name used by

*I am indebted to Dr. Brooke Derr for much of what I know in this area.

51

the troops) had never faced anything like this. It had been six months since the city manager's directive had integrated the two-person patrol teams, and it had produced six months of anger, fighting, dissension, and rebellion in the ranks. Three officers had threatened to quit, and one of the new female officers was threatening Kim with a discrimination lawsuit. Nothing was working right. The two in the room now were representative of all that was ulcer-producing.

Mike spoke first. "Look, Kimbo, I gave it a good try, but I'm not going to get my head blown off because my partner here can't haul her keister over a fence. She drives me nuts with her jabbering in the car, then when there's action she runs around like a chicken with her head cut off. I'm fed up, and I'm not alone. There's a lot of your guys out there who are ready to quit, and we want to know what you're going to do about it?"

Sharon responded, "Listen to Captain America! He spends half the night asleep while driving, never allowing an original idea to pass between his ears. And then when he wants to wake up, he hops out of the car and rips off down some dark alley chasing some Puerto Rican kid on the way home from a dance. Where does it say in the small print I've got to follow the bionic man here every time he decides to get his evening exercise? If you can't put me with one of the nonbigots—I take it on faith there is one in this precinct—I may just join Rita in her lawsuit!"

Adrian Kim stared past the two officers to the pictures on the wall, with squad rooms full of smiling (male) officers from those halcyon days now gone. "I wonder if it's too late to reenlist," just slipped out.

FUNCTIONAL TYPE   Adrian Kim is a police sergeant. This situation might be similar to problems experienced by a military leader, a sea captain, or a railroad conductor.

LEADERSHIP FACTORS   The principles involved in this case include conflict, frustration, stress, group climate, and male/female relations.

QUESTIONS TO CONSIDER

1. What are the male/female issues involved in this case? How might they be approached to minimize the confrontation and conflict?
2. Is it possible that real dangers exist with these integrated two-person patrol teams? If so, what should be done?
3. What are the lose/lose dynamics of the current situation? What would have to be done to move to win/lose? to win/win?
4. What role does communication play in defusing this situation?
5. What rewards could be created for those who help make the new approach work? What behavior should those rewards be tied to?

ANALYSIS   Adrian Kim can begin by dealing with content or process in this situation. The content issues here have to do with men and women in the world of work. The dynamics of those relationships should be reviewed and considered.

There are several process issues here. One has to do with directing the integration, a unilateral authoritarian approach, rather than getting everyone involved in the whys and the hows of the process. The next has to do with the conflict resolution techniques and moving from lose/lose to win/win dynamics. Consideration needs to be *given here to the stress built into this type of work and the institutionalization of approaches to cope with it. There is also the possibility that the law ought to be reexamined to see if in fact the integrated approach does create additional, real dangers. If these are present and ignored, disaster is inevitable.*

For the people involved, training could be provided in more effective communication and human relations techniques. Skill at empathetic listening, speaking clearly, and giving effective feedback could diffuse some of the negative energy in the situation. The system should provide real and valued rewards for those who are successful in making the new approach work.

You will sometimes find that it is not possible (or desirable) to work through the conflict with the members involved. Calling in a skilled third party to assist in the process can have several advantages. This person (or group) can help the parties discover mutual interests, assist in balancing the power, synchronize confrontations, heighten integration, change existing norms and traditions, reinterpret communications, and keep tension at an optimum level. In a power struggle, this person may control outcomes. If bargaining, she can act as mediator; and when collaborating, she can be a facilitator.

As the leader of the group, if your efforts or those of a subordinate to whom you have delegated this important task are directed at resolving conflicts and frustrations and developing an open, trusting, collaborative climate, everyone can win.

COMMUNICATION THEORY AT WORK, OR YOU CAN'T GET THERE FROM HERE

Communication is the single most important leadership skill and the most important organizational topic to be discussed in this book. Civilization is created through communication; culture is transmitted to future generations, problems are solved, relationships formed, all that makes us human is wrapped up in our ability to communicate effectively.

Communication can be defined as a two-way transfer of meaning. Each part of this definition contains meaning that aids in understanding what communication is and does. *Two-way* implies that communication is an interactive process with information both being sent and returning. The term *transfer* in the definition implies that the meaning must get from one person to another. There is no current "Mork from Ork" technique for touching another person and instantaneously transferring information. Therefore, your message must go through a medium. There are problems in getting the message through that medium.

The third part of the definition is the concept of *meaning.* The definition could read "a two-way transfer of *information, ideas, concepts,* or *feelings.*" Any of these definitions would have been adequate, but the word *meanings* was chosen because several concepts associated with the term *meanings* aid in the understanding of communication.

First, meanings come from two places: inside the communicator and from the context (environment) of the communication. When you are communicating with a different person, or the same person in a different environment, the meaning will change. Telling employees to get a job done immediately will sound different to them on a Friday afternoon than it will on a Tuesday morning.

Secondly, people develop meanings for communication symbols based on their experience. Since no two people have the same experience, no two people will have the same meanings. A client may call you and say that his check was incorrect. What you think of as a check may not be what he means by a check. In fact, he could be referring to an invoice, a receipt, or a bill of lading.

Third, and the most important concept to understand: Words do not have meanings, only people have meanings. If you want your brain filaments to burn out, consider the fact that the word *word* is a word. What does the word *word* mean? It does not mean anything. It is just a collection of squiggly lines. I know what *word* means to me. You know what *word* means to you. If we share a common meaning we can communicate.

I have tried to show the importance of this concept by beginning each section with definitions of the key terms. By doing this, my intent is not to insult your intelligence. You may say, "Well, everybody knows what *motivation* means." The point is that people know what *motivation* means to them. Communication that leads to understanding, however, requires effort at developing some *shared* definitions.

Fourth, to change people's meanings for things, you must change their experiences. People will relate to the concept of stress management from working under stress quite differently than they will from just reading about it in a book.

Fifth, as experiences change, people's meanings change. That is to say that the person we meet today will not be the same as the one we knew in college ten years ago or the one who is represented on the resumé. Records and memory may "freeze-frame" people at some past point, but they are living today and they are changed. This will affect our communication with them.

Communication that leads to understanding involves a successful two-way transfer of meaning. The problem is that there are numerous barriers that consistently get in the way of success.

Barriers to Effective Communication

The two stick people in Figure 24 represent the two parties in this transfer-of-meaning (communication) situation. The *sender* is the one initiating the symbolic transfer; the other party is the *receiver*. The message is transferred through some type of *medium* and the response comes in the form of *feedback*. Each of these four parts of the process contains several components in which communication can break down. The ones to be discussed here are identified in this figure.

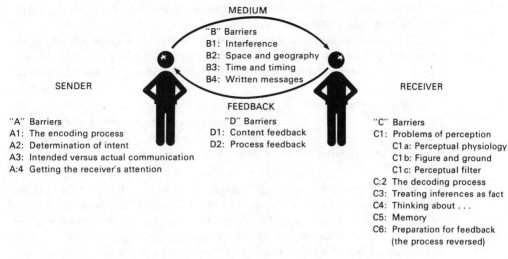

FIGURE 24. Major barriers to an effective communication process

Problems Experienced by Senders

A1 ENCODING: SELECTING A SYMBOL TO ASSIGN MEANING TO. Assuming that you begin life as a clean slate, the first communication challenge you face is related to perception, or gathering a meaning that you can transfer. The problems associated with perception are the first barriers confronting the receiver. This analysis begins with the assumption that the senders have some meaning in their brains that can be transferred. In the illustration the meaning is represented by a star (since I am not adept at drawing movie stars or linguine). The sender must select some symbol system as the vehicle for the transfer. The problem is that there are so many

FIGURE 25. The menu of communication symbols

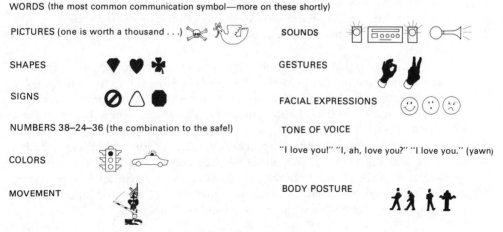

symbol systems, and the sender must make assumptions about which will be most likely to work with this receiver.

The most common symbol is words, but as you have already seen, words do not have meanings. So when a person uses a word, how do we know what he or she means by that word? This analysis will ignore the problems of:

different languages	*C'est faite rien?*
different dialects	Pig in a poke (do you know what a *poke* is?)
special jargon	The plumber's spider (do you know what a *spider* is?)
and generational differences	Careful in asking your teenager to cut the *grass*.

The focus will be on the English language. In any library there is a large, dusty book titled *Unabridged Dictionary of the English Language*. The book contains in excess of 300,000 words. "But, Mr. Bothwell," you protest, "except for William F. Buckley, most of us do not talk like unabridged dictionaries." That's true. We have a working vocabulary of 2,000 words and a core vocabulary of about 500 (I, you, go, he, she, it, etc.). However, if you assume that we can communicate and share definitions for those 500 core words, you assume incorrectly; for if the 500 words are taken back into the unabridged dictionary, you will find that they have over 14,000 different definitions.

A2 DETERMINING THE INTENT OF THE COMMUNICATION. Obviously, there are many different reasons for communicating. As the sender, it is important for you to be clear about what your intent or purpose is in sending your message. If you are confused about what you intend for your communication to do, or if you have intentions that conflict with one another, your communication will probably not be successful. The result may be a receiver who is frustrated, confused, or defensive.

A3 A GAP BETWEEN THE INTENDED AND ACTUAL COMMUNICATION. People often send double messages. A double message is a statement in which there is a discrepancy between what one intends to communicate and what one actually communicates. This is sometimes done intentionally, but more often is due to lack of clarity or mixed feelings on the part of the sender.

An example of a double message is a person shouting "I am not mad!" and slamming a fist on the desk. The words say one thing; the actions, facial expression, and tone of voice say something else. Which message do we believe? Studies of this phenomenon have shown that where the words and actions contradict each other, the receiver will usually believe what you do over what you say. We often hear a sender lament, "But I told them . . ." (that is, "I said the words"). But when the boss says, "That's all right, it's five o'clock—go ahead and go home," the boss's tone and manner may be saying, "If you cared about this company, you wouldn't run out on me." The employee ends up somewhat confused and perhaps resentful.

A4 GETTING THE RECEIVER'S ATTENTION. Most people live and work in a world of noise, confusion, and interference. There are countless distractions competing with you for your receiver's attention. If the receiver is not tuned in when you broadcast, the message is not likely to be received.

The standard techniques for gaining someone's attention include eye contact, touching, dramatic gestures, using the person's name, and raising your voice. The problem is that when everyone in the environment uses these attention-getting techniques, the result is heightened chaos.

An alternative is getting attention by challenging ("I'm about to tell you something you will never forget as long as you live!"), by giving your message a dramatic buildup, by speaking slowly and quietly, or by giving a message that requires thought. (The participants in my leadership training programs can tell you that they have never forgotten that "Some dinosaurs were as small as chickens.") These techniques only work if they are infrequently used. Use them today on your boss and you will have his or her undivided attention. But come in every day for a week and begin by saying, "I'm about to tell you something that you will never forget as long as you live . . ." and you will lose the boss's attention (and possibly your job).

Barriers in the Medium
Through Which the Message
Is Transferred

B1 INTERFERENCE BETWEEN SENDER AND RECEIVER. The only pure (interference-free) communication environment I recall seeing is the scene in *West Side Story* where Tony and Maria meet at the youth-center dance. Their eyes meet across the crowded dance floor, and as they walk together the rock band is replaced by two hundred violins, and dancers go from leaping to slow motion before disappearing, and the lights fade until they go out. But not to fear, because a spotlight comes on, illuminating Tony; another spot illuminates Maria. As they stand there nose to nose in the quiet darkness, he says something to her. She responds to him. This is a moment of pure communication.

The question you must ask yourself is how much this scene resembles your office, factory, or home? Most people say their working environment is more like the original dance scene: bright, noisy, and totally confusing. As a sender in such a scene, you have to be sensitive to the competing distractions (often other senders) vying for your receiver's attention. These distractions can include office talk, ringing phones, phone conversations, machinery, noisy air conditioners, and outside traffic. If you are fortunate enough to have some control over the communication environment at work, you may wish to consider methods of minimizing or separating competing message sources.

B2 THE INFLUENCE OF SPACE AND GEOGRAPHY ON COMMUNICATION. There are four aspects of communication space that deserve attention. These are: 1) personal life space, 2) the office environment, 3) the physical plant, and 4) geography. Each will be examined in turn.

Personal life space refers to the piece of turf that people carry around with them, surrounding their bodies. The most interesting discovery of explorations into cross-cultural business is that this social distance varies from culture to culture. For North Americans, the distance is about a foot and a half. For South Americans, the distance is more like six inches. Observers have been amused to attend a cocktail party with representatives of both continents present and watch a North and South American talk themselves across a room, with the latter advancing to close the distance and the former retreating to widen it.

The point here is that you need to be sensitive to this distance when involved in interpersonal communication. Issues of how far apart you are, whether the parties are sitting or standing, which sex each party is, and what emotions are being conveyed will all influence the eventual success of the communication.

The second space consideration has to do with the office environment. In large offices in Europe the most important people are put in the middle of the room; in the U.S. they are distributed around the outside. Barriers such as desks, tables, and counters will determine whether or not the message gets through. When I worked as a social worker, my supervisor wanted to know the secret of why people would open up to me more than to others. It was a secret I had discovered quite by accident in my previous job, when I taught at a college where the president's office was designed something like this.

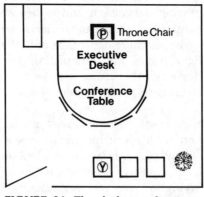

FIGURE 26. The desk as a barrier to openness

Somehow I never felt like opening up in that office. So when I went to work for the Department of Welfare I changed my office from this to this:

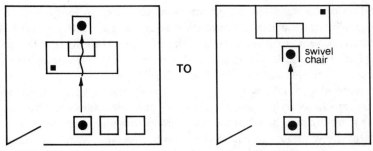
FIGURE 27. Removing the desk as a communication barrier

It did, and does, make a difference. Look around your office (and home) for barriers you have constructed to understanding.

B3 COMMUNICATION: TIME AND TIMING.   As discussed elsewhere in this book, time is *not* a constant. The quality of time differs dramatically from favorite movie to dentist's chair and from corporate president to rest-home resident. The message from sender to receiver passes through an environment of time. How that time is perceived by each party will influence the quality of the message as to whether it is developed, rushed, or garbled.

A related matter has to do with the timing of a message. Requests for action from the boss are not heard the same way by employees at 4:45 on Friday as they are at 10:00 on Tuesday. If you communicate to someone an error they've made in their work and, in an apparent overreaction, they run crying from the room, what may not have been apparent is that someone just called and said the employee's aunt just died or that you're the twelfth person in fifteen minutes to point out a mistake. You cannot always know the timeliness of your message in advance, but it is an important factor, and you should consider it before sending a message.

The relativity of time and space is shown in the story of the Texan who wanted to give a New Englander an idea of how big his ranch was relative to the New Englander's farm. "Ya see that old limousine of mine?" the Texan said. "I can begin driving at one end of my ranch in the morning and spend the whole day in that car and just barely reach the other end of my ranch by sunset." "I know exactly what you mean," the New Englander replied. "I had a car like that once myself." With such totally different concepts of distance, the two could not hope to understand one another.

B4 IS IT POSSIBLE TO WRITE RIGHT?   Writing has many advantages. It helps the writer to clarify intents and thoughts. It often adds power to the message to be delivered (the "mailgram!"). It provides a record of a message as to time and content. But as it solves some problems, it creates others. Four are discussed here.

Many communicators have assumed that they could avoid all the communication problems discussed so far by putting their message into writing. But one major drawback of any written message (memo, letter, note) is that it is untimely. No matter how promptly the message is delivered, the spontaneity is lost, the world has changed, and part or all of it may not be true. (I will resist here all jokes about the U.S. Postal Service.)

A second problem with the written message is best understood by reflecting on the earlier comment about double messages. In a verbal message the meaning may be 60 percent in the tone of voice, gestures, etc., and 40 percent in the words; whereas in the written message, all of the meaning is contained in the words. Therefore, if the words are not meaningful to the reader (receiver), understanding is hopeless. The reader cannot interrogate the letter and ask, "What do you mean?" And even if the message is clear to the reader, what if that assumed meaning is not what the writer meant?

A third problem with the written message has been created by the electronic copier. In the age of carbon paper, which I grew up in, the difficulty of corrections placed a limit on the number of copies made of any message. But with the ease of copying today, everyone is copied in on the original, based on the fear that someone might be missed. Someone estimated that the federal government alone uses enough sheets of paper every year to fill 110 buildings the size of the Washington Monument. The most omnipresent objects in any office, public or private, are the rows of gray file cabinets. Has communication improved?

FIGURE 28. Does "The Word" get through the system? (Reprinted by permission of Tribune Company Syndicate, Inc.)

Finally, there are the challenges of trying to gain understanding in the thicket of indecipherable handwriting and errors of punctuation, spelling, and grammar. (Be honest—all of us but the editors of this book slept through high school English classes.)

Barriers on the Part
of the Receiver

C1 THE PROBLEMS OF PERCEPTION.   Perception is the process by which the five senses take in messages from the environment. Much of the meaning we possess has come through this process. (Additional meaning is created through our own internal thought processes.) Several problems on the part of the receiver, however, are due to the differential and imperfect functioning of our perception. Three examples will be analyzed briefly here: (1) differential physiology, (2) the problems of figure and ground, and (3) the perceptual filter.

The first perceptual challenge is based on the good news and bad news of each person's unique physiology. In no two people do the eyes, ears, nose, taste, and touch function (perceive) exactly the same. Do we all see the same red? (or do we see red at all?) Do we all hear the same B flat? Do we all smell the same zesty aroma? One might respond, "Who cares?" And yet the differences cited could be very important to an interior decorator, a concert pianist, or a cook. Two people in the same situation can, in good faith, report hearing and seeing two very different things.

The second challenge has to do with our perception of figure and ground. In a perceptual situation, the figure is the stimulus from which we take the meaning; the ground is the background against which that figure stands out. If you look at a word on this printed page, the figure is the dark printed letters that make up the word. The ground is the white page behind that provides contrast. The importance of that contrast can be seen if you write a word on a page of typing paper with a bottle of typing correction fluid.

We have been conditioned to perceive figure and ground in certain ways. That is why many people have trouble perceiving the meaning of this:

FIGURE 29. The challenge of figure and ground

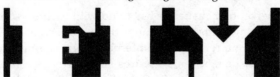

or this:

FIGURE 30. Would you recommend
this person for a blind date?

The problem in the former is that the figure and ground have been reversed,
providing difficulty as the brain attempts to gain meaning from the dark
objects it perceives as figures, which are actually background to the white
letters. The problem in the second is an ambiguous figure that can actually be
perceived in two different ways. (This well-known young girl/old woman
figure helps explain why you seldom trusted your roommate to line you up
with a blind date.) Again, two people can perceive the same situation very
differently. This, as any attorney knows, can become critical with witnesses in
a court trial.

This figure/ground problem can become very important in any situation where it is necessary for people to listen to you and really hear what
you're saying. If you speak so fast that the words (figure) run together, it
becomes increasingly difficult for the listeners to gain your meaning. Background interference can likewise blur the clarity of your words. You must
take these problems into account if you are interested in the listener's understanding.

The third perceptual challenge has to do with each person's perceptual
filter. As you assign meaning to the things that you perceive, this meaning is
filtered through and altered by your internal programming, including your
needs, goals, values, beliefs, fears, desires, and physical state. The hungry
student hears a lecture differently just before lunch. The high-need achiever
perceives an assigned project differently from one who is trying to avoid
work. Every person you communicate with is unconsciously (and sometimes
consciously) distorting what you say. And it helps to keep your frustration
level down if you realize that you are distorting the messages of everyone
who is trying to communicate with you.

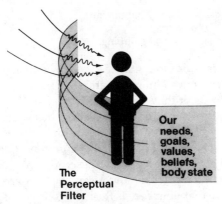

The Perceptual Filter

Our needs, goals, values, beliefs, body state

FIGURE 31. The perceptual filter

An example of this process would occur when you give instructions to two of your employees, Nancy Newperson and Loretta Longtimer. Nancy is eighteen, a recent high school graduate, and in her first job. She is interested primarily in the fun and social contacts of the job. Loretta has worked for you for fifteen years. Her greatest desire is to be promoted to supervisor.

You come to each employee and say, "I have a project here I want you to work on. If you do a really good job I will have an important surprise for you." Do both employees hear the same message? Highly unlikely! Why? You're the same, the words are the same, but their internal filter changes the message.

C2 DECODING: ASSIGNING MEANING TO THE PERCEIVED SYMBOL. Once the receivers have perceived the message, they will assign their own meaning to each of the symbols. The meaning assigned will be used on the person's experiences, education, and understanding. It will obviously vary not only from receiver to receiver, but also from sender to receiver. Here again, I must remind you that the meaning is not in the words or symbols, but in the heads and hearts of the people communicating.

C3 WHEN YOU ASSUME ... One of the most challenging aspects of communication is separating fact from inference. After one of the communication exercises I frequently use in my management development programs, the participants often reflect on their inadequate performance and say that one of the important lessons they have learned is that one should not make assumptions. This insight is not only improper, it would be impossible to implement. Everyday experiences are filled with assumptions and inferences necessitated by living. Every time you approach an intersection with a green light, you bet your life on seven unverified assumptions. You assume that:

1. The opposing light is working.
2. It is red.
3. The driver of the oncoming car can see the light.
4. The person can see the color red.

5. The person knows what a red light means.
6. The person intends to stop.
7. The person's car is capable of stopping.

You have to assume in order to live. The key is to compartmentalize what you "know" from what you have "inferred" and, whenever possible, to check out these assumptions to see if they are verified or refuted.

Chris Argyris, in his writing and teaching, has stressed the importance of building all of your communication around directly observable data (DOD). This means that instead of dealing in emotions, guesses, assumptions, or inferences, you provide people with observed behavioral data. Instead of saying "I know just how you feel and I can see you are really upset," you might say, "I perceive that your face is flushed, your hands are trembling, and you're raising your voice. When I am like that it's because I'm very angry." Now the person has something tangible to confirm or refute.

C4 THINKING: THE PROCESS OF MULLING OVER THE MEANING.   I said earlier that much meaning comes from the environment through our perceptions. But human beings also have the ability to create and modify meanings through the process of thought. Thinking is discussed in detail in Leadership Technique Section 4. The importance of mentioning it here is to stress how much our lives (and the world) could be improved through more thoughtful communication. Too often as a leader you find yourself in a pressurized environment where you feel a need to respond quickly. Sometimes just taking a deep breath and giving yourself a few moments to think through your response can make all the difference in the quality of your message and the listener's response. Sometimes a message of great importance or heavy emotional content needs considerable study and perhaps the time to sleep on it.

C5 DO YOU REMEMBER? ... WHAT?   ("How long have you had this memory problem?" "What memory problem?") The mind must do more than just perceive stimuli, process thoughts, and produce messages. It must also provide a vast storehouse for all the person's accumulated meaning. This storehouse is called the memory. Many people speak of having a poor memory; some claim to be memory experts. Wherever you are along that continuum, memory, like all other parts of this process (speaking, listening, reading, thinking), can be improved. Suggestions for improvement are found in Leadership Technique Section 4. As a leader, if your memory is poor or rusty, you will be at a distinct disadvantage in communicating, both as a sender and as a receiver.

Barriers in the Feedback Process

D1 GIVING AND RECEIVING CONTENT FEEDBACK.   The act of *feeding* information *back* to the sender is usually thought of in terms of the content of the communication. In other words, if a person has commented on your report or asked you what you think of the weather, your response to the comment or about the question is content feedback. It is essential if the communication-feedback cycle is to continue. Communication is often painful, but silence kills the process. The now-famous response of the negotiator, "The two parties are still talking," reflects the wisdom that when the talking stops, the shooting starts (in international relations, in business, *and* in marriage).

The content feedback is often blocked and disrupted by many factors. A person who has given honest feedback in the past and been rebuffed may be reluctant to respond. Where there is differential status (the boss asks, "How do you like my new clothes?"), there may be a concern about the feedback. Where the feedback could bring retaliation, it may be blocked by fear. Laziness, indifference, emotions, and confusion can all block the giving of quality feedback.

The sender also has some responsibility for the effectiveness of the feedback exchange. Asking for feedback, attentively listening to the response, acknowledging and rewarding the response can all promote better feedback. Leadership Technique Section 4 presents a method for improving the quality of feedback.

D2 HOW AM I DOING? PROCESS FEEDBACK.   There is another level of feedback just as important as the first. This has to do not with the content of the exchange but with the communication process itself. With every message sent, there is also broadcast an implied question: "How did I do as a communicator?" Contained in this question are the subquestions: "Did you hear me?" "Did you understand me?" "Do you agree with my message?" Life and time do not allow for these questions to be dealt with at the overt level. The sender usually listens to the response, watches the eyes and gestures, and infers the answers to these questions. If the coach asks, "Why did you make that shot?" and the player responds, "I've got to get a new gym locker," an assumption can be made that the process has broken down somewhere. In this case the process may need to be brought to the surface and dealt with as content:

> "Did you hear what I said?"
> "Did you understand what I meant?"
> "Do you agree with my message?"
> "What is your response?"

As with the previous type of feedback, silence and nonresponse (ignoring the sender, no gestures or facial expressions) are serious barriers to understanding.

An appropriate conclusion you might draw at this point is that it is amazing that anyone ever understands anyone else. Communication that leads to understanding is the rare and beautiful exception; misunderstanding and confusion are the rule. You may also conclude that to communicate clearly and effectively is hard work and requires a real understanding of the basic techniques. Some of the more important ones are presented in Leadership Technique Section 4.

Chapter Summary

"The fish is always the last to recognize the water." The objective of this chapter is to sensitize you as a leader to the larger environment that surrounds and affects every one of your leadership acts. You might think of this environment as being a mine field. This chapter has provided you with insights into a number of mines that could explode your best efforts to produce results and be successful. Spend some time planning before an act and analyzing after the act the challenges and problems of your bureaucracy, its built-in constraints, the group climate, and the communication network. This ongoing process can spell the difference between failure and success.

Leadership Technique #3
OD—ORGANIZATIONAL DEVELOPMENT, NOT OVERDOSE

Organizational development is a process of planned, organization-wide change that utilizes behavioral science, applied by internal or external change agents, to create a self-renewing organization that can solve problems and adapt to environmental changes. That sentence is a mouthful, but each part is essential to describe this important approach to leading an effective, thriving organization.

Qualities of Organizational Development (OD)

1. OD is a process of planned change. What this means is that the effort involves a series of changes, or interventions, in the ongoing, normal activities of the organization. These interventions are carefully planned and executed to bring the organization from a currently less desirable state to a state of more effective functioning. This effort becomes an ongoing process, not an event or series of events.

2. True organizational development occurs organization-wide. In management development the client that is changed is the manager. In organizational development the client that is changed is the organization. While the process and techniques discussed here can be used on a smaller unit, such as a department or work group, they are usually applied to whole organizations.

3. OD utilizes behavioral science knowledge. The change strategies that are applied to the organization are based on concepts developed in disciplines such as psychology, sociology, management, and organizational behavior. These concepts have been developed and tested in real-world settings using an action research model.

4. The concepts are applied by internal or external change agents. A change agent is a person who is a facilitator of change. In many situations an external consultant is used to guide the process. OD consultants come in three varieties: excellent (5 percent), adequate (15 percent), and those who create more problems than they solve (80 percent). You can tell the good ones because their goal and the results of their efforts will be to develop processes in your organization so that it can help itself. As

the organization becomes self-renewing, internal OD personnel are often used on an ongoing basis.

5. The goal of OD is to create a self-renewing organization. Such an organization has developed the systems and processes to use its people in processes of planning and problem solving that help the organization adapt to internal and external changes and successfully accomplish its goals. Self-renewing organizations are discussed in more detail later in this section.

Assumptions and Values upon Which OD Is Based

Unlike the "value-free" social sciences (which, of course, aren't value-free), organizational development is a normative behavioral science. That is, OD is based on a set of openly held assumptions and values. Organizations that would not subscribe to these values would probably not want to engage in the OD process. Here are a few of the more significant concepts that form the foundation of OD:

1. Individuals have drives toward personal growth and development.
2. Needs and aspirations of people are reason for organized effort in society.
3. All people have value, and their welfare should be a concern of the organization.
4. Work and life are richer and more meaningful if feelings, hopes, and needs are a legitimate part of the organization's culture.
5. People wish to be accepted by and to interact cooperatively with at least one small reference group.
6. People are capable of increased effectiveness, and they can contribute to their reference group's solution of problems.
7. Leadership and maintenance functions must be shared with group members.
8. Suppressed feelings and attitudes have a negative effect on the group's problem solving, personal growth, and job satisfaction.
9. Decentralization or power equalization is to be valued and attained.
10. Win/lose strategies are not as optimal to the solution of most organizational problems as win/win strategies.
11. OD takes time, patience, and a long-range time perspective by key organizational leaders.
12. Improved performance from OD needs to be sustained by changes in the total human resource system of the organization.

Basic Organizational Concerns

There are certain questions that every organization must answer if it is to survive and thrive. Some of the key questions include:

1. What are our mission, our goals, and our objectives?
2. What goods or services will we produce?
3. Who will be our key people?
4. How will these people be structured to get the job done?
5. What facilities, materials, and technology will we need?
6. What will be our values, norms, rules, and policies?
7. What will our division of labor, positions, and roles look like?
8. How will we recruit, select, orient, and train our people?
9. What informal and formal rewards will we provide those who are productive and contributing?

10. How will we communicate information to get the job done?
11. How will decisions be made and implemented?
12. How will responsibility, authority, and power be distributed?
13. What control systems will be employed?
14. How will problems be detected and resolved?
15. How will conflicts and disagreements be resolved?
16. What is the market for our goods and services?
17. How will we price and market our products?
18. How will we monitor and adapt to environmental changes?
19. What will be our ongoing management (planning, organizing, doing, controlling) process?

If the organization is to move from surviving to thriving it must accomplish three broad goals, suggested by the sequence of questions above:

1. The *maintenance* of internal processes and problem solving.
2. *Adaptation* to external (environmental) changes and forces that affect the organization.
3. Development of a favorable method and rate of *exchange* with the marketplace.

In every organization there are a set of built-in tensions. They will always exist, and both sets must be adequately dealt with if the organization is to be effective.

FIGURE 32. Two sets of organizational factors that need consideration

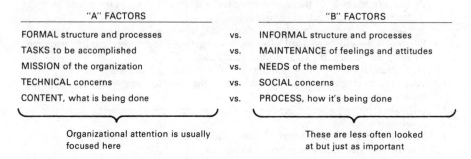

"A" FACTORS		"B" FACTORS
FORMAL structure and processes	vs.	INFORMAL structure and processes
TASKS to be accomplished	vs.	MAINTENANCE of feelings and attitudes
MISSION of the organization	vs.	NEEDS of the members
TECHNICAL concerns	vs.	SOCIAL concerns
CONTENT, what is being done	vs.	PROCESS, how it's being done

Organizational attention is usually focused here

These are less often looked at but just as important

The two groups of factors are intertwined, and both must be attended to. The skillful leader is concerned with both and has designated people and processes within the organization to attend to both.

The OD Goal:
A Self-Renewing Organization

An organization would be self-renewing to the extent that:

1. People affected by the organization (primarily members, but possibly some outsiders) feel a sense of community and perceive themselves to have power and influence and thus to be able to take actions and effect changes in their own interest.
2. Those people have that power and influence and in fact exercise it.
3. There exists a structure and climate that allows organizational members to

exercise and develop their competence; work toward solving individual and group problems; be open, honest, and collaborative; develop an enhanced self-image; have control over their environment to an increasing degree.

4. When all of the above are operating, the organization would have systems that are responsive to forces within and without that are dysfunctional, and would take appropriate action to modify or eliminate them and promote counterforces of development and growth.

Specifically, the objectives of a self-renewing organization would include the following items (you might use these as a yardstick against which to measure your own organization):

1. A climate in the organization that promotes trust, openness, honesty, shared feelings, and mutual respect.
2. A system of communication that provides for the sharing of relevant, helpful, timely information.
3. The location of problem-solving and decision-making responsibilities as close to the information sources as possible.
4. The authority associated with position and role, or complemented by authority, based on knowledge and ability.
5. A feeling of ownership in the members for the goals and objectives of the organization.
6. Collaboration between managers and members in developing plans and controls on objectives and results.
7. Involvement by members in job-related problem solving and decision making, self-direction, and self-controls.
8. An emphasis on conflict resolution, collaboration, and win/win approaches to disagreements.
9. A reward system that recognizes both the achievement of the organization's goals and the development of its members.
10. Systematic procedures for monitoring the external environment and the internal organizational status, for planning and reestablishing goals, for coordinating units and individuals, and for optimizing member involvement.

It's not possible in a general written work to draw a picture of a self-renewing organization. A generic picture would be of little use. An organization's specific picture would require familiarity with a specific organization. Perhaps it's most important to get commitment from all organization members to the values and objectives outlined in this section. A collaborative effort can then be undertaken to create the appropriate structures and processes.

The Organizational Development Process

It should be kept in mind that the purpose of this process is to help an organization develop—that is, to improve (but not necessarily to grow). If an organization is not renewed, either with external assistance or through internal processes, it will eventually develop dysfunctions, atrophy, and die. The plains of bankruptcy are strewn with the bones of once-healthy corporate bodies. OD is designed to take an organization from its current state, be it healthy or ailing, and develop it until it has internal, self-renewing systems. The process is outlined in this figure.

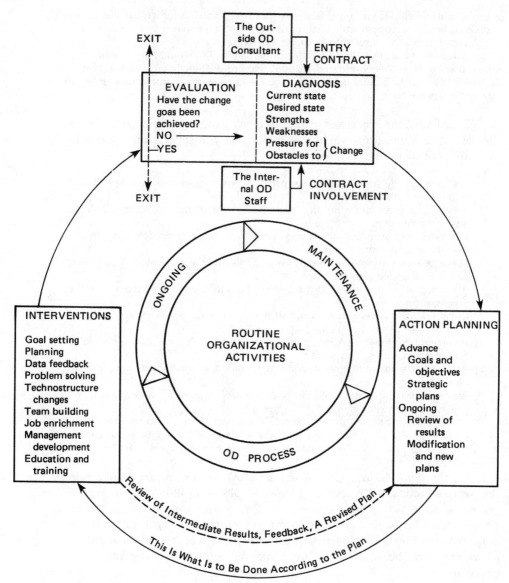

FIGURE 33. The organizational development process

Organizational development is usually undertaken when a need is apparent in the organization. This can include major problems of motivation or lack of productivity, the challenges of a merger, a change in leadership or policy, a desire to modify the structure or the internal processes, or when there is an apparent need for improved planning or communication. Some part of the organization, hopefully top management, will perceive the need and make the contact with the OD specialists, either internal or external. (This description will look at the external OD consultant, though the principles apply

70

equally well to both.) The first step in the process is called *entry*; it involves the consultant actually coming into the organization. How entry is handled is critical to the success of the process. The ground rules, the contract (written or implied), and the initial contact the consultant has with the members of the organization will set the stage for the success or failure of the following steps.

Once the consultant has made entry into the organization, the next step is the *diagnosis* of the current state of things. Clarification is made of the organization's strengths and weaknesses, where things are, where people would like them to be, the pressures for and obstacles against change. (Lewin's force field analysis is a helpful model for this type of diagnosis.)

The next step in the process is *action planning*. There are two types of planning involved in the OD process. The first is an advance component that has to do with establishing goals and objectives and planning strategies for the action steps to follow. The second form of action planning is related throughout the process each time an intervention (change of action) takes place. I worked for a year as an organizational development consultant with the New York City school system. Members of our consulting team would carefully plan each trip and the steps to be taken. Some things occurred as expected, and yet there were many surprises and unexpected events. This required us to meet each week in a debriefing and repeat-planning session.

The planning that takes place is for one or more *interventions* that will be introduced by the consultant. An intervention is a change in the normal activities of the organization. If the members are making automobiles or hamburgers and someone comes in to analyze and feed back what's going on, or to change the organizational structure, or to take everyone away to a three-day planning session, that's an intervention. (I know the term is not a normal part of most people's vocabulary. During the New York project I hung a sign in my office reading "One year ago I didn't even know what an intervention was, and now I are one.") Figure 33 shows nine of the most common interventions. Reference to any of the outstanding OD books in the bibliography will outline in detail how they are to be carried out.

When the interventions are considered completed an *evaluation* is conducted to determine if the planned goals of the change have taken place. If the answer is yes and the organization has now established internal systems for ongoing process maintenance, the OD consultant can (should) exit the system. If the organization is self-renewing, there should be processes and procedures integrated into the new normal activities for periodic diagnosis, action planning, intervention or fine tuning, and evaluation. If the changed goal has not been achieved, the organizational development cycle commences again.

Conditions that Facilitate Successful Change

Any effort to create organizational change is more likely to succeed if:

1. Leaders and top management recognize the problems and believe that applied behavioral science can help.

71

2. Personnel and reward systems in the organization are modified to support the change.
3. Involvement of organizational members in every phase of the process is widespread.
4. Assumptions, values, theories, and practices are shared openly and carried out visibly.
5. Those involved work for early, visible success and build upon those successes.
6. Efforts are made to internalize the processes of the "action research" cycle: diagnosis, data gathering, feedback, action planning, action (intervention), and evaluation (diagnosis).

ILLUSTRATIVE CASE C

The Case of Chris Laine

Chris Laine leaned against the fender of the silver Porsche and stared out at the rows of waves marching endlessly against the base of the Palos Verdes cliffs. It had been eighteen months since Chris had started his own business, a small electronics firm, in the garage that stood separate from the home. At first it had just been family and friends working together to manufacture and market a small hand calculator. But Chris had developed an interesting twist for his calculator, and during the past few months sales had soared. The operation had been moved to a small plant, forty new employees had been hired, and still the orders came in faster than they could be filled. But this was only the beginning of the challenges. Chris had turned the organization and supervision of the employees over to an uncle, and this had turned out to be a disaster. Several employees had complained about Uncle Fred's dictatorial methods and ambiguous policies—before resigning. Now there was talk of forming a union. Production had fallen off, and back orders were piling up. Worst of all, Chris had lost the zest for the job. It just wasn't fun anymore. As the sun slid into the Pacific, Chris repeated the same question over and over: "What should I do? What should I do?"

FUNCTIONAL TYPE   *Chris Laine is the president of a small manufacturing business that is experiencing rapid growth. The situation might be similar to that of a hotel owner, restaurant owner, head of a retail or service firm, or operator of a large-size farm.*

LEADERSHIP FACTORS   *The principles involved in this case include or-*ganizational development, management, *and* team building.

QUESTIONS TO CONSIDER

1. *What basic management principles have been violated in this case?*
2. *What would it help Chris to understand about stages of organizational growth?*
3. *What should be done about the situation with Uncle Fred?*
4. *What steps could be taken to head off the unionization movement?*
5. *What part could a team-building effort play in this situation?*
   What part could a corporate goal-setting and planning effort play?

ANALYSIS   *Chris Laine needs to begin by gaining an understanding of how organizations grow. The field of organizational development offers a number of* books and courses that would be helpful to persons in this situation who want to increase their own understanding. As they grow, organizations, like people, go through stages that have been quite clearly defined. Each stage will bring certain benefits and be accompanied by certain problems. The rapid-growth phase that Chris's organization is in requires the development of competent management and a good delegation and accountability system. Chris's feelings are not unusual for an entrepreneur who has had the thrill of starting a new business, only to become less enthusiastic as the business grows and becomes more bureaucratized. Many entrepreneurs will bail out as the organization moves into departmentalization and will begin a start-up process again.

The employees of this organization need a good **team-building** session. The content of this session would focus on goal and objective setting and a planned division of labor. Accountabilities would be established, an appraisal system agreed to, and a system of informal and formal rewards designed. The process outcomes of such a session would include clearer communications, more group unity, and increased esprit de corps.

It would be helpful to establish a corporate planning procedure that moves forward on a routine basis and monitors growth in relation to goals. These team-building sessions should be repeated on a semiannual to annual basis to ensure that all parts of the train are running on the same track. A good organizational development consultant might be involved on an as-needed basis.

Summary

Organizational development, if clearly understood and successfully practiced by the manager and the organization, can lead to the achievement of goals, the early identification of problems and their creative solutions, and developing an organization that continues to develop and self-renew. This process of organizational development does not have to apply just to large corporations or government agencies. The same process is equally appropriate for a school system, for a classroom within that school system, or for a church within a community. All of these principles apply to that most important organization, the family. Parents would be well advised to follow the process that is outlined in the first two chapters of this book: establishing clear goals for their family, consistently monitoring whether or not those goals are being accomplished, and occasionally using this organizational development process to diagnose problems within the family and to develop ways of creating changes that are likely to lead to a more successful accomplishment of the family's goals.

Leadership Technique #4
HOW TO GET THE WORD
THROUGH THE SYSTEM:
COMMUNICATION IN PRACTICE

The last section in Chapter 2 identified sixteen major barriers to communication understanding. Presenting solutions on how to resolve each of these barriers would require another book. Some solutions are obvious, such as "Get the receiver's attention," or "Make your messages timely." Some solutions require additional knowledge and practice. This leadership-technique section focuses on five approaches to improving your communication:

1. Developing clarity in what you say and write.
2. Improving your listening skills.
3. Thinking clearly.
4. Improving your memory.
5. Giving effective content feedback.

"Is That Clear?" "Huh?"

Whenever our sending a message results in misunderstanding, we find it easier to blame the problem on the receiver rather than on ourselves. There are several specific actions that can be taken to enhance the possibility of sending a clear signal.

First, clarify your own meaning before trying to send it on to someone else. This will include not only the content of what you wish to send, but also the purpose and intent. What are you really trying to accomplish with this meaning? What is the scope of the message? A more-focused communication has a better chance of being understood.

Second, code your message in the most understandable form. Use words and sentence construction appropriate to the listener (nine-year-old child versus Ph.D. friend, for example). Try to be concise, while giving an appropriate amount of detail.

Third, consider the person or audience with whom you will be communicating. What is their level of preparation to receive this message? That can be a question of both their knowledge and of their listening skill. If the message is an order or instruction to a subordinate, does he understand why he's being asked to do this thing? Have you defined the appropriate standard of performance? Will there be follow-up? What kind and how much? Some of your people just need a general sense of what is needed and they will take it from there, whereas others need a step-by-step explanation in minute detail.

Fourth, consider the environment in which the communication is taking place. Are there sources of interference that you will need to deal with? Are there physical barriers to being understood? Will your relationship in time and space be helpful to your message, and if so, where can it best be found? Are there any norms, traditions, or values that must be taken into account?

Fifth, consider your method of communication. Would this message be sent verbally or in writing? If in writing, in what format: memo, note, letter, contract? If orally, should it be delivered one on one, to a small group, or to a large audience? Would any audiovisual materials help others to understand? Could someone assist you in giving this message? (Could someone else do it better?)

Sixth, consider the feeling climate of this communication. Are there feelings of mutual trust and respect, or will you encounter suspicion or opposition? What emotional tone will your message have? Will what you say and do be seen as consistent?

These six areas are part of the planning and preparation essential to sending a clear message and getting your meaning across. If you are unwilling to consider these questions, you must ask yourself if you are really serious about being understood.

Improving Your Listening Skills

Research has shown that you spend most of your day communicating. Of that communication time, half is spent in listening. The other half is divided between speaking, reading, and writing. For students or trainees, the listening time may increase to 75 percent.

Research further shows that you only understand 50 percent of what you hear, and that your "active forgetting process" removes much of that half within a day. This lack of understanding is extremely costly. In dollar terms, consider a twenty-dollar "misunderstanding mistake" made by each of your employees each working day for a year. The total cost is staggering. The social costs of lack of understanding—when you look at divorce, suicide, employee sabotage, crime, alcoholism, racial conflict, and mental illness—are enormous.

The sad thing about these statistics is that everyone can learn to listen with much greater efficiency. Unfortunately, this skill is rarely taught in the public schools. To improve your listening ability, here are some key rules:

1. Convince yourself that listening does not come naturally and that you're going to have to work at it.

2. Begin with the attitude that everyone has something important to say. Find out what there is in their communication that is helpful and interesting to you.

3. Avoid judgment on either the content of the message or the method of transmission. Prejudging often turns to bigotry—that is, a closed mind.

4. Examine your motives. Do you only listen to what has value for you? Could you listen to help the speaker, even if your listening did nothing more than communicate, "I value you and what you say"? Better still would be a motive of using what you hear to help the other person.

5. Try to minimize distractions. Shift the site of the exchange, if possible. Where distractions can't be avoided, increase concentration with eye contact and posture.

6. Do something active. Note taking can assist in fixing ideas in your mind. But you must work at developing an effective note-taking system or part of the message will be lost in the process.

7. Ask questions. This maintains the attention of both sender and receiver. It also requires activity on your part to formulate good questions. Your questions give process feedback to the sender that you were hearing and understanding.

8. Try to summarize or restate what you have heard. Reflect back the sender's content and emotional tone. Summarize the message and check to see, "Is that what you mean?" Go over your notes with a couple of reviews to fix ideas securely in long-term memory.

These eight rules, if consistently applied, can increase your understanding and professional satisfaction in communication situations. Learn them and teach them to those you communicate with. The savings could be enormous.

Look at the following two puzzles. Which one bothers you more?

FIGURE 34. Puzzles for the left and right brain

A.	B.
Three men checked into a hotel. The clerk told them the cost of their room was thirty dollars, so each man paid ten dollars. After they had left for the room, the clerk discovered that he had made a mistake, that the room was only twenty-five dollars for the night. He gave a bellhop five dollars to return to the men. On the way to the room, the bellhop reasoned that there was no way that three men could divide five dollars. The bellhop pocketed two dollars and returned one dollar to each man. Each man had therefore paid nine dollars for the room. Three times nine is twenty-seven, plus the two dollars the bellhop kept makes twenty-nine. What happened to the other dollar?	
If this one bothers you more, you are possibly an analytic, left-hemisphere thinker.*	If this one bothers you more, you are possibly an intuitive, right-hemisphere thinker.

Because of current attention given to the subject, many people are now aware that they carry inside their skulls not one, but two brains. The right and left hemispheres of the brain each perform important, if separate, functions. Without getting into the issues of redundant abilities and shared information between the two hemispheres, I'd like to present a basic description of the two and the implications for one's thought process.

The left hemisphere of the neocortex (outer brain) is concerned with the ability to read, write, speak, calculate, analyze, and evaluate. The left hemisphere processes information in series. This side seems to be more involved with the conscious, rational side of nature. This is the source of analytic thought.

The right hemisphere is concerned with the ability to recognize patterns, view objects three-dimensionally, understand music, rhyme, recognize faces, do holistic reasoning, construct objects, do art, and engage in nonverbal thinking. The right hemisphere processes information in parallel. This side seems to be more involved with the emotional, subconscious, and dreaming side of nature. This is the source of intuitive thought.

The powers and results produced by these two sides of the brain vary from person to person, from situation to situation, and from moment to moment. It is evident that progress requires some integration of the products of the two. This has two implications. First, you should determine where your strengths lie (math versus art, for example, or speaking versus composing).

*Before you burn up your brain filaments trying to solve the puzzle on the left, you should recognize that it involves nines, which often work as "magic numbers." If you follow the logic of the puzzle exactly as presented there is no solution.

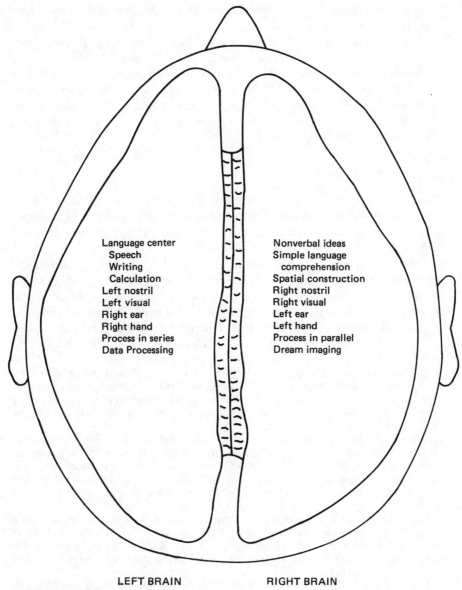

Language center	Nonverbal ideas
Speech	Simple language
Writing	comprehension
Calculation	Spatial construction
Left nostril	Right nostril
Left visual	Right visual
Right ear	Left ear
Right hand	Left hand
Process in series	Process in parallel
Data Processing	Dream imaging

LEFT BRAIN   RIGHT BRAIN

FIGURE 35. The hemispheres of the brain

You may then want to team your efforts with those whose strengths proceed from the other hemisphere. The analytic person needs the artist to enhance creativity; the intuitive thinker needs to expose his or her ideas to scrutiny and application.

The second implication has to do with you as an individual expanding your ability to utilize the full capacity of your brain (both hemispheres). If you are the analytic type, you might consider instruction in art, sculpting, music, brainstorming, and poetry. If you are the intuitive type, you might consider writing prose, public speaking, math puzzles, law or business cases, computer programming, or science.

As the leader of a work group, team, or family, you have a responsibility to see that the group's approach to problem solving, decision making, communication, planning, and use of leisure time involves the strengths of both analytic and intuitive skills. Without one, the result is chaos; without the other, the result is sterility. In either case, the chances of surviving (never mind thriving) on the part of the family, the team, or the business are significantly diminished.

Remembering to Remember

The story is told of the man who went to the psychiatrist and said, "Doctor, I have been experiencing a real serious problem with my memory." The doctor said, "How long has this problem been with you?" The man replied, "What problem?"

Successful functioning on the part of a teacher, executive, quarterback, mother, maître d', engineer, or cab driver is unlikely without a good memory. Remembering, like listening, can be improved. It's a cop-out to say, with resignation, "I just have a poor memory." It's also evident, from the previous section, that some will remember faces better than numbers and vice versa.

Here are a few memory devices that can assist you in keeping track.

1. Repetition is a key to remembering. What is 12×12? How do you know? How did you learn the multiplication tables? Rote learning is a key to the success of schools, advertising, and political rhetoric. Can't remember a name? Repeat it immediately upon hearing it. Ask how it is spelled. Say it again. Use it immediately in speaking to someone else.

2. Visualization requires connections to be made between the right brain and the left brain. Thinking of the number 111 as three candles on a cake, or picturing Mr. Bristle with porcupine quills coming out of his coat, helps to fix the name or number in your mind. Develop a visual picture for each number, zero through nine, then associate the pictures to remember with addresses, area codes, and other important numbers.

3. To aid in remembering names, associate the first name with the last to form a picture. The more exaggerated and comical, the easier it will be to recall. Bill Fisher might conjure up an image of a person who has dumped all his bills into a pond and is now trying to retrieve them with a rod and reel. Mary Green might be two aliens at their wedding. You get the idea.

4. When you have to remember a list of items, try linking them together. For example, think through the sequence of breakfast relative to your grocery list and picture eggs, milk, flour, pancake syrup, orange juice, napkins, dishwasher soap. Or try tying your number visuals into the list. The numeral 1 might be a soldier, 2 a cobra, and so on, through 9, a balloon on a string (make up your own visuals). Now, at the gas station you need to:

1—Check the tires (a soldier shooting air into the tires).

2—Check the wiper blades (a snake coiled in the windshield), through . . .

9—Fill 'er up (a balloon filled with gasoline).

5. Details such as points in a speech can often be recalled through the use of acronyms and key words.

S uccess is something we all desire. It requires four things on our part.
E nthusiasm for the product and the benefit it can be to the customer.
L earning about the product and how it meets a need.
L eading the person to the closing question, where he or she can choose between the two options you present.
S incere service as a follow-up to the sale.

(The content of ideas and stories would fit in between each of these five main ideas.)

The keys to a better memory, then, are:

Repetition
Visualization
Association
Exaggeration
Linking
Acronyms
Key words

Think you can remember them?

Giving Effective Content Feedback

When a person asks "Did you read my report?" or "What did you think of that shot?" or "Do you love me?" they are asking for content feedback. The feedback process can be blocked for many reasons, including fear, indifference, differential status, and previous bad experiences with giving open, honest feedback. If the feedback process is blocked, the two-way transfer of communication stops and relationships die. Assuming that you desire to give effective feedback, this section will present several principles you must consider.

Objectives of Effective Feedback

To be of value to the person receiving it, feedback should be:

1. HEARABLE.   As presented in the theory section, the two major sources of interference are internal and external. The major internal barrier to hearing feedback is the person's own defensiveness. Using the approaches in the human relations section of this book and the communication techniques discussed below will go a long way toward overcoming that defensiveness. The external noise that interferes with hearing needs to be avoided, minimized, or talked over.

2. TESTABLE.   Feedback is of more value to the person receiving it if it can be tested, verified, and confirmed or denied by others. To meet this criterion it must be presented in the form of directly observable data (DOD). Feedback

based on DOD presents to the other person what you saw and/or heard along with any inferences you made from that. This information can be confronted or confirmed by the person receiving it.

3. USABLE.   Feedback is obviously most helpful if it can be used. But this criterion is difficult to determine. If people say that they want and can use the feedback, it is not necessarily so (they may be too defensive). If people do not want the feedback, they may still need it and may be able to use it. One possible guide is to ask yourself, "If I give this feedback, who's more likely to benefit, them or me?"

4. BASED ON INCREMENTAL CHANGE.   People mostly change in small, imperceptible ways. The chance of any feedback you give another person causing major changes in his or her views or personality is virtually nil. Aim for small but important, specific information the person might need. Over time, these can accumulate to major alterations in the individual. As you are about to give feedback to anyone, ask yourself, "Is it hearable, testable, usable, and based on incremental change?" If the answers consistently come out "No," you can predict that in the long run you will pay some interpersonal dues.

Techniques of Effective Feedback

As important as knowing why you are giving the feedback is knowing how to give the feedback. Listed below are five standards to keep in mind if you wish your feedback to be effective.

FIGURE 36. Techniques for giving more effective feedback

Feedback will go from *INEFFECTIVE* to more *EFFECTIVE* as it goes from . . .

GLOBAL $\longrightarrow$	SPECIFIC

Feedback that is vague and sweeping.
   "You're stupid."
   "You're a lousy employee."
	Feedback that is incremental, founded in DOD.
	   "When you don't get the report done at three o'clock as you promised, I feel angry and disappointed."

MAXIMALLY EVALUATIVE $\longrightarrow$	MINIMALLY EVALUATIVE

Feedback that connotes right or wrong, good or bad. Positive evaluations are not necessarily helpful because they imply the possibility of being withheld or replaced by negative.
   "You did a lousy job of scoring tonight."
   "You did a great job of scoring tonight."
	Reduce the evaluation or judgments you make of the person's behavior. Feelings should not be judged: They are not right or wrong; they just are.
	   "Members of the team who cannot score consistently will not be able to play."

MAXIMALLY ATTRIBUTIVE $\longrightarrow$	MINIMALLY ATTRIBUTIVE

Guessing at another's thoughts, feelings, motives, values, put in the form of feedback.
   "I know you're very angry at me and I know exactly how you feel, because you always . . ."
	Provide DOD and your inference. This can be denied.
	   "When I hear you raise your voice at me and see your face get flushed, I asume you are very angry."

DELAYED ⟶	TIMELY
The "carpetbagger" approach—saving up negative feedback to dump on the other as a counterattack. Deals with the "there and then."	Not necessarily immediate, but as soon as possible after the incident, under the appropriate circumstances (such as privately). Deals with the here and now.
"You've said several times over the last six months that you would never . . ."	"When you came in late last night, I was upset because . . ."

UNWANTED ⟶	WANTED
If you perceive that the feedback is not wanted, you should test it.	Obviously the value is improved if it is asked for and accepted.
"Do you want me to tell you why . . ."	"Since you asked and I assume you really mean it, I want to tell you that . . ."

To be sure, there are pressures as part of the heat of battle. In the midst of an argument or heated discussion at work or at home, it is not always possible to remember and use all of these guidelines. But after a less-than-successful feedback exchange, if you will sit down and review these rules, you will usually see why your feedback was less than effective, and how to do it better the next time. Over time, your ability to give feedback successfully will improve.

3
Whom: The Leader's
Followers

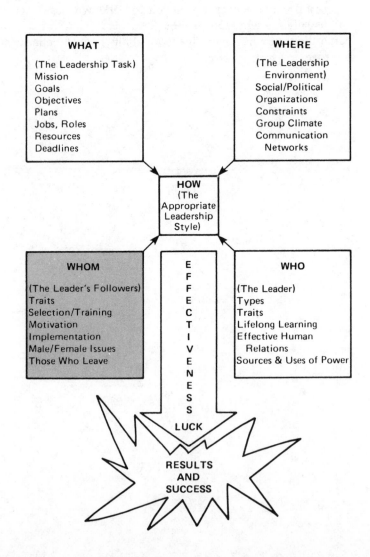

WHAT	WHERE
(The Leadership Task)	(The Leadership Environment)
Mission	Social/Political
Goals	Organizations
Objectives	Constraints
Plans	Group Climate
Jobs, Roles	Communication
Resources	Networks
Deadlines	

HOW
(The Appropriate Leadership Style)

WHOM	EFFECTIVENESS	WHO
(The Leader's Followers)		(The Leader)
Traits		Types
Selection/Training		Traits
Motivation		Lifelong Learning
Implementation		Effective Human
Male/Female Issues		Relations
Those Who Leave		Sources & Uses of Power

LUCK

RESULTS
AND
SUCCESS

The close relationship that one would expect between a leader and his or her followers often does not exist. Leaders are often threatened by strong followers who fear they may be displaced. More often, leaders are confused by behavior of their followers that does not meet their expectations. "I don't understand why these people at PDQ don't respond to me; my way of dealing with people always worked when I was at XYZ!" "Those Boy Scouts drive me nuts! They never show me the respect I get from my people at the office." These expressions of frustration and puzzlement are typical of leaders who have not sensitized themselves to the sometimes subtle, often dramatic differences in followers. Even if the other variables have been taken into account, if the leader does not adjust the style of leading to the differences in the followers, the results can be disastrous.

FIGURE 37. The challenge of leadership (By permission of Johnny Hart and Field Enterprises, Inc.)

Figure 38 enumerates a number of key traits that ought to be carefully considered by each leader in making a decision as to what is the appropriate leadership style to use with a particular group.

For the purpose of analysis, each trait may be examined along a continuum of possibilities, with the worst possibility on the left and the best possibility on the right. It is obvious that one would lead a subordinate who is rebellious, not overly bright, and of questionable loyalty differently than one would lead a subordinate who is cooperative, creative, and dedicated to the cause.

The problem with applying this insight in any pure sense is twofold. First of all, there is the complexity of individuals. What of the person who is made up of a disturbing mixture from the two extremes?

Second is the further complexity of groups of subordinates. Within a given group, the leader will find a challenging mixture of individuals who range from loyal to disloyal, from experienced to wet behind the ears, from motivated to those whose hand must be held on every project. This is the

FIGURE 38. A simplified continuum of followers' traits

TRAITS OF THE FOLLOWERS	UNDESIRABLE	ACCEPTABLE	MOST DESIRABLE
Intelligence	Low	Average	High
Experience	Limited	Moderate	Considerable
Ability	Limited	Moderate	Extensive
Loyalty	Low	Average	High
Attitude	Poor	Fair	Good
Knowledge	Limited	Moderate	Extensive
Cooperation	Poor	Fair	Good
Trustworthiness	No	Somewhat	Unquestionably
Willingness to follow instructions	Seldom	Usually	Always, with insight
Decision-making skill	Poor	Fair	Good
Problem-solving skill	Limited	Moderate	Extensive

challenge of leadership in the real world as opposed to the abstract leadership of the textbooks. Remember, I promised you that there would be no simple cookbook solutions to this complex art of leadership!

However, there is value in the insight on the differences in sub-ordinates. The leader must make an effort to get to know each follower personally, to make a realistic assessment of the strengths and weaknesses, needs, interests, and ambition of each. This will provide concrete guidelines for leadership approaches that are most likely to work with that person. It will be of great assistance in the areas of motivation and personalized rewards. It can be done, but it requires caring, effort, listening, thoughtfulness, and time. Many leaders feel they are just too busy for these qualities, and they pay a heavy price.

In dealing with the group, while the individual differences will be noted, some generalizations can usually be made about the types of followers in the group. There will be certain stereotypical characteristics to a group of Ph.D. engineers, versus a group of laborers digging a ditch, versus a group of preschoolers, versus a group of new recruits. Each will have some generaliza-ble characteristics which, when considered in conjunction with the task, the environment, and the leader's proclivities, will provide guidance in a leader-ship style that is most likely to work.

More will be said about the impact of the follower's traits on the leader's style in Chapter 4. The point here is to recognize the importance of getting close to "the troops" and being observant of each of them. It is helpful in this regard if the leader is involved in the important processes of recruiting, selecting, orienting, and training new group members.

RECRUITMENT AND SELECTION OF FOLLOWERS

Recruitment is the process a leader of an organization engages in to create a pool of possible new members. *Selection* is the process that is used to screen that pool of potential members and make the important decision of who will be invited to join. The importance of effective recruitment and selection cannot be overemphasized. Mistakes made in this initial stage of creating an organization, group, or marriage will have long-range negative implications on everything that follows.

However, the process by which organizations and future members come together is ethereal at best. Sometimes the contact is initiated by the member, often by the organization. Sometimes each side is clear about exactly what they are looking for; at other times they are fuzzy and vague. Sometimes there is a clear understanding of what each has to offer; whereas at other times, the case is understated or oversold. Mistakes at this point will continue to produce negative consequences on into perpetuity.

Consider the case where the organization is going out looking for warm bodies. This can be done publicly through advertising, semipublicly through personal networks and contacts, or privately through the use of headhunters. In each case the assumption is that the organization is clear about what it is looking for in a new member and what it will have to offer when it finds the right person. In reality, both of these turn out to be optimistic assumptions. If the job description is vague, it is hard to find the right person to fit it. This can produce a waste of time and emotion on both sides during this process. A second problem is that the organization, in trying to attract the best possible members, will often overstate the attractiveness of the position, oversell the glamor of the organization, or overdramatize the cause. This obscures the chances of getting the best "fit" for the position and can lead to disappointment (and possible sabotage) later on. Problems are created for the new member, but even greater headaches can be experienced by the leader, which is why the person who will be the eventual supervisor should be involved in this process. The best policy is one of clarity and honesty. If the leader/organization sets this example, the applicant may respond in kind.

Once the pool of potential new members has been created, the leader/organization has to make a selection. Having created the greatest group in the world to choose from is not useful if the wrong person is subsequently selected. It is helpful to keep the objectives in mind. One objective is to insure that the experience, abilities, and skills of the new member will fit the existing position. A second concern is how the new member will fit with the leader and the group. A third objective is to assess whether the position will fit the needs, interests, and goals of the individual.

Fitting the person to the job is important, but difficult. One reason is that it's hard to determine exactly what the person is able to do. We try to make predictions from the documentation provided by the candidate, but how helpful is this, really? What is learned from an examination of a transcript, for example? Sam Jones has a 3.95 GPA and Ron Ross has a 2.60. Which of the two is more intelligent? Which one studied harder? Which one learned more? Which one knows better how to take standardized tests? Which one cheated on exams? Which one was dating the college president's daughter? See what I mean?

In addition to the transcript, the applicant will usually provide a resumé or vita. In the premodern era these were unattractive but readable and honest. Today every applicant has read one of the how-to books, and we are in the age of the Madison Avenue resumé. I have sat on many search committees and looked at hundreds of these resumés. One sent a cover letter that began, "If you are not interested in hiring the most brilliant, talented, personable individual in the world, throw this in the trash!" You guessed it, right in the round file. Another applicant, wanting to have a resumé that would stand out, printed it on bright orange paper. When photocopied, however, all of the copies came out black. I dutifully stapled all the black sheets together and circulated them to the committee members with the attached note: "Do we really want to hire this person?" We didn't! Another applicant sent in an impressive resumé for a position in marketing. The committee was impressed and authorized me to invite the person in for an interview. Just as I was about to do that, we received a second resumé from the same person, for a completely different position in finance. Same person, same life, but totally different presentation of experience. The obvious point here is to try to disregard the window dressing and look for content with substance.

The process is supposed to be further assisted by obtaining letters of recommendation. When was the last time you saw a letter of recommendation written in any but glowing terms? And with the new laws opening all these "confidential" letters to the applicant, the recommendations have become even more glowing. If one were to believe these letters, we are in the age of the "bionic applicant."

Those who survive the paper screening are invited in for interviews. This process at least enriches the data. We now have some idea of the person: sex, race, age, physique, dress, personal style, speaking ability, problem-solving ability, and the ability to respond under pressure. (All those things we were not allowed to find out on paper. Anyone who thinks these factors are not major considerations in the selection process is living in a world of cotton candy!) The interview should probe to confirm or reject the documented experience. It should, if properly conducted (it seldom is), establish those more ethereal but very important qualities of thinking, speaking, relating, dealing with pressure, and so on. This does not mean you have to follow the model used by recruiters at the Harvard Business School, which most resembles a scene out of *Marathon Man,* but you must keep in mind that if you are hiring this person (as opposed to obtaining someone for a volunteer position) you could be making a $200,000 decision.

The interview also allows you to deal with the second objective of determining the fit between yourself, as leader, and the potential new member. All of the science aside, the key is how you feel about one another. The existence or nonexistence of mutually felt good vibrations is not to be discounted. You cannot entirely let your heart rule your head, but if you don't get a good feeling, you may want to trust that instinct regardless of how good the person looks on paper.

Furthermore, if you choose really excellent people, you can cover a multitude of your own weaknesses. Good people always hire better people;

bad people always hire worse people. One multimillionaire said that he discovered early in life that he was not very bright or hard-working, so every chance he got he hired people who were brighter and harder-working than he was. He then created an environment in which those people could do their thing, and they made themselves and him very wealthy. You can do the same.

In terms of the person's ability to do the job, the bottom line has to do not with resumés or with interviews, but with doing. The best process, if the organization has the time, money, and ability, is to provide some type of an assessment center. Here the applicant is placed in a simulated environment (low-cost and low-risk with mistakes) and asked to perform under expert observation. The results the person can produce are good, bad, or non-existent.

The final objective of the selection process is to look at the decision through the eyes of the potential new member. To paraphrase the old marriage axiom, "If you find the perfect person for the job, will he or she be satisfied with you?" It is important that you and the applicants be clear about what they want and need to get from a job, their interests, goals, and ambitions. Being clear about this at the front end of the process can save frustration, wear and tear, lawsuits, sabotage, and turnover down the road. Promises made should be kept. The reality of the job should fit the recruiting hype. If not, watch out. You may have a million-dollar quarterback who never plays!

ORIENTATION FOR NEW MEMBERS:
WHAT IS A NICE PERSON
LIKE YOU DOING
IN A PLACE LIKE THIS?

The ideas that follow are focused on new employee orientations, but the principles apply to new members coming into any new setting. The basic thrust of orientation is to lower the new members' anxiety sufficiently so that they are able to concentrate on what needs to be done and become contributing members as soon as possible.

The traditional approach to orienting new employees ranks somewhere between useless and counterproductive. A large organization will bring fifty new employees, total strangers to one another, into a large auditorium. On the stage will be half a dozen VIP's from the organization. The new members will be welcomed and then shown a frothy twelve-minute propaganda film on the organization, complete with band music, and designed to persuade the uninitiated that all employees working here love their jobs and that the organization is saving the world. The VIP's will then take five minutes each to tell stale jokes and to describe their areas of responsibility (all totally meaningless to the initiates, since they have no idea why this information is useful at this point). The personnel director then passes out the employee handbook, a three-by-five-inch blue book with 120 pages of policies and

87

rules. The group members will then be asked if they have any questions. None will be asked. No one has the slightest idea what an intelligent question might be at this point, and they're not about to make fools out of themselves asking a dumb one. The personnel director concludes the meeting: "Seeing no questions, we'll adjourn with the reminder that our doors (waving to the VIP's) are always open to you." (The VIP's will yawn and look at their watches.)

The new members, with anxiety levels now triple what they were prior to orientation, will go to meet their supervisors (or employees to whom this "distracting" task has been delegated). If the supervisors and new employees are meeting for the first time, the anxiety will be further increased. The bewildered persons will be led down a maze of halls to the new office. There they will be introduced to seventeen co-workers, instantly forgetting each of their names. This will be doubly anxiety-producing, because from this point on each of the co-workers *will* know the new employee's name. The new workers will be given a cursory tour, shown to their desks or machines, given some work to do, and told to "come and see me any time you have any questions." The paralysis caused by the increasing anxiety now approaches catatonia. Research indicates that the anxiety lasts for months, resulting in lowered productivity and other problems such as absenteeism.

Better approaches to orientation are available. They have been developed through research at corporations that are innovative leaders in personnel management, such as Texas Instruments Corporation. The process begins by asking the questions, "What causes anxiety in new employees, and what is the best way to lower it?" Anxiety is caused primarily by confronting the unknown, in this case unanswered questions. The new approach to orientation may begin in the same traditional way, but when the new employees are brought into the office they are instructed that their initial task is to ask as many questions of as many co-workers as they can. This question asking may take two hours or two days. The rest of the staff has been instructed to cooperate by answering frankly and completely anything they are asked.

Initial questions are usually safe ones, such as where is the rest room or the drinking fountain. As the new workers feel more comfortable, they will get down to the nitty-gritty questions such as, "What is the boss like?" and "What do I do if I get sick?" Since many of the important questions that need answers are not intuitively obvious, and many of them are cyclical during the year, you can assist the new employees by providing them with sample questions that they need to seek the answers to. These questions can be in the form of a lengthy checklist or on a form with a few questions for each day and a place to review and check off with the supervisor at the end of the day.

Does all of this question asking really make a difference? Where the new orientation approach has been used, the results have been dramatic. Not only was productivity higher and attained in less time, but these individuals showed higher morale and lower rates of tardiness, absenteeism, and turnover. Every company, agency, church, school, club, and team would benefit from adopting some form of this improved approach to new-member comfort and productivity.

Once upon a time in the world of work, people learned how to do by doing, not by going to school. If you wished to learn how to bake bread, make a carriage, draw up a contract, or perform surgery, you apprenticed yourself out to an experienced master and watched, assisted, copied, and mastered. Today the apprentice/master model of training has largely vanished, often to our loss.

Training in industry commenced in a major way during the two world wars. Many new employees, including thousands of women, were coming into the work force with no experience. They had to get their skills up to speed quickly. Most of the standard approaches to vocational education and training were adopted during this period. These practices are still found in offices and factories today.

There is a distinction between teaching and training. Learning forms a continuum that goes from knowledge to attitudes to behavior (performance) to skill. Using that concept, the distinction between the two might be viewed as follows:

TEACHING

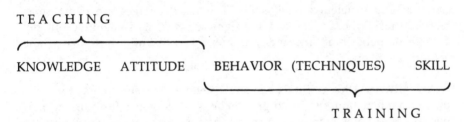

KNOWLEDGE   ATTITUDE   BEHAVIOR (TECHNIQUES)   SKILL

TRAINING

A further distinction might be made in that teaching is often concerned with knowledge for knowledge's sake, whereas training is concerned with passing on information and techniques that have immediate practical application. There is much overlap between the two, and the distinction is often lost on the trainee. Leaders must function as both teachers and trainers. The following section deals with the role of the leader as a teacher.

Training provides benefits for the organization in higher productivity, less waste, increased safety practices, less turnover, and better communication. Training benefits the leader by reducing problems that have to be solved, increasing the amount and quality of delegation, providing more satisfied workers, and developing group cohesion and morale. Training helps the employee to be better prepared for the job, decreases his chance of injury, increases her chance of promotion, and leads to increased job satisfaction and self-esteem.

Approaches to Training

There are many different ways that people can be trained. Each method has advantages and disadvantages. Some of the more common approaches are analyzed here for your benefit.

ON-THE-JOB TRAINING is the oldest type of training and is still found in many organizations, especially the trades. It has the advantages of limited expense, low cost and risk; it is directly relevant to the work to be done; and it integrates the employees and provides trainer and trainee with a feeling of accomplishment. The disadvantages include the possibility of creating resentment, jealousy, and fear on the part of the trainer; the difficulty of finding qualified employees to do it; and the limitation to individuals or small groups.

THE LECTURE METHOD is more a form of teaching and is often found in educational organizations. It provides information in a quick, efficient manner, and it can be well-organized and follow a logical sequence. The disadvantages are that it can be boring and irrelevant, it may not meet the learner's needs, there is a lack of involvement on the part of the learner, there is often no opportunity for feedback, and it usually has no affective or behavioral component.

THE CASE METHOD is used in many business schools and some organizations. It has the advantage of dealing with real problems and real situations; it teaches that there is no one "best" answer; and it develops the learner's analytical and problem-solving skills. The disadvantages are that it may frustrate those who are looking for right answers, it is cognitive but not affective or behavioral, and many trainers do not know how to use the method effectively.

SMALL-GROUP DISCUSSION can show several different points of view; it stimulates interaction, can build group cohesion, provides for different perspectives, and helps members to refine their values. The disadvantages are that it can be dominated by one person, it may miss the point or issue, it may lead to erroneous conclusions, it may not be practical, and it can become "the blind leading the blind."

LARGE-GROUP DISCUSSION also clarifies points of view, helps members to answer questions, gets members involved in the learning, and develops the individuals' strength in defending themselves. The disadvantages are that it may waste time and wander, it may be dominated by one or two members, it may miss the point of the discussion, it may confuse instead of clarify, and the members may have little to contribute.

SIMULATIONS (sometimes called simulation games) pique the interest of the learners, provide for learner motivation, provide instant feedback, are often low-cost, and can be constructed to resemble the real process. The disadvantages are that simulations may be complex and difficult to administer, may be costly, can be limited in scope, and the learners run the risk of mistaking simulation for reality.

PROGRAMMED INSTRUCTION can be in a written form only or can be used in conjunction with a computer program. It has the advantages that the learner can proceed at his or her own pace, the information comes in small units, there is immediate feedback, it is logical and well-organized, and it develops the learner's problem-solving skills. The disadvantages are that it requires the learner to be motivated, it can be costly, it is abstract and cognitive only, there is a lack of interaction with others, and it may not be relevant.

ROLE PLAYING involves the learner in taking the part of another and seeing how that person might handle a problem situation. It provides interest and involvement, it involves learning by doing, it creates empathy for others, it creates options that have to be dealt with, and it includes affective and cognitive components. The disadvantages are that it is very threatening to some, the point may be missed, the learning may not transfer to the learner, and it can lead to game playing instead of sincerity in the real situation.

PROJECTS are a form of learning by doing. They get the involvement of the learner, having affective and behavioral components, allow new perspectives, and provide for new experiences. The disadvantages are that there is a need for leadership and direction by someone experienced, those learning may not have the skill to do the project, and it may lead to unnecessary specialization.

The Leader as Trainer

Leaders and managers must view training as one of their main responsibilities. While the actual training may be shared or delegated, the responsibility for seeing that it is done, and done well, cannot. The leader who does his or her own training will have an important opportunity to develop a rapport with the follower that cannot be gained in other ways.

The preparation for conducting training consists of covering the four bases suggested by this book. *What* is the purpose of providing the instruction? What is to be taught? Learning objectives should be established for the overall program and for each individual unit of instruction.

Where is the training to take place? What is the climate for learning? What resources are available? To be effective you need to be sensitive to those for *whom* the instruction is provided. What are the learners' innate abilities for learning? How much knowledge and experience do they already have to build on? What is the person's learning style? Chapter 4 presents the Kolb theory of four distinct learning styles based on abilities with abstract conceptualization, active experimentation, concrete experience, and reflective observation. Figure 39 presents a picture of those four styles; Figure 40, discussed in the final part of this section, shows the relationship of learning style to teaching method.

Finally you must consider *who* you are as the trainer and what you bring to the learning situation. Your training style will often be based on your own learning experiences over the years. After twelve years of public school and ten years of higher education, I had to make a major effort to change my style when I began training in 1970. My only experience had been with the

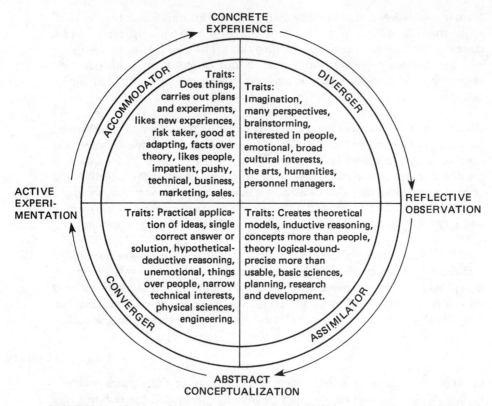

CONCRETE
EXPERIENCE

ACCOMMODATOR

Traits:
Does things,
carries out plans
and experiments,
likes new experiences,
risk taker, good at
adapting, facts over
theory, likes people,
impatient, pushy,
technical, business,
marketing, sales.

DIVERGER

Traits:
Imagination,
many perspectives,
brainstorming,
interested in people,
emotional, broad
cultural interests,
the arts, humanities,
personnel managers.

ACTIVE
EXPERI-
MENTATION

REFLECTIVE
OBSERVATION

CONVERGER

Traits: Practical application of ideas, single
correct answer or
solution, hypothetical-
deductive reasoning,
unemotional, things
over people, narrow
technical interests,
physical sciences,
engineering.

ASSIMILATOR

Traits: Creates theoretical
models, inductive reasoning,
concepts more than people,
theory logical-sound-
precise more than
usable, basic sciences,
planning, research
and development.

ABSTRACT
CONCEPTUALIZATION

FIGURE 39. The experimental learning model and four learning styles (Model designed by the author after the theory in Kolb, David A., Irwin M. Rubin, and James M. McIntyre, *Organizational Psychology*, 2nd Ed., Englewood Cliffs, N.J.: Prentice-Hall, Inc., 1974)

lecture/discussion/note-taking method of learning. I had to adapt myself to experiential methods without fearing the loss of control. Methods of instruction can be changed. Your method will be based on your personality, learning style, experience, and teaching philosophy.

Consideration of these four factors will lead you, the leader, to your final decision: "How will I present the information and evaluate to see if it has been learned?" Referring to Figure 40 you can see that there are several instructional methods that can be used. Each will be well suited for certain learning styles and not well suited for others. That means you have to test and identify the styles and then divide the larger group into smaller, homogeneous learning-style groups. Each group could then receive a different mode of instruction. The other option is to use several different training methods, on the assumption that each group member will gain some things from the session.

Once the information has been presented, the control step is exercised. This consists of critiquing the group in some way and providing reinforcements that strengthen desired performance. Your goals in training are to change behavior in an improved way and to provide positive attitudes and

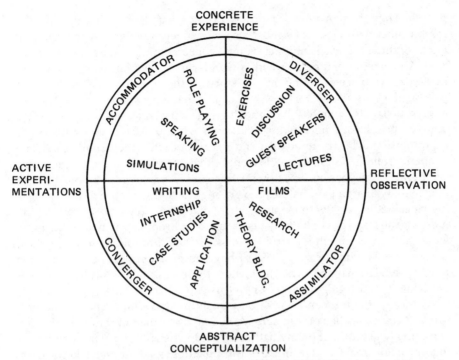

FIGURE 40. Teaching/learning techniques associated with Kolb's four learning styles (from *Organizational Psychology*) (Model designed by the author after the theory in Kolb, David A., Irwin M. Rubin, and James M. McIntyre, *Organizational Psychology*, 2nd Ed., Englewood Cliffs, N.J.: Prentice-Hall, Inc., 1974)

self-concept. The standards established and methods of critique should strengthen the learner and provide quality future results.

Training is essential to any collective endeavor. Reviewing the methods and mode of instruction is a reminder of the challenge training presents. The implications of good or poor training will stay with leaders, coaches, and parents for a long time. Training is a key to whether the leader and the group will succeed or fail in achieving their established objectives.

HOW TO GET MOTIVE/ACTION RATHER THAN MOVEMENT

Motivation is one of the most important tools in the leader's kit, and it's probably one of the most misunderstood areas in all of the leadership and management literature. To understand what is being talked about when the topic is motivation, it is helpful to begin by understanding the word *motivation* itself. Take the word and split it (MOTIV /A TION), then add an *e* to the first word and a *c* to the second to get two words, *motive* and *action*. A motive is a reason for doing something, and an action is the doing. Each of these qualities must be present in the doer if you are going to have motivated people. They must have a reason for doing what they are doing, and the reason must be theirs. They must also be actively involved in the doing. If either of these aspects is missing, you've got something, but not motivation.

An example of a person with a wonderful motive but without any real doing taking place is found in the story of the woman who goes to the psychiatrist and says, "Doctor, my husband has a problem." (Note that it's always the spouse who has the difficulties!) The psychiatrist says, "Well, since your husband isn't here, why don't you explain to me your husband's symptoms, and I'll try to see if I can figure out what the problem is." The woman replies, "I'd love to. I would love to talk about my husband's symptoms." She goes on, "Doctor, my husband is employed as a door-to-door salesman by a large national firm. Every night when we retire to bed, he sets his clock radio for five A.M., and when that clock goes off at five in the morning, he leaps out of bed, rushes into the bathroom, switches on the light, looks at himself in the mirror and says, 'You are the world's greatest salesman!' " The doctor says, "Well, I have no problem with that; he sounds fine to me." The woman says, "Just listen; there's more. You understand that I'm lying in bed trying to sleep when this clown comes back into the room, gets down on the floor and starts doing pushups, and with every pushup he's saying, 'You can sell! You can sell!' Well, I take as much of this as I can take, and I finally get up, put on my bathrobe, go downstairs, and start cooking his high-protein breakfast. He finishes the pushups, goes in and takes a cold, bracing shower, gets out and gives himself a good rubdown with a coarse towel, puts on his very best three-piece sales suit, gets his sales kit, and comes downstairs to eat his breakfast. He pops in his three vitamin C pills and proceeds to the living room, where he selects one of our John Philip Sousa marching albums, places it on the stereo, and immediately begins marching around the living room saying, 'You're a salesman! You're a salesman! You're a salesman!' " The psychiatrist, perplexed, responds, "Well, madam, I really don't understand what the problem is. It sounds to me like your husband is a highly motivated salesman. What is the problem?" The woman replies, "Doctor, I can't get the man to leave the house!"

The challenge that managers and leaders have is that many times the reason for doing is theirs, not the doer's. In fact, they envision their responsibility as getting people to do something. I think practicing managers have been misled in this regard because they often take their questions from social scientists. If the social scientists ask dumb questions of a theoretical nature, the managers tend to follow their example by asking dumb questions of an applied nature.

For example, for a long time psychiatrists and psychologists were asking the question, "Why do people move?" It has been my experience that every time a person goes to a leadership or management development training program, when the subject of motivation comes up, participants rub their hands together gleefully and say, "Oh boy, we're finally going to find out how to get our people to do something!" Let me now answer that first profound question of the social scientist. The reason people move is because they are alive. If you have some people in your office or shop who are not moving, bury them—they are deceased. Therefore, it is superfluous to ask, "How do you get people to move?" If you have people in your organization who are alive, they will be moving.

This concept was forcibly brought home to me when I took a job as a social worker for the Department of Welfare in the heart of the Appalachian poverty belt. I was given a case load and was told that my responsibility was to get out to my clients and to get them doing something. So I marched out into the "hollers" with my middle-class value system to get these people to do something, and I found that my clients were very actively involved in doing. Actually, it was the things that they were doing that were creating some of their most serious problems.

So a second type of question that a social scientist might ask is, "Why do people move where they move?" In other words, "Why do people do what they do?" And the question that the manager or leader might ask is, "How can I get people to do what I want them to do?" In order to understand how to get people to do things and what it is that moves people to act, consider Figure 41.

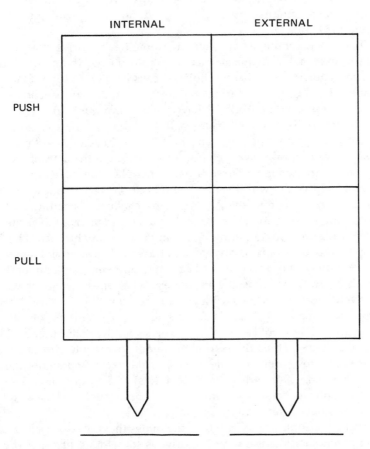

FIGURE 41. Model for analyzing why people do what they do

There are two columns in Figure 41, Internal and External, and two rows labeled Push and Pull. Within the four panes of this little window can be diagrammed all the possible reasons why anyone does anything. People act because they are internally pushed; they act because they are internally pulled. They act because they are externally pushed or because they are externally pulled. Now let's look specifically at the labels for the categories contained in each of the panes of this window.

Those things that internally push people to do what they do, to move, the psychologist labels *drives*. A drive is an inner urge or feeling that we must move, that we must act, that we must accomplish a certain thing. No one knows exactly what a drive is or where it comes from. Perhaps the best lay description that has been given is the one given by Flip Wilson in his Geraldine routine. Geraldine has just come home from the store, where she has purchased a fifty-dollar flaming red dress. The boyfriend, Killer, is very attracted to the dress until he finds out the price. At that point Killer, who is about to kill her, says, "Why did you spend fifty dollars of my hard-earned money on that dress?" Geraldine's instantaneous response is, "The devil made me do it!" The implication is that when we have a drive inside us there is a devil (or something) with a pitchfork prodding us or pushing us along to do the things we do.

When the psychologist talks about people having drives, he is talking about a process that for the normal person is controllable. If the drive is out of the person's control, then the psychologist calls it a compulsion. One of the great labels that I acquired during my graduate studies in psychology was "obsessive-compulsive neurotic." I have used this phrase on myself many times; it has been used on me by others. If it is too viciously applied to me, I immediately respond by pointing out that all of us have our own little areas about which we are obsessively compulsive. There are those in life who are compulsive hand washers. These are the people who suffer from germ phobia and feel that the world is filled with bacteria that are out to get them. For the compulsive hand washer, life's greatest challenge is getting out of the rest room without touching the doorknob, sometimes referred to as the Lady Macbeth Syndrome. Some people are compulsive straighteners. These are the people who come up to your desk and are always straightening and putting everything in order. They feel a need to line things up and make sure that they are parallel to the sides of the desk. Then there are those who are compulsively messy. I worked with an attorney one time whose desk was piled four feet high with manila folders full of legal briefs. Once I had identified myself, he would walk slowly around his desk, and then suddenly leap in and pull one of the folders from the middle of the pile. Amazed that he was always able to retrieve my file when I could never find anything in my own alphabetized, color-coded file system, I asked him one day, "How are you always able to come up with my file immediately?" His wonderful answer was, "I have a sense of the layers."

Internally, people are pulled to do the things that they do on the basis of what the psychologist calls *a need*. If a drive is something inside of you that is pushing you or prodding you to accomplish or achieve, then a need is like a series of containers that, when not filled, contain a vacuum which you are moved to fill. For example, every night when you dream, even though you do not often remember your dreams, you engage in a number of Walter Mitty activities in which you are kind, wonderful, gracious, courageous. In fact, in our dreams each of us is a perfect "ten." While dreaming, you fill up all of your internal containers so that your needs are satisfied. However, as you launch out into the day, you might arrive in the office and have someone storm in and point out that you made a mistake on the report you filled out the previous day. You suddenly find out that you are down a pint of self-respect. You might then feel a need to go around and get strokes from other people, saying, "Am I not wonderful? Wouldn't you like to say something nice about me?"

Understand that needs, like drives, are simply concepts that have been developed to explain why people do what they do. You cannot cut a person open and say, "There is the liver, there is the pancreas, and there is the need for achievement." It isn't in there; it doesn't exist, in fact. It is very difficult to identify people's real needs by observing their behavior. Sometimes people's behavior will suggest exactly the opposite of what they really need. People who have a real need to be ignored will find themselves dancing on the tables and those who have real needs for attention will often sit quietly in the corner. Most of the major motivational theories are "need"-based. The reason for this is not because it is the most accurate way of describing human behavior, but because most of the major motivational theories were developed by people who had a psychology background.

Referring back to the analysis "window," notice that the second column looks at the external factors that move people to do what they do. From the study of people it is apparent that it's not just forces inside individuals that get them to move and to act, but also a number of external forces in their environment. The right-hand column of Figure 42 lists some of those external forces that push people to do what they do.

If you wanted to get an individual to move from Point A to Point B, what are the ways that you could go about doing that? The first possibility is that you could physically push him, force him to do what you wanted him to do, or move him where you wanted him to move. The problem with using external force to get people to do things is expressed by the law of physics that says, "For every action, there is an equal and opposite reaction." When you push people, there is a very real possibility that they will push you back, and if their force is greater than your force, you lose. Externally pushing or forcing people to get things done was given the clever acronym of KITA by Fred Herzberg. KITA stands for a "kick in the lower back." Herzberg points out that in the world of work there was a great deal of negative physical KITA that was used to get people to move, to do something. He pointed out that this has slowly fallen into disfavor and is not found much in the American work force today. Physical KITA has two very distinct disadvantages. Number one, when you force or push people to do certain things, the bruises, the evidence of your forcing, shows externally, so the technique you have used is obvious to others. Secondly, as just pointed out, when you push people, since

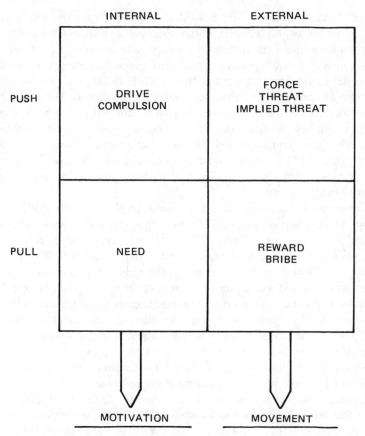

	INTERNAL	EXTERNAL
PUSH	DRIVE COMPULSION	FORCE THREAT IMPLIED THREAT
PULL	NEED	REWARD BRIBE
	MOTIVATION	MOVEMENT

FIGURE 42. A model of why people do what they do and what leads to motivation rather than movement

their reaction goes through their autonomic nervous system, which is the reflex system of the body, there is a very real possibility that they will push you back.

So, because this is not a very sophisticated way to get things done and because there is likely to be a reaction, today, Herzberg says, we have changed our approach to getting people to move, and we're now more likely to find people using negative psychological KITA. You find out what it is that people want and need, what their fears are, and then, in Herzberg's words, "You play a tune on these, and they'll tell you where the gold is buried." Negative psychological KITA has two advantages over its older counterpart. First of all, when you hurt people using psychological KITA, the telltale evidence is not there. When they bleed, they bleed invisibly. And secondly, when you use this approach to get the people to do things, if they accuse you of using psychological KITA on them, you can accuse them of being paranoid. (There is the poster that shows these two are not mutually exclusive. It has eyes peering out of the dark, and says, "Even though you're paranoid, it doesn't mean they're not out to get you.") In classic economic terms, this approach was known as the stick approach. The classical problem was how do you get the donkey to pull the cart of wood to market when the donkey has no interest in pulling the cart of wood to market? The answer was that you get one of the logs out of the cart, walk up and hit the donkey between the eyes. The donkey says, "Nobody ever explained it to me that clearly before," and begins to pull the cart.

Is there a more subtle way of using an external push to get people to do what we want them to do? The answer is yes. This second external push approach is called a threat.

One of the things we know about human beings is that they are averse to pain and would prefer to avoid it. A threat, then, is a promise of future pain based on the person's action in relation to what you want him to do. So let's go back to the original example. Let's assume that you want to move someone from Point A to Point B. Let us also assume that she has no need or motive or drive to want to make that kind of move. You ask her to move; she refuses. You then open up your briefcase and take out your 250-volt electric cattle prod. You plug it into the wall and say, "I really think you ought to want to move over to that other place," and then you zap her with the cattle prod. She comes a foot and a half out of her chair, shouting, "No one ever explained it to me that clearly before," and then she moves to the other point.

Once you have zapped her a few times with the cattle prod, and she understands that there is pain associated with not doing what she's asked to do, you and she can move to an advanced form of external push, a more subtle approach, and use an implied threat. Suppose you have a visitor from the regional office and you want to demonstrate how highly motivated your employees are. You go to the person who understands the threat of the cattle prod, which you have hidden in your briefcase, and you ask him to move from Point A to Point B. He smiles, pants expectantly like Pavlov's dog, and trots quickly to the other side of the room. If he should hesitate at all, all you have to do is glance at the briefcase to remind him of the implications of not carrying out your request.

Obviously, in real life you don't use cattle prods to get people to move, but our world is filled with negative external pushes (threats). Threats of being fired, threats of being reprimanded, threats of having your pay cut, threats of being transferred to another place, threats of not getting the promotion that you want—all types of threats are used to get people to do the kinds of things others want them to do. So there are very powerful negative sanctions that can be used to make sure that you respond to these external pushes. Research has indicated that this approach to movement is the *most commonly used* and the *least effective* of any of the approaches. (I think it is interesting to note that if you take a look at our child-rearing practices, this approach is most commonly used there too.)

There is a different way you can externally get people to move, and that is by pulling them, by providing something attractive to them on the basis of their needs and wants. You can provide them with a reward, a golden ring that will cause them to ride again and again on the merry-go-round of life, trying to capture that ring. This seems to be a more positive approach, but as

Herzberg points out, "All you've really done is change the source of KITA from negative to positive. You are still kicking the people, but now you're doing it frontally." This, in classic economic terms, is known as the carrot approach. Instead of hitting the donkey continually, which tends to broken down donkeys and people, the idea is to attach a carrot, a desired object, on a string, put it on a stick, and dangle it in front of the donkey to get it to pull the cart to market. (You never really hear the end of the story to find out whether or not the donkey actually gets to eat the carrot.)

A negative term can be attached to this concept of reward: *bribe.* If a threat is a promise of future pain, a bribe is a promise of future pleasure or satisfaction.

When I talk to people in the world of work today I ask them if they see any difference between those who are coming into the work force today and the kind of people that they saw in the work force twenty years ago. Their answer is "absolutely yes." And I say, "What do you see as one of the major differences?" Their response is, "When I came to work twenty years ago, if my boss told me to jump, I jumped, or if I was real assertive I said 'how far?' And then I jumped." These managers continue, "When I come to my employees today and tell them to jump, their response is 'Why? What's in it for me? What will I get if I jump?' " Where have employees internalized this idea that they are to be rewarded, that they are to get something for their good behavior or their good choices? I think it comes from several sources. Perhaps it comes from an approach to child rearing that says there must be an explanation for everything that is done. These days we cannot just say to the child, "Don't set fire to Daddy's foot!" Instead, we have to go through an explanation that says, "You really ought not to set fire to Daddy's foot because if Daddy's foot is burned, he'll have to go to the hospital. And if he goes to the hospital, he can't work. And if he can't work, he won't get paid. And if he doesn't get paid, you won't be able to get the chewing gum that you wanted at the store."

Secondly, it has something to do with the results of what might be called the supermarket syndrome. The supermarket syndrome is a relationship occurring between parents and their children that begins to teach them about the way the world works or the way they can expect the world to work. The first phase of this training occurs the first time the parents take their three- or four-year-old to the supermarket. Children are very curious, and they can find a number of ways to destroy anything they can get their hands on. The first thing that Junior is curious about is what happens when the bottom can in the pyramid of tuna fish cans is pulled out, and he finds out. He is also curious about what happens when he takes that long row of carts in the store and charges it toward the front plate-glass window. So after a very bad set of experiences at the supermarket, the next time the parents go, the second phase of the training occurs. The parents say to Junior, "I'm going in the store to do the work that I need to do. You stay here in this car and don't you touch anything." The parents remind him that they still have the electric cattle prod at home. The parents go in the store and do their twenty minutes of shopping, and when they return to the car they find out that the child has dismantled the AM/FM radio, has let the air out of all four tires, and is in the process of removing the windshield.

During the third trip to the store the process of bribery begins. The parents say to the child, "I am going into the store to go shopping. I want you to stay here in the car. Don't touch anything. If you are good and haven't touched anything when I come out, I will bring you a treat." When they return to the car, this time the child is sitting angelically on the front seat, hands folded, eyes gazing toward heaven, singing "Ave Maria." The first time this approach is used, the parents can get away with paying off the bribe with a one-cent gumball. If you ever wondered why all those penny and nickel machines are sitting by the door in the supermarket, that is the bribery section of the store.

The problem with this approach is after a few repetitions the child is a little older and a little smarter and now begins the process of escalating demands. When you ask the child to stay in the car and not touch anything and you'll bring a treat, the child says, "What's the treat? What's the payoff? What am I going to get for being good?" And when the parent responds and says, "I'm going to bring you one of those gumballs," the child responds, "That's not good enough." The parent asks, "What is it that you want?" The child responds, "I want a package of Hubba Bubba." Now the parents accede to this demand and say, "Well, you know that's only twenty-five cents—what the heck." What they don't realize is that the demands have just escalated by 2500 percent, from a penny to a quarter. This procedure can keep up indefinitely. The next time the child will want the entire candy section, and eventually will be demanding everything, including the blonde clerk working at check stand number three.

So it shouldn't be surprising that after having gone through a child-rearing practice like this for so many years, following the same procedure in the school system, where the gumballs of grades are dangled in front of them, by the time people get into the work place they have developed the orientation that they will not do anything that is right or anything that is required of them unless some appropriate reward payoff or some sort of bribe is provided.

By now a most important insight should become clear. Looking down the two columns of Figure 42 on page 98, what must be understood is that any actions that are produced in people by external forces, whether they be positive or negative, are going to lead those people only to movement. Such forces will never lead to motivation. The reason for this is inherent in the definition of motivation that started this section. In motivation the motive or the reason must be internal, must be part of the doer. Therefore, it is only when people are acting on the basis of their needs or wants or drives that the leader is going to get motivated individuals. The task of leaders or managers or supervisors or coaches or parents, then, is to get to know their people extremely well and find out what they want and what they need to get from the situation they're in and the kind of work they are doing. Then they must find ways of creating mental, emotional, and actual links between the wants and needs of those people and the goals and objectives of the organization.

To the extent that people can see a way of meeting their needs as they help the organization achieve its goals, you will have successful organizations and happy, satisfied, and fulfilled people. When people do not see a relationship between the fulfillment of their own needs and the accomplishment of the goals of the organization, the leader must resort to threats or bribery. The question leaders have to ask themselves is, "Am I interested in having motivated people working with me and for me, or am I only interested in movement?" Most claim that they are interested in motivation, but by the way they act it is evident that all they are interested in is having people move and do the things that *they* want them to do. Motivated people in an organization move and act in very different ways from those who are operating on an external stimulus because the motive, the locus of action, is located inside each individual.

Motivational Theories

The three most famous motivational theories are all based on the concept of needs. This is not because needs are the best or the only appropriate way of explaining human behavior, but because all three of the theorists who developed these views of motivation were psychologists or had a psychology background. I refer to Maslow's hierarchy of needs, Herzberg's two-factor theory, and the research done by David McClelland of Harvard University. This section of the book will present the Maslow theory and the McClelland theory. The Herzberg two-factor theory is discussed in detail in Leadership Technique Section #2, on job enrichment.

Abraham Maslow's widely quoted hierarchy of needs gives the leader some important insights in terms of how to work with and motivate followers. It also has some difficulties and some cautions related to its use. Maslow identified five major areas of needs which all human beings have. He showed further that these major categories of needs arrange themselves in a hierarchy, an ordered ranking in which some are more important or more basic than others. (Refer to Figure 43.) The most basic level of needs, the base of this triangle that Maslow used to represent the hierarchy, consists of the physical needs of the body: breathing, the need for water and food, rest, exercise, and so on. All of these needs are basic demands for physical survival, and the statement "Man does not live by bread alone" applies only when man has all the bread that he needs. When there is a lack of bread, the thing the person is more interested in than anything else is being able to eat. So at any time people experience deprivation at this lowest level, their concern is going to be for the things of that level and not for the higher-level needs.

The second level is the level of safety, of security. People want to be sheltered. They want to be protected. They want to know that their lives can be relatively predictable. All of the norms, customs, and traditions that we have in our culture, which are discussed in Chapter 2, are designed to give life that structure and predictability which is so important to people.

The third level of needs Maslow presents are what he calls social needs. Man has the need to give love; to receive love; to belong, to be a part of, and to be included in things that are going on. One would assume that by the time this third level of needs is reached we would be pretty well beyond concerns of physical survival, yet the information received from many of the orphan-

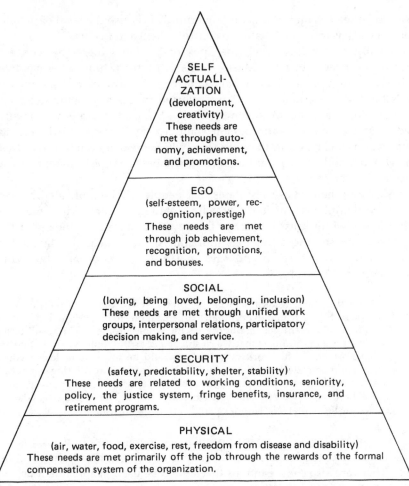

FIGURE 43. Maslow's hierarchy of needs and its relationship to the work place

ages in Europe following World War II indicated that children would often lie down and die, not from the lack of food or warm clothing, but from a lack of love, from a lack of belonging. This is a very strong and powerful motivating force in the lives of many people. One need only remember the testimony given by John Dean in the Watergate trials when he indicated that he knew what he was doing was wrong. He knew it was illegal, yet he felt that not to do these things would exclude him from that circle of people who had access to the President.

The fourth level of needs is the level of ego or self-esteem needs. This has an internal component where persons want to feel good about themselves, to have self-confidence and self-respect. It also has an external component in which people want to receive recognition and praise and honor from other individuals. This is also a very powerful motivating force in people's lives, and many of the positions they occupy, the roles they play, and the physical objects that they are able to accumulate are all symbols of this desire to be seen as important and powerful. This is also the level of people's control needs, wanting to be able to control others and events.

Finally, the highest level, the apex of Maslow's hierarchy, concerns those needs related to what Maslow calls self-actualization. This has been probably the most misunderstood and controversial of all of the basic moving needs Maslow presented. Some have referred to this as a being need, and some as a spiritual need. Most commonly it is referred to as a developmental need. If at the ego level the person wants to say "I'm okay," then at the actualization level he wants to be able to say, "I know that I can improve, that I can get better and grow. I want to become the best possible person that I am capable of becoming."

Maslow's theory basically states that people will be motivated by each level of need until it is satisfied, at which point their concerns will come at the higher levels within this hierarchy. Taking this assumption initially at face value, you can see the difficulties individuals often encounter in modern organizations. Robert Townsend says in *Up the Organization* (New York: Knopf, 1970, pp. 139–140)

> We know that these first three levels are pretty well satisfied in America's work force today. So we would expect man's organizations to be designed to feed the ego and development needs. But there's the whole problem. The result of our outmoded organizations is that we're still acting as if people were uneducated peasants. Much of the work done today would be more suitable for young children or mental defectives. And look at the rewards we're offering our people today: higher wages, medical benefits, vacations, pensions, profit sharing, bowling and baseball teams. *Not one can be enjoyed on the job.* You've got to leave work, get sick, or retire first. No wonder people aren't having fun on the job.

The value of Maslow's theory is to provide a general sense of what it is that motivates people, the basic needs they have, and a rough ordering of those needs. There are also some cautions that should be used in applying Maslow's hierarchy of needs too directly to specific individuals whom you lead. The first caution has to do with the overall theory of the hierarchy itself. The concept, when it is presented in the form of the triangle, gives the impression that until the needs at a given level are completely satisfied, the person's attention does not turn to the other, higher levels of needs. This is unrealistic, especially when we're looking at people in a relatively normal situation where there is not, for example, serious deprivation of physical needs. You might conceptualize the theory differently, as shown in Figure 44.

Looking at the concept in this way, you can see that all of the levels of needs are functioning simultaneously, although at any given point along this continuum one level of needs is going to be more significant in the focus of the individual than the others. This helps you to better understand where people are, and also to realize that they have concerns and issues at other levels of needs besides the areas of their primary concerns.

A second caution that needs to be given concerning Maslow's hierarchy of needs has to do with the fact that in looking at this hierarchy, you would always believe that an individual would be primarily motivated by his or her concern for safety and security much more than by concerns relative to

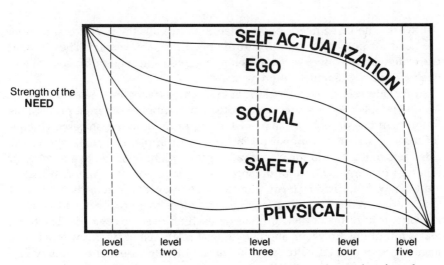

FIGURE 44. A reconceptualization of Maslow's hierarchy of needs

actualization, for example. When the hierarchy is used in this way, it simply is not able to explain the behavior of an individual such as a martyr, a person who would give up his or her life to be actualized—for a principle or for a particular valued objective. Yet history shows that this behavior has occurred on a number of occasions, and therefore there are certain circumstances under which the hierarchy is turned absolutely upside down.

The third and final caution has to do with a warning to leaders and to managers and parents not to apply this model of needs too directly to any given individual. Each person is going to be different, and his or her own particular internal hierarchy and the complex relationships between her or his various wants and needs are going to be quite different. You must find out what the person's particular "hot button" is and then design a system of incentives and rewards that particularly appeals to the individual. If the person is looking for opportunities to advance, you are not going to motivate him with guarantees of security; but if the person is more concerned with safety and security, offering him opportunities to advance is only going to frighten him and is not going to get out of him the desired behavior you are looking for.

The other motivational theory to be examined is David McClelland's theory of the need triad, the three basic need factors, which, if related to Maslow's theory, constitutes the three higher levels of Maslow's hierarchy of needs.

McClelland, a Harvard psychologist, is most noted for his work with the need for achievement. The reader would be well advised to read the literature indicated in the bibliography pertaining to McClelland's interesting work in this field and the type of training and socialization that develop people McClelland identifies as "high-need achievers." My purpose here will not be to explain that theory in depth, but rather to look at the three needs that he identifies and to show how these can create interesting profiles for people in various positions and for looking at various individuals with whom you work. The three needs he has identified he calls the need for affiliation, the need for power or control, and the need for achievement. These would correlate with Maslow's social or belonging needs, his ego or his self-esteem needs, and his self-actualization needs.

An interesting way of looking at these three needs and the patterns they form in people's value systems is to look at a number of different professions in terms of the stereotypes that exist, some of them based on research conducted on various vocational positions. For example, Figure 45 shows the three sets of needs and the classifications that might be given to a number of different positions within an organization. Again, you are cautioned that in working with individuals you cannot stereotype them according to what "secretaries are like" or what "engineers are like"; you really need to look at individuals in terms of their profiles on each of these three needs. The thing that is intriguing, however, about looking at relationships in this way is how a manager with a need pattern as shown might work most effectively with a secretary with a need pattern as shown, a need pattern quite different from the manager's own. This would help the leader or manager to understand how best to motivate subordinates, and to know what kinds of rewards and incentives could be offered to get the best performance, and to provide the most satisfaction to them.

FIGURE 45. Analysis of various occupations using the McClelland need triad

OCCUPATION	AFFILIATION NEED	CONTROL NEED	ACHIEVEMENT NEED
Accountant	Low	High	Moderate
Attorney	Low	Moderate	High
Clergy	Moderate	Moderate	Low
Coach	Moderate	High	Mod./High
Custodian	Low	Moderate	Low
Doctor	Low	High	High
Engineer	Low	High	Moderate
Executive	Low	Moderate	High
Farmer	Low	Mod./High	Low
Govt. administrator	Low	High	Mod./High
Manager	Low	Moderate	Moderate
Secretary	High	Low	Low
Teacher	High	High	Moderate

ILLUSTRATIVE CASE D

The Case of Fran McEwen

Fran McEwen feigned a small smile at each of the volunteers heading home as they passed by on their way out of the building. Fran envied them, knowing another long night lay ahead, trying to catch up on all that had not been done. As the heavy door was closed, the interior of the building seemed quiet and free from the day's confused hassle. Fran slumped at the table behind the piles of envelopes waiting to be stuffed with fliers and brochures. After many years as a supervisor in the private sector, this opportunity to head up a voluntary political organization presented a new challenge. The workers, all volunteers, showed little interest in efficiency and schedules, and spent much of their time socializing on the job. They often reported late and left early. And what was to be done? You couldn't fire them. "Ah, for the good old days," Fran muttered, remembering how the appearance of the supervisor in the office used to produce an electric response, a mingling of fear and respect. But now all of that was gone. These people were at best indifferent and at their worst indolent. "How do I influence these people and get the job done?" The empty room produced no answer.

FUNCTIONAL TYPE   *Fran McEwen is the head of a voluntary political organization. This situation might be similar to that experienced by the clergy, association heads, club presidents, or recreation directors.*

LEADERSHIP FACTORS   *The principles involved in this case include* motivation, reward systems, *and* uses of power.

QUESTIONS TO CONSIDER

1. *In what significant ways are volunteer organizations different from other places where people work?*
2. *What are the major challenges of managing volunteer organizations?*
3. *What positive and negative sanctions are available to the head of a volunteer organization?*
4. *Can volunteer jobs be enriched? If so, how?*
5. *What sources of power are most applicable to a volunteer situation?*

ANALYSIS   *The key element in this situation is the voluntary involvement of those doing the work. A different set of rewards, management techniques, and approaches to motivation needs to be used with these people. The informal positive and negative sanctions are much more likely to succeed. All the Herzberg factors apply. The work should be made interesting, challenging, and achievement-oriented. There should be recognition and opportunities for enlarged responsibility for those who do well.*

    A second ingredient in these situations is that the sources of power must be altered. Authority and formal sanctioning power are less important. More important in getting things done are charisma, expertise, knowledge, respect, and liking. These situations require more leadership skill than brute force, and those who handle them well should be commended.

Summary

Leaders, managers, and parents will always be concerned with the subject of motivation. The two keys to approaching it properly are, first, to get to know your people well and try to tie their wants and needs to the goals of the organization (group, family). The second goal is to try to create an environment in which the work is interesting, challenging, involving, recognition-oriented, achievement-oriented, and one in which there are opportunities to enlarge the scope of one's responsibilities. In such an environment people will motivate themselves and make themselves (and you) very successful.

TO HELP OR NOT TO HELP:
THAT IS THE KEY
TO INTERDEPENDENCE

One of the oldest recorded questions is also one of the most profound: "Am I my brother's keeper?" Most of the discussions of this question center on the concern, "Who is my brother?" This is an important issue, but because of its widespread treatment will receive only brief attention here. The focus of this analysis will be on the role of keeper or helper.

Whether you take a creationist view of the human race or an evolutionist view, the same conclusion can be drawn: We are all discended from the same source. All lines of genealogy, traced far enough back, will begin to converge. The answer to the first question then is stunningly simple: "We are all brothers and sisters." No one of us is an island; we are all parts of the whole. Every person you associate with is a relative, whether near or distant.

Simply establishing kinship, however, does not define the quality of the relationship. Do you have an obligation to your brothers and sisters? If the answer is no, then a course of *independence* is implied. Since this path has been taken by so few, and since the concern of leaders is with the connectedness of the group, the focus here will be on paths leading to *interdependence*.

Do members of the group have obligations to be keepers of others? A keeper is defined as a guardian, protector, or custodian. These roles on the part of the leader lead not to the desired interdependence, but to *dependence*. A dependent relationship provides short-term satisfaction for both leader and follower, but provide neither with long-range self-actualization.

The process of understanding will commence by defining the three terms and describing their relationship.

FIGURE 46. Three approaches to relationships

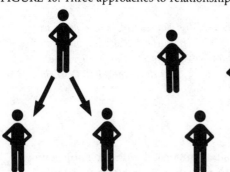  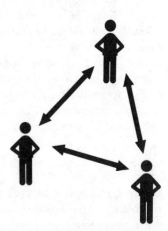

DEPENDENT

to be influenced, controlled, determined, or supported by someone else.

INDEPENDENT

to be free from the influence or control of others, hence self-governing, self-ruling, not connected with others.

INTERDEPENDENT

A mutual dependence that is not uneven. Doing what we can do for ourselves, getting help when appropriate, helping others when appropriate.

The process in relationships is normally to work from dependence to independence to interdependence.

Two questions must now be addressed, substituting the word *helper* for *keeper* in the question "Am I my brother's/sister's helper?" The first question: Do I have an obligation to help others? The second question: Is it always helpful to help? Each will be examined in turn.

The question of whether or not you have an obligation to help is related directly to what end you are trying to achieve. If that end is independence, then it can be argued that the less help you give, the better. You should help others only to help themselves. This end implies that each goes his or her own way, unconnected by helping relationships (either giving or receiving).

The concept of a self-made person is really a myth, an egotistical illusion. No matter how independent you have been, you are indebted directly to dozens of others for what you have become, and indirectly to millions. For example, what have electricity, printing, the internal combustion engine, shoes, bread, the scientific method, automation, the economy, eyeglasses, agriculture, and the concept of how to write a resumé contributed to your current "self-made" status?

On the other hand, if the end of your efforts is connectedness, whether in the form of dependence or interdependence, then a helping relationship is one clear possibility for achieving either.

To help is to aid, assist, give, share, remedy, relieve, or make easier. But will doing any of these things automatically lead to interdependence? Not necessarily. The question that must first be answered is whether or not to help, then concerns with motives, actions, and techniques can be addressed.

Figure 47 explores the key question of whether or not to help and the related questions of why, how, and to what end.

The potential helper must first deal with two questions: "Have I been asked to help or not?" and "Am I going to help or not?" There is a relationship between these two questions, and that relationship is further complicated by the fact that the related questions can be answered for the "right reason" (symbolized by the + on the diagram) or for the "wrong reason" (symbolized by the − on the diagram).

Look at the upper-left quadrant, as an example, and suppose that someone (a child, an employee, a team member, a follower) asks you to help him or her, and you decide that you will not. Good reasons for making this decision might be that you know he has the ability to do it himself, that you want to give her a chance to grow, or that you know someone else is more competent to help him than you are. The wrong reasons for arriving at this decision might be that you are uncaring or selfish or preoccupied or too busy to sacrifice.

So the first significant issue is, "Are your motives or reasons for helping the best?" Even at this stage of the analysis, it is obvious that the answer to my second question is that it is not always helpful to help.

You next have to concern yourself with the right actions in carrying out the help, if you decide to help. Some of these are listed on the chart, including listening, observing, sensitivity, empathy, and accountability.

FIGURE 47. An analysis of the helping relationship

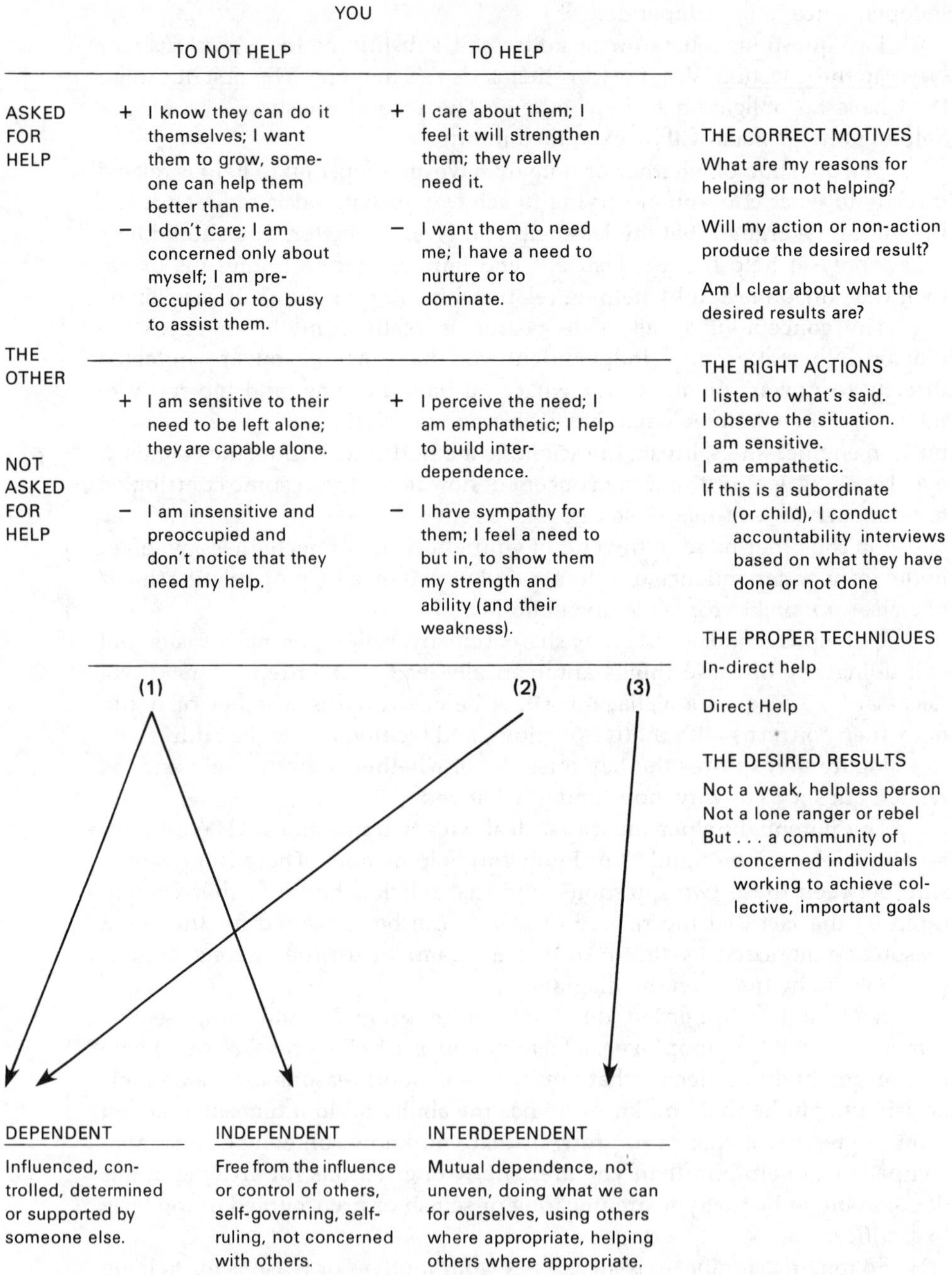

YOU

	TO NOT HELP	TO HELP
ASKED FOR HELP	+ I know they can do it themselves; I want them to grow, some-one can help them better than me. − I don't care; I am concerned only about myself; I am pre-occupied or too busy to assist them.	+ I care about them; I feel it will strengthen them; they really need it. − I want them to need me; I have a need to nurture or to dominate.
THE OTHER		
NOT ASKED FOR HELP	+ I am sensitive to their need to be left alone; they are capable alone. − I am insensitive and preoccupied and don't notice that they need my help.	+ I perceive the need; I am empathetic; I help to build inter-dependence. − I have sympathy for them; I feel a need to but in, to show them my strength and ability (and their weakness).

(1) (2) (3)

THE CORRECT MOTIVES

What are my reasons for helping or not helping?

Will my action or non-action produce the desired result?

Am I clear about what the desired results are?

THE RIGHT ACTIONS

I listen to what's said.
I observe the situation.
I am sensitive.
I am empathetic.
If this is a subordinate (or child), I conduct accountability interviews based on what they have done or not done

THE PROPER TECHNIQUES

In-direct help

Direct Help

THE DESIRED RESULTS

Not a weak, helpless person
Not a lone ranger or rebel
But . . . a community of concerned individuals working to achieve col-lective, important goals

DEPENDENT	INDEPENDENT	INTERDEPENDENT
Influenced, con-trolled, determined or supported by someone else.	Free from the influence or control of others, self-governing, self-ruling, not concerned with others.	Mutual dependence, not uneven, doing what we can for ourselves, using others where appropriate, helping others where appropriate.

If the decision is made to help, a second-order decision must be made in terms of employing the proper helping technique.

Proper communication is one of the key actions in helping, and while this could be discussed in the communication section, it fits most appropri-

110

ately here. Here are my two lists of the Ten Most Helpful Phrases and the Ten Least Helpful Phrases. Ask yourself how many you consistently use from each list.

THE TEN MOST HELPFUL PHRASES

1. I care.
2. I'd like to understand.
3. How are things with you?
4. Let's define the problem.
5. This is what I heard you say.
6. Let me hold you close.
7. Where does it hurt?
8. How does it hurt?
9. Can I do something?
10. (Silence, with concern)

THE TEN LEAST HELPFUL PHRASES

1. You shouldn't feel that way.
2. Why did you do/say that?
3. That's not important.
4. I know exactly how you feel.
5. I know what you're going to say.
6. How come you're not as good as . . . ?
7. Do you want to know what I think? or, Here's what you should do.
8. I told you so.
9. Any phrase that contains the words, *always, never, all the time, everyone,* or *permanently.*
10. (Silence, without concern . . . indifference)

You usually think of helping directly, with advice, assistance, aid, a gift, a loan, or by actually doing for the other person. But direct help is not always helpful, again, if your desired result is to produce people capable of doing for themselves. Benjamin Franklin said, "When you do for a man what he can and should do for himself, you do him a great disservice."

As a helper, you might wish to consider sources of indirect help which ironically might be more helpful. These could include just listening, prayer in the person's behalf, anonymous service to the person so that he or she does not feel indebted to anyone specifically, creating an opportunity for the person, and connecting him with others who might be most helpful. Selecting the proper technique can go a long way in determining the failure or success of the help.

Finally, you must look at your decision to help or not, your motive, your actions, and the techniques in terms of whether or not it produces the desired result. The four arrows under Figure 47 give a rough analysis of the relationship of these to the three possible outcomes. If you do not help people, for whatever reason, at best they will become independent and go on successfully but unconnected (at least to you). At worst they will fail due to your nonassistance.

If you help people for the wrong reasons, they will likely become

111

dependent on you and never develop their own internal strengths and abilities. But if you help people for the right reason and with the proper actions and techniques, then you have the opportunity of developing the most desirable interdependent relationship, one that provides both support and growth.

The theme of helping people for the right reasons and in the right way and of doing for yourself whenever possible runs throughout this book. The final chapter of the book explores the consequences of our ability or inability to create an interdependent, peaceful world.

EVERYTHING YOU ALWAYS WANTED TO KNOW AND SOME THINGS YOU PROBABLY DIDN'T: MEN AND WOMEN IN THE WORLD OF WORK

If you are going to be successful as a leader, it is important that you be able to develop the full potentiality of all of the resource people that you have, regardless of what "categories" they may fall into. People tend to think categorically and to view others in stereotypes, whether positive or negative. They group the people they know according to nationality, race, sex, religion, age, physical health, and so on; discrimination can be the result. A leader must set the tone in avoiding even subtle discriminatory behavior or else pay the price in lowering employee morale.

All of us are members of majorities as well as minorities. This section will focus on one major minority group. Using the word *minority* is actually inappropriate, because the focus group will be women. Women have always been a significant portion of the American work force. In fact, there have been periods of time when in various occupational groups they have constituted the majority of those who were working. There is absolutely no question of the discrimination that women have faced in their work. There is plenty of evidence to document discrimination in pay, in promotion, in status, in opportunities and fringe benefits, executive perks, and so forth. This section speaks specifically to some of the problems and difficulties encountered by men and women working together.

My concern with minority issues probably derives from my parents' perverse sense of humor in giving me a name that is used both in the Anglo-Saxon as female, and also in the spelling as Oriental. I remember an early shock in my life occurred when, at a young age, I won a national contest and was the first boy on my block to have a brand-new, expensive English racing bike—girl's model. Another major blow was getting two weeks into my basic training at the Air Force Academy and receiving a large brown envelope from the Department of Defense inviting me to join the Women's Air Force. Needless to say, my request to carry out this invitation from the Department of Defense was refused.

Perhaps such experiences have made me unusually aware of problems of sex discrimination. But it was a particular college class that upset many of my simple assumptions. The first semester I was at Harvard one of the professors offered an elective course on the subject of Sex and Social Roles. In this class we had an opportunity to study the ways that society conditions us to play the roles of males and females. One of the first things that the instructor asked us to do in order to get a very good basis for what we were going to be studying and talking about was to spend a couple of weeks in the Harvard Medical School library looking in depth at some major medical texts that talked about the physiological and genetic bases of sex. In the process of this study I really learned more than I wanted to know about the differences and similarities between males and females.

Up to that point in time I had gone through life on the naive assumption that the world was basically divided into two sexes. I was one of those people who had been confused regarding the furor in the 1960s about testing the sex of the women on the Russian track team. It seemed to me that a simple anatomical examination would quickly determine which sex a person belonged to. The study in this class helped me to understand that there are actually many sexes, forming a continuum that goes from super-male on one end to super-female on the other end, with a totally indeterminate sex in between. The importance of this discovery will become clear in the discussion that follows about what is "male behavior" and what is "female behavior."

The Harvard class helped me to begin clarifying my own thinking on this important leadership topic. My experience over the past decade in training over eight thousand managers, more than half of whom were females, has helped me to gain an even greater understanding of the attitudes, experiences, difficulties, and challenges that men and women face in working together. The following are some of the conclusions I have drawn from my study and experience.

PROPOSITION 1.   Men and women are different. I know that this is a very unpopular view in this unisex age in which we live, but I am prepared to argue the point with anyone who wishes to disagree. Genetically, physiologically, in most cases anatomically, emotionally, intellectually, and spiritually, men and women are different. Each of the sexes, male and female, has its own particular strengths and weaknesses. Women excel in a number of areas, men in some others.

PROPOSITION 2.   The sources of differences between men and women are difficult to identify as to whether they have a genetic or a socialized basis. In other words, if you say that men are more aggressive than women or if you say that women are more emotional than men, are you talking about something that has a basis in glandular hormonal activity or are you talking about something that has a basis in the type of training and socialization received by the two sexes? Please be careful before you reveal your own assumptions about these questions, because these are very difficult issues to sort out. They make a big difference, because until total success is achieved in manipulating the genetic code, in changing genetic characteristics, if you look back at the source of these differences you will find that there are some that something can be done about and others that cannot.

PROPOSITION 3. This is a very important point and needs to be considered very carefully. The differences within the sexual grouping, male and female, are greater than the differences between the two groups. In other words, to say that men on the average are more aggressive than women on the average, or to say that on the average women are more emotional than men is not to say that all men are aggressive and that all women are not aggressive or that all women are emotional and all men are nonemotional. Here again, within each of the sexes you will find a continuum that goes from nonaggressive men to very aggressive men; and you will find a range from very aggressive females to nonaggressive females. You will discover that the women on the aggressive end of their scale are much more aggressive than the men from the moderate to nonaggressive end of their own scale. Therefore, it's virtually impossible to indicate which of these two characteristics a specific man or woman is likely to demonstrate.

PROPOSITION 4. If you consider the fact that women make up roughly 50 percent of the working force today, at least in the free world, it seems to me absolutely ludicrous to ignore and hold down one half of the brain power that is available to solve so many of the tremendous problems that confront this globe.

I have felt and have publicly espoused for years the doctrine that one of the most underutilized and underdeveloped resources we have in the American work force is the modern-day secretary, especially executive secretaries. It's been my experience in working with executive secretaries that they spend much of the time functioning as executives—making decisions, signing contracts, making resource allocation decisions, and generally running things while their male executive bosses are out kissing babies and playing golf. Therefore, I started a movement called SASS which was usually received with a great deal of shock and initial consternation at my training program for secretaries. SASS stands for the Society to Abolish Secretarial Services. When I would share this information with secretaries, they would immediately be shocked and many of them would say, "But we like our work as secretaries; we don't want to have it abolished." My response would be that I have never in my experience found a secretary who wakes up every morning, leaps out of bed, and says "I can hardly wait to get into the office and lick stamps, fold letters, and put them in envelopes." My thinking is that we should seriously adopt in the work place the motto that IBM was using in their advertising a few years ago. It said, "Machines should work, people should think." Therefore, we ought to use executive secretaries as executives—making decisions, doing planning, forecasting, managing, delegating, and accomplishing significant management leadership tasks. Leave the grunt work that needs doing to the R2-D2's in the work place.

PROPOSITION 5. Militant feminism, especially in the work place today, is often misdirected and usually counterproductive. It's been my experience in dealing with a number of militant feminists that they have really missed the mark. For example, great energy is poured into the use of proper pronouns and titles while ignoring issues that have to do with power and compensation, which to me are much more central. I'm tired of having the experience of being rebuffed by females when I try to help them on with a coat or hold a door open or help them carry a heavy box. It gets a little old to have to continually justify my help by saying "Yes, I would do the same thing for one of my male colleagues." I think that it is important for women, whatever form of discrimination they feel they are facing, to consider the range of options they have as a recourse, not to see all men as their enemy and not to go out of their way to offend those who are trying to be helpful and show them the kind of common human courtesies that make life worth living.

In conclusion, you as leaders have a responsibility to get to know each one of your subordinates as individuals and to treat them as individuals. You should assess their idiosyncratic strengths and weaknesses and make their strengths productive. To do anything less than to fully utilize the great resource that we have in all of our minority groups, whether they're based on sex, race, nationality, religion, or age, is not to fully mobilize the problem solvers available to confront the massive problems and the very survival of this planet.

The most effective, most productive, most satisfying way to deal with human beings is to treat them as individuals, to try to move past your biases, prejudices, and stereotypes and to find out what a specific individual is really like. Then if you are a manager or leader, you should create a system of motivation, challenges, and opportunities designed specifically to deal with the person's special needs, characteristics, personality, traits, and behaviors.

If you consider Maslow's hierarchy of needs, discussed earlier in this chapter, you can see that the highest level of needs individuals have are for self-actualization. When this need has been blocked, rebellion, protest, and outrage are the result. Women, blacks, Hispanics, native Americans, the handicapped, the aged, and others have been told, "We are not going to allow you to progress, not because you lack the confidence, the brains, or the ability, but because you belong to some specific group or category which we are going to classify as unfit." Individuals who hold back others and do not allow them to reach their level of full potential do themselves a great disservice, create significant problems within the organization, and deprive a problem-filled world of a much-needed resource.

One final note, whenever I have discussed this point with the hundreds of groups of managers I have trained—groups that were all male, all female, and mixed—I have always found it interesting to watch their reaction as I pointed out at the end that I have had careers in more than a dozen different organizations. I have worked at many different levels, in government and the private sector and for a number of different supervisors and managers. Far and away, the two best managers I have ever worked for were both women. It's interesting to look at the expressions on people's faces as this fact is brought out and to consider the various and perhaps erroneous conclusions they might draw. Any of the following reactions are possible: (1) The women listening to me make this point might say, "Well, it's obvious that women make better supervisors and managers"; (2) the men listening to me make this point might say, "But you're only one individual with very limited experience, and the fact that you worked with two good female managers might only have been an anomaly, an experience that would not be repeated for other people." There is another possibility that needs consideration: In a male-dominated world of work, perhaps a woman has to be just a little better, try a little harder, work a little longer, and be a little more sensitive in order to climb the organizational ladder to success and achieve the things that might come a bit easier for the man facing that same corporate ladder.

ILLUSTRATIVE CASE E

The Case of Brooke Gionelli

Brooke Gionelli slammed the door to the office and kicked the roll-away chair against the wall. The noise of the five o'clock traffic could be heard outside on Commonwealth Avenue. Brooke had worked for the Environmental Quality Agency for twelve years, and for the third time had been passed over for promotion. This time the middle manager's job had gone to Eddie Lucero, the biggest boot licker and back stabber in the office. Mr. Evans, the bureau head, had mumbled some things about problems with Brooke's supervisory style and management attitude. Brooke knew that this was baloney, that the reasons were far more subtle. Again come the angry thoughts of quitting: "That would show them! This place would fall apart in two days without me here." Then came the darker thoughts of sabotage or withdrawal, while staying around to watch the suffering. It was clear that something needed to be done, but what?

FUNCTIONAL TYPE *Brooke Gionelli is a supervisor in a large government agency. This situation might represent that of a supervisor in the private sector, an engineer, or an academic department head.*

LEADERSHIP FACTORS *The principles involved in this case include* bureaucratic survival skills, career development, communication, *and* male/female issues.

QUESTIONS TO CONSIDER

1. *What might be the actual causes of Brooke's consistently being passed over? Is there anything Brooke can do to find out the real reason?*
2. *What principles of power and organizational politics would apply in this situation? How would they apply?*
3. *Write a solution to this case based on each of the three alternatives.*
4. *What career options are open to Brooke?*
5. *What principles of good communication are being violated on both sides here?*

ANALYSIS *There are two approaches that Brooke can take to this problem situation. One is in terms of bureaucratic survival skills, the other is in terms of personal career management. The former approach would consist of reviewing and implementing the sections on power, conflict management, frustration, organizational politics, feedback, using available legal avenues, and building support groups.*

The approach in terms of personal career management might begin with reviewing the three options of accepting the situation, changing the situation, or getting out.

This might be a time to reevaluate career goals and the different ways in which they can be achieved. This may be the time to start the process of making a move to a new agency or perhaps out of government altogether. It might be a time for some honest reflection on personal strengths and weaknesses to see if there might not be some blind spots to reasons why the opportunities keep passing to others. And maybe it's a time for gaining new knowledge or skills.

GOOD-BYE, COLUMBUS . . .
THOSE WHO LEAVE THE CAUSE

Most organizations and groups begin with the (naive) assumptions that their cause is the most noble, that it has the greatest likelihood of success and that any member who signs on, signs on for the duration. It is tremendously frustrating when the leader discovers that all of these assumptions may be incorrect. This section focuses on how the leader might deal with the third incorrect assumption.

Followers often leave the cause, and they do so for a variety of reasons. Here are only a few:

Reasons Some Followers Are No Longer With Us

1. They have transferred somewhere else.
2. They have been laid off.
3. They have been drafted.
4. They got a better offer somewhere else.
5. They have gotten a divorce.
6. They have been excommunicated.
7. They got fed up, tired, sick, or are indisposed.
8. They have retired.
9. They have disappeared.
10. They have been imprisoned.
11. They are suffering from amnesia.
12. They have been fired.
13. They have run away.
14. They are in a coma.
15. They have been taken hostage.
16. They are dead.
17. They have been captured by aliens.
18. They left to start a cause of their own.

You can see from this rich and varied list that someone's leaving cannot always be viewed as a lack of loyalty or common sense. The key test for the leader is how to respond to one of the subordinates' decision to leave.

In my very mobile career, I have left many organizations for several of the reasons listed above. My leaders in these organizations have responded with varied reactions, ranging from indifference to helpfulness to concern to anger. I discussed the phenomenon of the anger over an employee leaving with one of the fine people that I worked for. He responded with this interesting observation.

In my early management experience when people would "desert" me, I used to respond by getting very angry at them. I found that it never brought them back and only made me tired. I decided to take a different approach and respond with happiness and helpfulness for their new opportunity. This new response created several positive possibilities. First, they might decide that I was so nice they would rather not leave. Second, their new opportunity might fall through and they might stay on, with good feelings continuing between us. Third, they might leave, but then decide this was a better place and return. Finally, they might leave for good, but reciprocate my concern by furnishing me with an outstanding replacement and/or additional help in the future.

In a similar vein, another wise leader I worked for said, "When my parents were raising me, they never controlled my behavior with guilt, so I have never found that to be a useful way to get others to do what is in my best interest rather than theirs."

As a leader, you will face this situation many times. You must choose your response and decide whether it serves the best interests of the organization, the person leaving, or yourself. However you choose to respond, one action that is very helpful at this time is to conduct an exit interview.

Your objectives in conducting an exit interview might include discovering why they are leaving, determining what could be done to correct any organizational problems they may have determined, seeing what you can do to facilitate their move, and seeking their assistance in obtaining a replacement.

If the person's reasons for leaving are organizationally based, and especially if they are based on negative feelings about you, they will be reluctant to have this discussion with you. If they are forced to face you, they may respond by saying little or nothing, by lying to you, or by blasting you. None of these responses will be terribly helpful (to you). It may be helpful to have the exit interview conducted by another party. If it can be arranged, you may wish to have them give you feedback anonymously.

Whatever their reason for leaving, and no matter how painful the feedback, if changes need to be made that are within your control you should make them before more valuable people are lost. If, on the other hand, the person leaving was not only not valuable but a pain in the lower back, this might also be cause for celebration.

Leadership Technique #5
RINGING THE BELL-SHAPED CURVE:
EMPLOYEE APPRAISALS
AND DEVELOPMENT

One of the most challenging tasks faced by leaders and managers, one that keeps many people from moving up into positions of management, is responsibility in the control phase of an organization's operation. Performance appraisal is difficult and often painful, both for those who are conducting the appraisal and for those who are being appraised. Leaders are often uncomfortable with this process because they don't know how to do it well. They know it's an unpleasant experience for their followers or subordinates and they try to avoid it as much as possible and to get it over with as quickly as they can.

It is also certainly an anxiety-producing and unpleasant experience for the subordinate. Many times the process used for conducting the appraisal is what you might refer to as the "hot dog" interview. If you picture a hot dog, the first part of this type of performance appraisal is the initial bun that goes on top. This is the positive part of the experience. Supervisors and leaders have been trained to put their subordinates at ease, so they usually start with a dialogue something like this: "Hello, Bill. How are you today? The old performance appraisal time is here again, huh? Gee, isn't this crazy weather we've been having? How's the wife and kids? Now, sit down and relax. Would you like a cup of coffee? Take your shoes off. Take it easy, we're just going to have a brief session here and we'll try and get this over with as quickly as we can."

Once supervisors have loosened the individual up and gotten him relaxed, they then get to the meat of this hot dog interview; this is the negative part of the experience. The supervisor opens a manila folder on top of the desk and says, "Bill, what I have here is a record I've been keeping. It contains a hundred and seventeen mistakes you have made during the last year, and I thought maybe we could just look at these one at a time and see if we can try and understand what could have gone wrong. Now, the first mistake listed here that you made was on June second. That was the day that at two P.M. you said to Mary, 'Who cares!' Now, could you tell me what you were thinking about at that time?" The person who is being appraised at this point has an anxiety level that puts him virtually in a catatonic state. Not only doesn't he remember that date, that time, or that comment, but he is suddenly very vividly aware that he's going to have another hundred and sixteen bad experiences before the appraisal is finished.

At the end of this horrible blood-letting experience, the final bun of the hot dog interview is added when the leader or supervisor says, "Bill, I want you to know that you are a wonderful human being in your own right. You're really a valued employee here, and you certainly make a great contribution to our organization. I hope that none of these things I have said today are going to upset you in any way, because I want you to be able to go out there and do a good job. Do the very best that you can, and I look forward to sharing this experience with you again." This kind of approach is sometimes referred to as "patting a person on the back with a knife in your hand" or the "Et tu, Brute" approach. People say to themselves, "If I'm so great and I'm getting patted on the back for all these wonderful things I have done, how come it hurts so bad?"

A different, more effective approach that can be used for conducting these performance appraisals will be discussed momentarily, but first, to put the problem of personnel performance appraisals in perspective, take a look at your group of followers or subordinates as an aggregate.

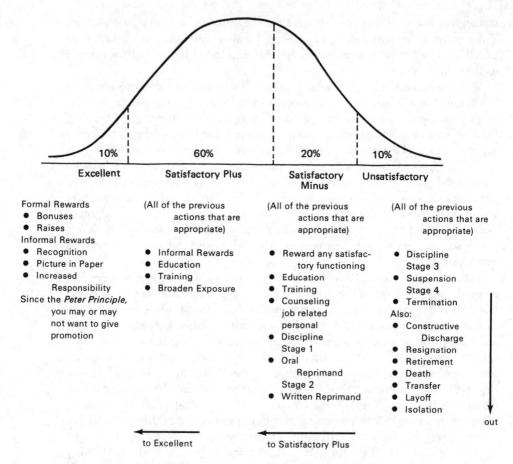

10%	60%	20%	10%
Excellent	Satisfactory Plus	Satisfactory Minus	Unsatisfactory

| Formal Rewards
• Bonuses
• Raises
Informal Rewards
• Recognition
• Picture in Paper
• Increased
  Responsibility
Since the *Peter Principle,*
  you may or may
  not want to give
  promotion | (All of the previous
  actions that are
  appropriate)

• Informal Rewards
• Education
• Training
• Broaden Exposure | (All of the previous
  actions that are
  appropriate)

• Reward any satisfac-
  tory functioning
• Education
• Training
• Counseling
  job related
  personal
• Discipline
  Stage 1
• Oral
   Reprimand
  Stage 2
• Written Reprimand | (All of the previous
  actions that are
  appropriate)

• Discipline
  Stage 3
• Suspension
  Stage 4
• Termination
Also:
• Constructive
   Discharge
• Resignation
• Retirement
• Death
• Transfer
• Layoff
• Isolation |

out

← to Excellent   ← to Satisfactory Plus

FIGURE 48. Distribution of people in an organization and corresponding sanctions and forms of reinforcement

Above is a picture of a bell-shaped or normal curve. This curve depicts a quality of human beings. If you take any given characteristics of human beings in the aggregate (their height, their weight, their intelligence quotient, the number of eyes they have in their head), these characteristics will tend to collect around some midpoint—some mean, median, or mode which is the central part of this normal distribution. Approximately 66 percent of the people will fall within the range from one standard deviation to the other.

Using the characteristic of people's height as an example, suppose the average height of human beings is five feet eight inches. You will find that if you look at people statistically, 66 percent of the population will have a height somewhere between five feet two inches and six feet two inches. As you get out to the extremes of this bell-shaped curve, you find those qualities of human beings that most often find their way into the *Guinness Book of World Records.* There are people who are nine feet four inches tall, and there are people who are two feet nine inches tall. There are people who weigh two thousand pounds and who will have to be buried in a piano crate, and there are women who have given birth to forty-five babies. But because these conditions are so extreme, so rare, and so unusual, most experience is with people in the central area of the curve. To be normal is simply to behave as the majority of people are behaving.

Now take this bell-shaped curve and divide it up differently, and then use it to examine four groups of followers. Refer back to Figure 48 and look at the group on the left (this is not meant to be a political statement). Ten percent of the followers in any situation could be classified as excellent or outstanding. These are the individuals who are the superstars. One of the first questions you must ask yourself as a leader is, "Do I want all of my followers to be in this category?" Your initial inclination is to say, "Of course—it would be great!" But would it really? How many times in history have we seen a winning team that was composed of all superstars? Stars, while they may be tremendous in their ability to produce, also have a number of problems and drawbacks. They can be egotistical and they can be prima donnas requiring a great deal of attention and deference. Stars can also be expensive. They can be very jealous and can create resentment among other team players. They are sometimes insensitive to others. All kinds of difficulties can come from having an entire group of stars. Certainly you hope that you have some of these individuals, but really, the next group is the glue that holds the organization together.

The next category, the largest group, the 60 percent listed on Figure 49, are those classified as "satisfactory plus." These are people whose performance is not outstanding, but they are the ones that do work that is good, steady, consistent, and dependable. These are the people who keep things going. One of the ironies in many organizations is that this group, the largest and most dependable, is often most neglected. While attention is going to the stars and the troublemakers, these people are just expected to do their job. If these people are ignored long enough, there is a real possibility that they are going to rise up some day and yell, "I'm mad as hell, and I'm not going to take it anymore!"

The next group over on the bell-shaped curve is classified as "satisfactory minus." There are two ways individuals can get themselves into this category. The first of these is to be a person whose performance is consistently poor, a person whose abilities are just subpar. No matter how hard these people try, no matter how hard they work, they are just not able to do the job. The other, even more upsetting way persons get into this category is through inconsistency. These are the ones who alternate back and forth between dependability and incompetency. These are perhaps the most difficult and challenging of all of the individuals that you, as a leader, have to work with.

The last category consists of those whose performances are simply unsatisfactory. They are not able to function in any way that meets the standards or requirements of the organization.

The basic approaches to dealing with each of these individuals is shown in Figure 48. In the first three categories, the approach is to reward all that employees do right, and engage in additional actions designed to move them toward more satisfactory performance. In the final category, after all else has failed, your primary effort should be to get them out. Several possibilities are listed. If the fit between person and job is wrong, getting them out can be the best thing for both the individual and the organization.

Your challenge as a leader is to determine which of these categories each subordinate falls into. That is a basic purpose of the performance appraisal: to determine the results the person has produced relative to the objectives and standards agreed upon between leader and follower. A second purpose is to use the appraisal as a developmental tool to reward and reinforce effective performances, moving the behavior consistently in the direction of more satisfactory.

ILLUSTRATIVE CASE F

The Case of Dana Wallach

Dana Wallach watched the beautifully executed pass from point guard to forward, and stood up in expectation of the slam dunk, only to have the forward and center collide and slam to the floor, with the ball dunked in the fountain at the end of the gym. The team exploded in gales of laughter and Dana exploded in unprintable words. Dana Wallach was in the first year of a high school coaching job that had been obtained directly after graduation from UCLA. Four years of playing on a well-balanced, dedicated, winning team had not been the right preparation for the frustrations of this fiasco. The Edgewood Eagles had not had a winning season in a decade, and this year looked as if it would be no exception. Every effort to teach the new four-point offense and to reward the most competent players had been a dismal failure. The team simply had no concept of playing together and winning. Dana's best player was also the biggest smart mouth on the team and often lazy. The fifteen players had fifteen different reasons for being on the team, from hoping for a letter jacket to getting out of sixth-period study hall. It was clear that "win one for the Gipper" would not work here.

FUNCTIONAL TYPE   *Dana Wallach is a basketball coach. This situation might represent that of a sales manager, scout leader, or director of a play.*

LEADERSHIP FACTORS   *The principles involved in this case include* goal setting, performance appraisal, discipline, *and* teaching/training.

QUESTIONS TO CONSIDER

1. *What is the problem with goal setting in this situation? What might Dana have learned at UCLA that seems to have been currently forgotten?*
2. *How might the learning ability of the players differ? What implications does this have for the leader?*
3. *What assessment and reward system would improve this situation?*
4. *What principles of good discipline would apply here?*
5. *How might Dana's concept of success be redefined in this situation?*

ANALYSIS   *The first problem that Dana clearly faces is that of working with the team to establish common goals. Unless all the horses are pulling in the same direction, the wagon is not going to move. The next step should be to assess the techniques for teaching and training this group, remembering that some will learn differently from others. The team needs to learn basics, especially the value of assists and teamwork.*

A system of appraising each member's performance needs to be established and understood by all. The formal and informal rewards that are available need to be identified and tied to the performance that you wish to reinforce (such as assists).

It would be helpful to review the discussion of methods of discipline in the performance appraisal section. Some people need recognition, some need training, some need to be reprimanded, and some may need to be kicked out. A team with no star can win; a star with no team cannot.

Dana should not forget the value of patience, long suffering, a sense of humor, and reasonable expectations. Enjoyment should come from the journey, not just the results.

An Approach to More Effective Appraisals

Premeeting Activity

Prior to the time you get together for the appraisal, you will want to make arrangements and communicate a set of appropriate ground rules (see examples in Leadership Technique #1, Leadership by Objectives and Results). These ground rules can be communicated verbally or in writing and should be agreed to by both parties.

It is also very important for the leader (appraiser) to consider carefully his or her own role. Some helpful questions to ask yourself might include:

1. Can I accept this person as he or she is?
2. Can I love (or respect) this person?
3. Can I listen empathetically in a way that will lead to understanding?
4. Do I appreciate and recognize the worth of each individual I work or live with?
5. Will my focus be on helping the individual to help him/herself?
6. Do I view counseling and development as an ongoing process and not an event?
7. If I see that it is necessary, am I willing and able to involve other expert "helpers?"

The Appraisal Meeting

Listed below is a set of techniques that follow in rough chronological fashion the process the interview should take. They are guidelines to an effective appraisal and should be adapted where appropriate.

1. Put the person at ease. This is also a process, the culmination of the premeeting activities. It is not an event accomplished by instructing the person to be at ease.
2. Ask good questions. The worst get only a yes or no response. For example, "Do you think you're a good employee?" The best are open-ended: "Tell me what you feel you do well."

3. Don't overtalk; you're here to listen. Avoid giving advice. Help people discover the solutions to their own problems. *Don't be afraid of silence and feel a need to fill it.* Silence will often follow a good question as the person is thinking.

4. Don't cross-examine. You are not the DA. This is not the inquisition.

5. If the problem is important to the person, it *is* important (whether or not it seems so to you).

6. Don't hurry the process. If done on an annual basis, you're making preparation for a whole productive year. Take the time to do it right.

7. Be straight about bad news (or good news). Don't send a double message, "You're a good employee, but . . ." Come out with it, "The problem is . . ." or "The mistake you made . . ." People are not made of china, they won't shatter. And think how excited they'll be to get a compliment with no "but" attached.

8. You will sometimes need to question the face value of things you are told. Read between the lines, be sensitive, be empathetic. Accept feelings, whether of joy over accomplishments or anger and disappointment. You may have to help people verbalize their feelings.

9. Develop a plan of action for the person to cover the next performance period (normally a year).

10. Summarize what has been agreed upon, get a commitment to the objectives and form a written "contract." Copies will go to the employee, you and your boss.

11. End at the end. Don't take forever with reentry. If it's been a good session, end it clean: "Thank you. We'll talk again soon."

12. Set the date for the first (usually quarterly) review and follow-up.

Meeting Follow-Up

If you talk to the employee consistently during the year, reviewing agreed-upon objectives and ongoing performance, and if you reinforce, recognize, and reward each result produced, the performance appraisal event becomes the appraisal process. The formal appraisal day can then become one of relaxed mutual congratulations for a job well done.

Leadership Technique #6
THE DELEGATION DECISION:
KEY TO SUCCESS

When I was a boy, my father taught me that my abilities to accomplish things would always be limited by my own talents, time, and energies. He said to me that I would never really be successful in my life unless and until I learned to "multiply my hands." At that time I didn't understand quite what he meant by this phrase. As I have gotten older and have learned more about leadership, management, supervision, and working with people, I have come to understand the great importance of delegating. The leader should accomplish specific critical functions which can not be delegated. In the section on time management I have discussed the difference between effectiveness and efficiency and pointed out that to be effective, a person must concentrate on doing the 20 percent of the tasks that produce 80 percent of the results. Delegation is a key to leadership effectiveness, which raises the question of why it's not fully utilized by more leaders.

The single most important factor that blocks human beings from accomplishing and achieving anything they want to do is fear. Fear is the most significant barrier that blocks delegating and transferring responsibilities to others.

A first type of fear is fear of the unknown. People are afraid of things that they cannot see or that they do not understand. In the delegation process, what this means specifically is leaders are always concerned that if they delegate a particular function to someone else, then they lose control of that function. They cannot know how it is going to turn out. They are not sure whether it is going to be done right (the way they would do it) or where things are at and, therefore, those with high control needs are very reluctant to assign responsibilities to others.

A second kind of fear that blocks many leaders from delegating is the fear of the loss of some vested interest. In every situation that exists, someone is benefiting from the status quo. To make any change is going to mean that some people are going to lose something they have valued. The leader, in transferring a responsibility to someone else, may be losing status, may be losing more than the ability to appear as a constantly overworked and harassed martyr.

A third type of fear that blocks leaders from delegating is a fear that the task is going to be done wrong, that mistakes will be made. Many times this fear is exaggerated by the fact that the leader is comparing the subordinate's ability to do the job with the leader's own ability to do the job. Obviously the leader can often do the job much better than any other subordinates because of greater experience or knowledge. But the only way those followers are going to get better and increase their capability is by practicing, by learning the very same way that the leader did. I have often pointed out to parents in family counseling situations that if mother continues to make the bed because she can do it faster than junior, the ultimate result is that the couple is going to have a twenty-two-year-old son whose mother still makes his bed for him.

Ironically, the fourth fear that often blocks delegation is just exactly the opposite of the one we just mentioned. Many leaders are fearful that the follower is going to be able to perform the function too well and that serious questions are going to be raised about why this particular leader is in charge if someone else is able to do the job as well or better.

These are the four major fears that block delegation. There are other fears that could be categorized, but the point is made that fear is a major obstacle to effectiveness.

A fifth barrier to delegation and effective time use occurs with leaders and managers who are not clear about what their role should truly consist of. These individuals often feel that they have been given a job to do, a job that they are being paid for. They feel that having someone else do even part of their job would be inappropriate, unethical, or immoral. Therefore, they tenaciously hang onto every little aspect of the job and diminish the results that can be produced because of their own limited time and energies.

A sixth barrier is a lack of clarity on the part of the leader as to exactly what it is that is to be done. If you have not commenced the enterprise by establishing goals and objectives as discussed in Chapter 1, then it is virtually impossible to pass on some of what you are vague about to someone else.

A seventh barrier to delegation is the lack of understanding of the concept of effectiveness. The problem here can be in not knowing of the 20–80 principle, of not believing the 20–80 principle, of not applying the 20–80 principle (in other words, of not taking the time to figure out what the significant tasks really are), or of wishing to be seen as a martyr by burying yourself with minutiae.

This leads to an eighth and final barrier. Many leaders and managers suffer from what was called earlier the Smokey the Bear approach to leadership. They direct a great amount of their energies to running around stamping out forest fires. This is called crisis management, and it is a pervasive problem in many offices. Because of poor goal setting, planning, and time use (delegation), the leader and staff are constantly moving from crisis to crisis, literally running around stamping out brushfires. This fire fighting consumes so much time and energy that no one ever bothers to ask why the fires are breaking out or what could be done to prevent them (like building firebreaks or seeding the clouds). Inevitably, one of these leaders is decorated for fire fighting by the higher-ups and then makes a career out of it. The really frightening part of it is that some of these individuals become arsonists, fomenting crises so that they will have brushfires to fight.

If you suffer from any of these ailments or a combination of them, you should carefully consider your methods and ask the following questions before reading the next section:

1. Am I interested in being busy *or* in producing results?
2. Which is more likely to get rewarded? (If the answer is the former, consider alternative employment.)
3. Do I really want to be a martyr? If not, why am I afraid of being more effective and having more free time?
4. Couldn't I use a healthy group of comers to push myself up the organizational ladder?
5. Would the world be better off if it were made up of four billion people just like me? Is it?

Overcoming the Barriers to Delegation

The process of overcoming fear is a simple one. It takes the form of an equation. Fear and faith cannot exist in an individual at the same time. The reason people are unsuccessful in using faith to overcome fear is that they misunderstand the meaning of faith. Faith is not an abstract principle. It is not merely believing in something; it is a principle of power. Action is involved in a correct application of faith. The formula, then, is: *Faith = Belief + Action*.

Consider the two parts of the equation. What is it that you need to believe in order to overcome fears? First, you must believe in yourself.

Second, you must believe in the help and support of others. You are not alone. Third, believe in the principles and ideas that will make you successful. If these principles are based on reality and truth, they are going to be operable and are going to overcome whatever superstitions and myths may be creating the fear.

The first principle of faith, then, is belief. But belief in and of itself is not enough. Belief must be accompanied by action. You must act to demonstrate belief in yourself, and you must act to seek and use the support of others. If faith, belief, and action are properly brought together, your faith has sufficient power to overcome whatever fears you might experience.

The person whose fear is one of losing control needs to take two specific actions. The first is to develop a control system so that the leader is in touch with whether the operation is meeting established goals and plans. The second act is to consider which need is stronger, the need for achievement or the need for control, and to convince yourself that the better road leads to achieving results.

The person whose fear is loss of some vested interest needs to do a cost-benefit analysis to weigh what will be gained by increased effectiveness against what one gives up (such as perceived indispensability or martyrdom).

The third fear is that the delegate will make mistakes. You would all like to believe that you, surgeons, and airline pilots constitute the only three segments of society that never make mistakes. Of course, this belief is a fantasy. As Townsend says (*Up the Organization*, New York: Knopf, 1970, p. 115), "Babies learn to walk by falling down. If you beat a baby every time he falls down, he will never care very much for walking." Traits of great leaders include a good memory for their own learning process, empathy, sensitivity, helpfulness, patience, and long suffering.

The fourth fear is that the delegate might be too successful and make the leader look bad. Great leaders attract great followers. Mediocre leaders attract incompetent followers. Great leaders are recognized by the number of successful comers they have right behind them in the organization. Such a leader's greatest contribution to the organization may be a team of successful leaders to whom the baton can be passed.

Dealing with the fifth barrier to delegation consists of refocusing the purpose of one's existence in the organization from doing the job one is paid for to producing desired results in the most effective way. Using others to produce these results is neither inappropriate nor unethical, it means one is "working smarter, not harder."

The solution to the sixth barrier is discussed in detail in Chapter 1: Begin *every* effort by stating clear goals and specific objectives. Then decide who could best achieve these objectives. It may not be you.

The seventh solution is bound up in understanding and applying the 20–80 rule. Make a list of all that you have to do. Now prioritize those items in terms of payoff. What is the top 20 percent, for which you are indispensable? Now look at the remainder. Which should be delegated, and which should be ignored? Act accordingly.

Finally, don't practice crisis management. People who play with fire eventually get burned. Which appeals to you more, thinking and planning or charred feet? Reread Chapter 1; then go and do likewise.

The Process of Delegation

Many people fail for lack of understanding. A leader came to me recently, very excited, and said, "I just realized that delegation is more than making assignments." So true! Proceed as follows:

1. Survey your stewardship, per the 20-80 principle.
2. Determine what you want the other person to do. Write this out in the form of a clear, specific, measurable, challenging, realistic accountability statement (objective).
3. Consider your delegates in terms of concerns such as how fast the assignment needs to be done, who is available, who can best do the job, and so forth.
4. Once the person has been selected, determine the means of presenting the assignment and "prepare the order."
5. Meet with the person, share the objective, define the related authority, explain the control system and deadline, and express confidence.
6. Follow up! Much delegation fails when it never goes beyond the assignment stage. Check up, encourage, help where appropriate. People don't do what you expect, they do what you inspect. This leads to the final step.
7. Meet face to face with the delegate for an accountability interview. (Parents take note.) Provide abundant praise and recognition for success, appropriate condolences for less than you both expected. Recommit, train, encourage, and reassign.

In conclusion, consider a couple of important principles. First, if you want motivated followers, you cannot delegate only the dog work and keep all the interesting tasks for yourself. Your people will spring to life when given the opportunity to solve a problem, make a decision, or think about something important. And they will be inspired if you occasionally empty the bedpans.

Second and finally, delegation provides you, the leader, with an opportunity to demonstrate one of your most important virtues—patience. Others will learn as you learned (though you hate to admit it or have already forgotten it), and that is by making mistakes. Don't jump in and play rescuer every time they are about to fall down; they will learn a lot from the natural consequences of falling. And don't beat them (verbally or otherwise) every time they fall, or you'll beat out of them all desires for risk taking—hence, the ability to be leaders. You're trying to train someone to take your place as you move up . . . remember?

Leadership Technique #7
TEAM BUILDING: SAME CLUB . . .
SAME BALL PARK . . .
SAME GAME

What is a team and what does it mean to build it? A team is another name for a group, which I have defined elsewhere as two or more people interacting in pursuit of a common goal. Using the word *team* in place of *group* implies, in addition to the above definition, a feeling of esprit de corps and a sense of wanting to excel in competition with other groups (teams).

By building a team, each person feels a part of the group or organization, the members understand where they are in the work environment, and they understand their business and the related rules. This all sounds straightforward enough, but it is amazing how many groups are not there. If you think yours is, ask the members the following questions:

1. Who belongs to this group (what are the boundaries)?
2. What is our purpose?
3. Describe our industry (league, conference, field).
4. What is our place in that industry (league, conference, field)?
5. What are our specific objectives?
6. What rules, values, and procedures do we operate by?
7. How do we measure our success?
8. How do we get along?

Such a survey (you'll get better results if they are submitted anonymously) can be quite revealing. Did yours produce any surprises?

Team building can be used with new groups just forming, with existing work groups (especially just before or after a major change affecting the group), and with temporary project teams. It can focus on content—how to get the job done and/or process relationships between members of the group, including you as the leader.

Before starting a team-building process with your group, it helps if you all have a shared perception of the basic characteristics of an effective work team. Those might include:

1. A clearly defined and shared sense of purpose.
2. A list of mutually created and agreed-upon objectives.
3. An organized structure that fits logically with the objectives to be accomplished.
4. Clearly defined roles and role relationships.
5. An open climate that fosters shared ideas and feelings.
6. A mutual concern that is demonstrated through empathy and support.
7. A willingness to observe how the group works and accept ideas for improvement.
8. A consensual decision-making process.
9. The sharing of power and leadership as appropriate to the task.
10. An accountability system that fosters responsibility, results, and follow-through.
11. A method for justly resolving conflicts and grievances.
12. A monitoring of the external environment and intragroup relations and a willingness to adjust as appropriate.
13. A commitment to the effective use of time and resources.
14. Feelings of comfort, accomplishment, and fun.
15. A satisfactory method for bringing new members in and allowing current members to leave.

The list could be expanded, but it covers some core concerns. No group is going to measure up completely. These are goals to be striving for.

The Process of Team Building

The process normally begins by taking the team away from the work (or home) setting. This removes the barriers of familiar irritants, interruptions, and a felt need to return to work.

It is usually helpful to use a trained non-team member as a facilitator. This person's group-process skills and objectivity can aid the flow of information and events. A skilled team member can sometimes assume this role, but this approach is more problematic. Professional consulting organizations that periodically go through this process have the wisdom to call in a consultant.

It is important to get everyone as involved as possible. This can often be done by alternating sessions between the large group, various mixes of small groups, and triads or dyads of individuals.

The first step might be a brief historical overview to give the team a sense of where they started, where they've been, and how far they've come. This is obviously not possible with a newly constructed group, but there is always a "prehistory"—possibly looking at the larger organization or how this group came to be formed.

The next step is an in-depth analysis of the present, looking at any one of the fifteen characteristic areas identified earlier. Questions such as "What are our objectives?" or "Why are we experiencing trouble in communicating?" can be explored from several perspectives through several techniques.*

Some cautions here. This is not meant to be a gripe session and should explore strengths as well as weaknesses. The atmosphere must support open expressions of concerns and feelings; otherwise, there is no purpose in getting the group together. This is *not* a sales meeting, staff meeting, or opportunity for the leader to present a new plan.

Identified problem areas can be worked on using the group problem-solving technique described in Leadership Technique Section 8 and the integrated decision-making approach discussed in Chapter 4.

The final phase looks to the future and consists of setting specific new objectives. Actions should be planned and a system for follow-up and review should be established.

These meetings can take anywhere from one-half day to three days. They may or may not include time for group socializing or individual time for reflection and personal commitment. The results can provide major benefits for you and your group.

---

*Any good book on organizational development will include sections or a chapter on team building. See the Bibliography for good sources.

4
Who:
The Leader

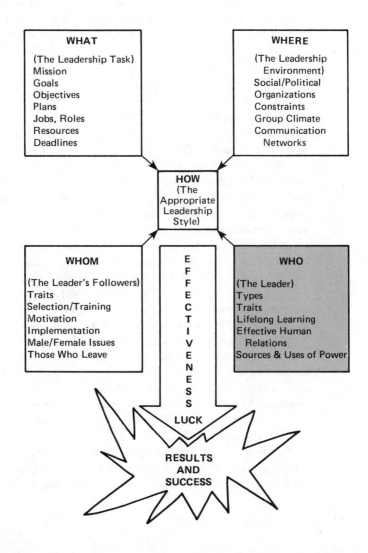

WHAT

(The Leadership Task)
Mission
Goals
Objectives
Plans
Jobs, Roles
Resources
Deadlines

WHERE

(The Leadership
    Environment)
Social/Political
Organizations
Constraints
Group Climate
Communication
    Networks

HOW
(The
Appropriate
Leadership
Style)

WHOM

(The Leader's Followers)
Traits
Selection/Training
Motivation
Implementation
Male/Female Issues
Those Who Leave

E
F
F
E
C
T
I
V
E
N
E
S
S

LUCK

WHO

(The Leader)
Types
Traits
Lifelong Learning
Effective Human
    Relations
Sources & Uses of Power

**RESULTS
AND
SUCCESS**

Now comes a most important part of the equation—the *leader*. This individual is certainly a central focus of concern, for without the leader there is no leadership, and all that has been discussed so far is meaningless. There is an additional factor, however, that makes the leader of central concern.

Given the complexity of leadership situations and the pressures to decide and act, many leaders ignore the stated goals, ignore consideration of the environment, ignore the qualities of the subordinates, and do what they feel most comfortable with. In this case Chapter 4 and Chapter 5 tend to blend. The leadership style chosen is not an outgrowth of considering many variables, but an extension of the leader's personality. Because of this, the effectiveness and results are much more unpredictable. If doing what you feel most comfortable with creates confidence, enthusiasm, and persuasiveness, the outcome might be successful. But if your personality/style goes against the stated goals, violates the organizational norms, and creates opposition in your subordinates, the effort—no matter how well meaning or well conceived— is usually doomed to failure. Because of the frequency with which the leader's personality rules, it is very important to understand the concepts discussed in this chapter, for they are often the heart of the leader's style.

TRAITS AND TYPES OF LEADERS

The oldest approach to understanding leaders is the trait approach. The earliest thinking held that leadership is inherent in the individual, that the individual is born with a set of traits or characteristics which, when exercised, would inspire others to follow. From the 1930s to the 1950s extensive studies were conducted to identify these key traits, notably at Ohio State University and the University of Michigan. This approach to understanding leaders was largely abandoned when the researchers came up with lists of several hundred mutually exclusive traits which, when related to actual leaders such as Jesus Christ, Abraham Lincoln, and Adolf Hitler, were completely different.

I discovered this dilemma in my three years of work in a state prison. On my first visit to the prison, I was attending a meeting in a minimum security facility. In this facility, inmates were allowed to wear regular street clothes. The meeting was to be attended by administrators, guards, and inmates, as well as outsiders such as myself. While I had taught criminology for several years, this was the first time I had actually been inside a prison. I was nervous. I presumed that I would be able to tell the inmates at the meeting because they would look tough, have tattoos on their arms and a scar on one cheek. (I found such an individual at the meeting, but he turned out to be a guard.) Upon entering the room, I stood off to the side and surveyed those in attendance. I spotted one individual who was tall, handsome, personable, and moving freely through the crowd, shaking hands and chatting. Concluding that he must be the person in charge, I walked over and said, "Hello, I'm Lin Bothwell, I'm in here for the meeting." He responded, "Hello, I'm Roger, I'm in here doing one to ten for armed robbery."

In working with dozens of inmates, I found that their lists of traits would make any employer anxious to hire them. They were intelligent, personable, hard-working, honest (among themselves), dedicated to their profession, skilled talkers, and so on. Their only problem was that they had one "tragic flaw": When they had three drinks they threw people out of second-story windows.

Listed below are the traits commonly identified by researchers as being most highly correlated with leadership. If you find that you don't have all of them, take heart; remember, there are 1,390 others that could describe you.

1. Intelligence.
2. Ability to get along well with others.
3. Skill in the area of technical competence.
4. Ability to motivate self and others.
5. Emotional stability and self-control.
6. Planning and organizing skills.
7. Strong desire to achieve task.
8. Ability to use the group process.
9. Ability to be effective and efficient.
10. Decisive.

Whatever the individual traits they possess, there are two qualities that set true leaders apart. One is that they have a dream they are determined to see carried out. They are often possessed with its accomplishment. George Bernard Shaw said, "The reasonable man adapts himself to the world, the unreasonable man persists in demanding that the world adapt to him. Therefore, all progress depends on the unreasonable man." (Shaw's dated quote obviously applied equally to women.)

A second quality of true leaders is that they are more than just dreamers, they are people of great action. Accomplishments do not come from those who dream great dreams, or even from those who have the potential to carry them out. Results are produced by action, action that often inspired others to act. Single acts that produce collective acts change the world.

To be a true leader, you must have a vision and act to bring it about.

Individual leadership traits are often combined into personality types in the current leadership literature. Examples of these leadership types might be seen from the creative titles of four prominent authors. Rensis Likert in his book *The Human Organization* (New York: McGraw Hill, 1967) classifies leaders as exploitive-authoritarian, benevolent-authoritarian, consultive-democratic, and participative-democratic.

William Reddin in his "The 3-D Management Style Theory" (*Training and Development Journal,* April 1967, pp. 8–17) analyzes leaders as executives, developers, benevolent autocrats, bureaucrats, compromisers, missionaries, autocrats, and dissenters.

Leonard Sayles in his *Leadership: What Effective Managers Really Do . . . and How They Do It* (New York: McGraw Hill, 1979) has three "lists" of leader types. The "A" list consists of the all-powerful boss, the complete bureaucrat, the sophisticated technician, and the rejectionist. The "B" list consists of thinking types, feeling types, intuitive types, and sensation types. The "C" list has rigid simplistic, adversary, super-sales-oriented, compromising, and creatively integrative types.

Michael Maccoby in his book *The Gamesman* (New York: Simon and Schuster, 1977) identifies four types of leaders: the craftsman, the jungle fighter, the company man, and the gamesman.

You can see from these creative titles that these four authors have identified and described some interesting leadership types. To gain a more detailed understanding of leadership types you would want to read any of these fine books.

My concern here is not to present a sophisticated analysis of leadership personality theory. You can explore personality theory in more depth through reading any basic text in psychology or social psychology. It should be obvious that you are who you are through a unique combination of heredity, experience, teaching, training, and reasoning. The concern in this section is to point out that you are you. Who you are, how you relate to others, your control and affiliation needs, your desire for achievement—all of these will *strongly* influence the personal leadership style you select, as discussed in the next chapter. And as has been emphasized throughout this book, how your personality and style fit with the goals and norms of the organization, the task to be done, and the personalities of your boss, peers, and subordinates will to a great extent determine your success or failure.

This leads to a most obvious and significant question: If the way you are has proved to be dysfunctional in some way, can your personality be changed. My opinion, and that of many others, is absolutely yes. The process of personality change is discussed in the psychology texts mentioned above. This is not to say that changing yourself is easy, or painless, or always successful, or even something that you can do by yourself. But it can be done. To have any hope of success, you must believe that. Then understand that there are many resources available to help you. All of the helping sciences—medicine, psychiatry, counseling, social work, education, training, and writing—are based on the premise that people can change. Part of the answer as to how you go about changing yourself will be found in Leadership Technique Section 8, and part of the process can be found in the following section on learning. Much of it will occur with or without your awareness, as you continue to live.

LEADERS AS LEARNERS

Most great leaders share one characteristic—a desire for continual learning and self-improvement. By definition, being a leader implies being out front, on the leading edge of knowledge and leadership techniques. This is one important quality that will make others want to follow a person. The leader must always be teachable and open to learning from others, *especially* his or her followers.

Over a decade and a half of teaching and training I have developed some theories on principles of good learning. This is not a scholarly learning treatise such as you would find in a psychology text, but my own set of practical ideas, ones that work. These ideas have value to you, the leader, both in your role of learner and also in your built-in role of teacher.

PRINCIPLE 1—THERE ARE DIFFERENT TYPES OF LEARNING.   Some people mistakenly believe that learning is learning is learning. This is not the case. There are different modes of learning and different styles of learning. For example, there is a difference between group learning and personal learning. Group learning occurs when you are experiencing, interpreting, and interacting with others and the external environment. Personal learning occurs when you are alone, thinking, reflecting, reasoning, pondering, problem solving internally.

There is a difference between longitudinal learning experiences and impact learning experiences. Longitudinal learning occurs, for example, in the college classroom where information is presented repetitively over time. It is like water dripping on a rock. (The reader may draw any appropriate conclusions relative to the analogy between the human head and the rock.) It is impossible to point to any one drop (in this case, a drop of information) as making an impression. Nevertheless, an impression is made. This process is often trial and error: It is slow, and often not firmly integrated into the person's behavior.

Impact learning experiences are brief and intense. They are often accompanied by a significant emotional reaction. Examples would include being fired from a job, contracting a serious illness, having a key subordinate quit, or being in an accident. These experiences are more deeply internalized, but often more painful than the longitudinal. Fortunately, we can learn much vicariously.

Another important principle is that there are different learning styles. I noticed this during my years of doing workshops. No matter how I structured the presentations, some of the participants loved the lectures and hated the exercises; others were just the opposite.

David Kolb and his associates presented their theory and research in *Organizational Psychology* (Englewood Cliffs, N.J.: Prentice-Hall, 2nd ed., 1974, pp. 27–34), indicating at least four distinctive learning styles. (Refer to Figures 39 and 40 for a visual presentation of the theory.) The styles were constructed from differences that ranged from an approach to learning that valued the concrete to one that valued the abstract and from an active approach to a reflective approach. The implications are that some learn best from lectures, texts, and films, while others learn best from exercises, role plays, and psychodramas. Some will value joining with others and tackling a project, while others will want to sit alone on a hill and make mental notes. The differences in these approaches have profound implications for leading, teaching, career planning, and perhaps even marriage.

The insight of this first learning principle is that in every situation where learning is occurring, each person will come to know in different ways. We learn differentially from experience to experience, from age to age, and from the marketplace to the attic.

PRINCIPLE 2—LEARNING IS A MUTUAL PROCESS.   Learning, at least group learning, involves interaction with others. When this is occurring in a teaching or training situation the learner often mistakenly assumes a very passive role which says, "You are the expert, I am the sponge. You provide all the answers and I will soak them up." I think this is a mistake. I point out in many of my management development courses that in the training room we have over five hundred years of management experience represented, as compared to my twenty. Then I ask, "Where is the expertise? Where are the answers?" I try to act as a facilitator to get class members to share their insights and ways of solving problems. As a learner, you should view everyone you meet as a potential source of important information. The active approach is also more likely to fix the learning in your mind for future use.

PRINCIPLE 3—LEARNING IS BASED ON SUCCESSFUL COMMUNICA-TION.   Learning requires an exchange of information. Presenting information clearly and being understood is one of the most difficult challenges in the world. There is not space here to analyze all of the impediments to good communication, so only two or three barriers will be presented.

A first serious mistake is to assume we are all speaking the same language. If you don't know why this assumption is absurd, you reinforce my point. I begin each class or session by working with the group to build common definitions. I show the class all of the different ways you can use the word *cat* and then ask them, "What is really meant by the terms *truth, empathy, democracy,* or *good human relations?*" The dangers of misunderstanding are best illustrated by the theory of the schoolteacher who was teaching vocabulary words to her students. Her method was to send the new word to be learned home the previous night to be studied. She would then check for comprehension by asking one of the children to define the word and another to use it in a story. This particular day the teacher said, "The word for today was *frugal.* Who can tell the class what the word *frugal* means?"

Little Sally in the front row raised her hand and was called on. "The word frugal means to save. A frugal person is one who saves." "Very good, Sally," replied the teacher. "Now, can someone use the word in a sentence so we are sure we know what it means?" Johnny, in the back row, waved his arm. Johnny loved to tell the stories. He was called on, and with dramatic flair began: "Once upon a time, a long, long time ago, a beautiful princess was picking wild flowers in the forest. Suddenly she heard a tremendous roar and turned around to see a fire-breathing dragon. Just then, on a distant hill, she spied a knight in shining armor on his white charger, and she screamed "Frugal me! Frugal me!" And the knight charged down the hill, leaped off his trusty steed and frugaled her, and they lived happily ever after." Johnny smiled and sat down. Moral: Be very careful how you use words.

A second serious mistake is to make assumptions and treat them as if they were facts. Many mistakenly assume that the insight here is to avoid making assumptions. This is not only not the point, it is impossible. We make one thousand assumptions to get through each day. The point is to keep the assumptions and facts separated in your mind, and continually to test the assumptions for validity and reliability. One very shaky assumption is, "I am being understood." How do you test for understanding? The worst way is to ask "Did you understand?" to which the answer 98 percent of the time will be "Yes." Better to ask to have things repeated or see some demonstration of comprehension.

Another mistake is to assume that communication and understanding come naturally, because we have had lots of experience talking at people. Communication and learning are hard work, and understanding is the rare exception. Without great effort and some skill, misunderstanding, confusion, and hurt feelings are the order of the day.

Principles 4 and 5 flow out of a common premise, that *learning is a difficult,* in fact, *painful process.* Learning requires us to do two things that we abhor.

PRINCIPLE 4—LEARNING REQUIRES THINKING. Thinking is something we seldom do. Because we are so unfamiliar with it we are uncomfortable and rusty when we have to do it. The educational psychologists suggest that Albert Einstein spent about .03 percent of his waking hours thinking, and that was about 100 times more than the rest of us. That means that you and I spend about .0003 percent of our life engaged in thinking. But you recoil, "What do those crazy psychologists know; my mind is working all the time." And you're right; it is. But what your mind is doing is called information processing, acting like an efficient secretary. It retrieves, sorts, labels, and stores information (perceptions). The true process of really struggling with an idea, trying to create something, trying to solve a complex problem is something we all too seldom do. Stimulate yourself to think in every way you can. Read a little of a difficult new book each day. Really think about your job. Take any problem, from hangnails to nuclear war, and think about it for five minutes without distraction. (You could save the world.) Work a puzzle. Write a song or poem. Really try to understand someone. When you stop thinking and learning you start dying (and quickly).

PRINCIPLE 5—LEARNING REQUIRES CHANGING. *Learning* and *changing* are really synonymous terms. If you can read and practice the techniques in this book and honestly say you are no different from when you started, then you haven't learned (no matter what you can repeat on a paper-and-pencil test).

I ask my students, "How many of you came here to learn?" All of them (who are conscious) raise their hands. I respond, "I believe you, or at least you're half right. Sitting in your chair is a split personality. One side of you says, 'I want to learn, to grow, to develop.' The other side says, 'I hope this guy doesn't tell me anything new, or I might have to change.' I have to come in on one side or the other of the battle between your internal status quo versus your desire for change. I choose to come in on the change side. It's me and you versus you."

We are all creatures of habit. Most of what we do we do habitually (including driving and making love—good grief!). Habits are a great asset because they allow us to do one thing while thinking of something else. For example, when you brushed your teeth this morning, were you consciously involved in the brushing? Aha, see? You can't even remember whether you brushed your teeth or not. With toothbrushing, that's fine. But too often your ways of managing, planning, and relating to others have been reduced to habit. You found something that worked—sort of—and used it over and over three thousand times!

To learn, to develop, to grow, you must change. You must root up those habits of practice and thought and reexamine them. Combine with Principle 4: *Think* about them. Do they still work? Can they be improved? Is there new information? Are there new techniques? Change involves risk. Leaders are risk takers. *Do it!*

Now, how much change is it realistic to expect? Look at the person who is sitting in your chair right now. Go ahead, look. That person has spent twenty, thirty, thirty-nine years "becoming." How much will you change having read this book? Don't call your associates around you, climb up on a table, and say, "You see before you the new me! I have just read Bothwell's book and I am a new person." Half of them will immediately throw up and the other half will collapse laughing. Because it isn't true. This book will not create a "new you."

But if you really read this book, thought about it, and applied parts of it, you might change as much as 2 percent. And if you do, that will be such a dramatic change that friends will come up to you and ask, "What's happened to you? You seem like a new person!"

I dare you!

PRINCIPLE 6—ADULTS CAN LEARN.   A startling statement? Not today, but it was twenty years ago. We have labored for a century under the theories of the psychologists who told us that the three significant events of our lives were our birth, weaning, and toilet training, and that anything worth learning had been learned by age five. Learning was something kids did. Adults had all that behind them.

Don't believe me? Then you weren't sitting in college classes twenty years ago. You never saw the two middle-aged homemakers come shyly into a classroom and sit down. All the students immediately got up and moved to the other side of the room (as though these women had a highly communicable disease). You could hear whispers of "What are *they* doing here? They're *old* people!"

Today all of that has changed, not so much because we repudiated Freud, but because educational planners are so poor. After World War II a large number of babies were born and began to flush their way through our society. The late fifties was the golden age of elementary education, the early sixties the golden age of secondary education, and the late sixties the golden age of higher education. Colleges were booming, buildings were going up left and right, and the educational planners projected this trend to continue forever.

It didn't. Suddenly enrollments fell as the boom matriculated. Classrooms stood empty, dorms were unused—and all those tenured professors! Oh my! Tuition from the "youth" could not keep the old alma mater afloat. There had to be a new market, and they discovered *you.*

Suddenly the boom was on. When I was at Harvard 1974–1977 the elementary and secondary ed training programs had vanished. What were the "now" courses?: continuing education, extension services, lifelong learning, recurrent education, corporate education, midcareer education, and so on.

Today adult education is a multibillion-dollar business. No longer is there an excuse to say, "I never got a chance to learn . . . or to obtain a . . ."

George Weathersby in his "Post Secondary Education" (*Society,* January/ February, 1976, pp. 60, 62, 63) states:

> One-eighth of the adult population was enrolled in some form of continuing adult education in 1972. In the broader view postsecondary education includes almost 78,000 institutions offering formal, organized instruction to about 24 million individuals.
>
> Demand for postsecondary education is strong and growing. While the adult population is growing at about 2 percent per year, continuing education enrollments are growing at about 7 percent per year—the same rate at which higher education enrollments grew during the baby-boom years of the 1960's.

Take advantage of all the great opportunities available to you today for lifelong learning. So what if it takes you thirty years to get a doctorate. You have something better to do?

In summary: To learn, you must consider your special style, share, seek to understand and be understood, think, change, and continue to develop. As you do these things you will stand out from the crowd and others will want to follow you as a leader.

Double-Loop Learning

Leaders are learners. One of the most important things a true leader will ever do is learn how to learn. If true growth and development are to take place, it is essential to apply the principles of double-loop learning.

What follows is complex because the mind, nervous system, and behavior are complex. (I am indebted to friends and scholars Chris Argyris and Don Schon for what I know of double-loop learning.) You can study the subject in depth in their *Theory in Practice: Increasing Professional Effectiveness* (San Francisco: Jossey-Bass, 1974). My presentation here will be brief and is meant to be understandable and usable.

Figure 49 presents an overview of the theoretical model. Some of the terms are a little difficult but should be understandable with the discussion that follows. Begin by walking through the diagram.

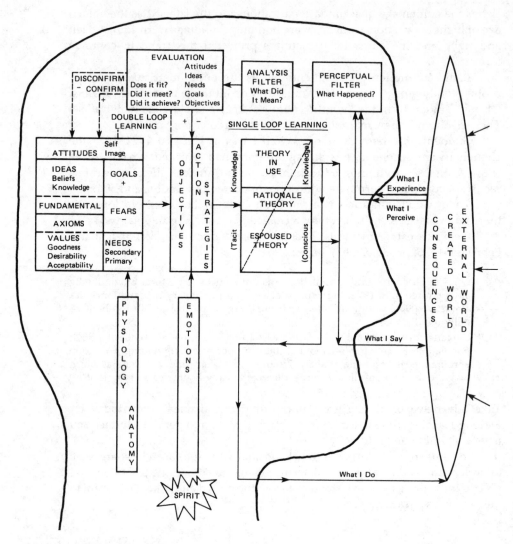

FIGURE 49. Theoretical model for a theory-of-action

Sparked by their spirit and moved by their emotions and physiology, people begin to gather information on the world around them and on themselves. Research indicates that this process begins before birth. Learning and growth proceed very rapidly in the years following birth, and the individual begins to develop basic ideas, values, goals, and fears. Primary needs are based on the physical survival of the individual, but as experiences continue, secondary or psychological needs are developed (love, power, growth). With everything that is experienced, the person develops basic attitudes or predispositions of how to react toward this "thing" when next encountered. These needs, ideas, values, goals, and fears make up the basic operating program of the individual.

To confirm the ideas, attitudes, and values; to meet the needs, avoid the fears, and achieve the goals, the person creates a secondary operating program consisting of goal/need specific objectives, and complex action strategies to see that these objectives are achieved.

The individual operates on the basis of three complex theories (programs): the theory in use, the rationale theory, and the espoused theory. The *theory in use* is the individual's basic operating program, and much of its content is tacit—that is, hidden to the individual. In other words, he or she is only conscious of part of the reasons why, and part of the knowledge of how things are done. The *rationale theory* is the explanation the individual gives himself or herself as to why and how something was done. This may or may not fit the theory in use. Part of the rationale theory is tacit, but much of it is conscious. The *espoused theory* is the person's explanation to others as to why he or she did something. This may be congruent with or bear little resemblance to the previous two. In fact, this will be determined by the person's action strategy (to be insightful and honest or to deceive). Most of the espoused theory is conscious.

As the person acts and speaks in interaction with the environment there are certain consequences. The external world of others partially comes to us, but is also created by us. For example, if we believe others cannot be trusted, and act as if they cannot be trusted, they may perceive this and respond in ways that are not trustworthy. This confirms our initial belief, but it is actually a self-fulfilling prophecy.

Through your senses you perceive and experience this external/created world. But the information that comes into you through this feedback process does not return unaltered. Your physiology will first filter much of what enters, distorting or selectively eliminating some of reality. You will then analyze, interpret, and assign meanings. Finally, the information that has now been filtered several times will be evaluated to see if it fits, meets personal needs and goals, and achieves your objectives.

You will notice from Figure 49 that this is a closed system, with the inside single loop going back to objectives and action strategies. These can either be confirmed or disconfirmed. If they are disconfirmed, you engage in first-order learning; in other words, you modify your objectives and strategies without altering the basic program (ideas, values, needs, goals, attitudes, and so on).

Here is the key. To engage in double-loop learning, you must go to the second part of the cycle. This second-order or depth learning requires you to reexamine and perhaps change your basic values, goals, needs, and attitudes. This process is more difficult, more painful, and often more frustrating, but is the only approach that leads to true learning and growth.

There are several reasons why double-loop learning is so difficult. First, valuing such a process must have become part of your basic program. Reaching just that stage is a challenge in itself. Secondly, many of these basic needs, goals, ideas, and values are buried deep and hidden to the learner. Uncovering them is not a simple process. Third, it is important to hold to basic tenets while evaluating them and incrementally changing some. Finally, some of these ideas and values (as the figure shows) are so axiomatic as to be virtually beyond change. This can provide both important stability and dangerous rigidity.

Two examples of the contrast between single-loop learning and double-loop learning may assist in clarifying this concept. Suppose a person believes that when you love people, and have a close relationship with them, you will inevitably end up being hurt. This belief may have come from several early (and perhaps idiosyncratic) experiences in the person's life. This belief has now become axiomatic. The person has several strong needs, including: I want to be loved (have relationships with others, avoid being lonely); I want to avoid this type of pain; I want to stay in control of my relationships with others. This person has a great fear of experiencing any more of this pain. She or he develops a goal of forming and carrying on relationships that cannot lead to hurt. To accomplish this the person develops some very complex objectives and action strategies, which include always keeping "loved ones" at an emotional distance, not letting others know him or her and what he or she cares about, and not caring too much for others.

The result of carrying out these action strategies is a series of relationships that lead to continual conflict, frustration, and pain. Others who care for this individual find their deep caring not really returned. They often respond to this defensively. When the individual is hurt by this response, she or he engages in single-loop learning and reinforces the belief that letting others get too close inevitably results in pain. She or he continues to create distance from others, which continues to lead to counterattacks, which continues to reinforce the basic belief system. The result can be disastrous.

To engage in double-loop learning in this situation, the person—with the help of one who truly cares and/or with the help of a therapist—would have to dredge out and confront the basic belief. Was it based on the loss of a parent? A pet? A friend? All of the above? Is every relationship likely to lead to the same conclusion? Is living without love and close relationships, without taking the risk of letting someone get close to you, really worth the loneliness and isolation? If not, the belief, some of the needs, the fear, the goals, the objectives, and the action strategies all have to be altered. This can lead to new, warm, satisfying relationships that can confirm the new belief: There is value in letting others get close to you.

A second example. Suppose a leader has the belief that the most important principle of a leader/follower relationship is that of *obedience*. This person has several needs. He or she wants: to be secure, predictability, to control, to run things, to produce results, to be successful. The person has several fears: losing control, having others question his or her authority, having some act differently than he or she instructed, being seen as ineffective. The goal is to be an effective, dynamic, powerful leader. The objectives and action strategies include giving orders, keeping track of every detail, closely supervising everything subordinates do, punishing deviation, rewarding conformity and dependence.

The negative results of the implementation of these action strategies could be several. Subordinates could tend toward apathy, power struggles, and sabotage. There could be high rates of turnover. In the absence of the leader, all productive activity might cease; subordinates might be confused as to what to do next. As these results unfold, the leader is only confirmed in the initial belief, and bears down harder and supervises more closely. The experience is unpleasant for everyone concerned, including the leader.

For this person to engage in double-loop learning, again the elements of the basic operating program would have to be questioned. Is obedience the most basic principle? What could be equally important? Love? Concern for the followers? Teamwork? Learning from others? Developing others? Might it not be, in fact, that if these other principles developed into action strategies, the desired obedience might flow as a natural consequence?

It would be difficult for this individual to learn to give up or share control, to let others explore their own ideas and methods, and fail, and try again. It would require a change in focus from being in charge to producing results and to having everyone, including the leader, receive more satisfaction from the working relationship.

Double-loop learning is the only method that leads to true change, growth, and development in a person. As these two examples have shown, it can be demanding, difficult, and disturbing. Without the help of others it is extremely difficult, but it can be done. The alternative, as I have shown, is to continue with self-defeating actions that lead to negative self-fulfilling prophecies and unhappiness.

Here is how you can begin the process. Use the model in Figure 49 to begin your analysis of yourself. Construct an inventory of your beliefs, values, needs, fears, goals, objectives, and action strategies. Be as honest and complete as you can. You may want to get feedback from those close to you in how they perceive you in some of these categories.

You may then want to construct a short life history. In writing the major events of your life, try to discover where some of your needs, goals, and fears have come from. Who were the people who were models in your life? What action strategies did they employ to get what they wanted?

Now consider which of your specific actions are dysfunctional to the achievement of your goals. This is where the involvement of other caring persons can really be helpful. Explore the goals, needs, and values that they may wish to change. Look for substitute action strategies. Take one piece at a time and work on it. Don't expect overnight miracles. Remember—you have taken twenty, thirty, thirty-nine years becoming who and what you are. If you find you could use professional help in making these difficult changes, then by all means seek it.

Double-loop learning is worth the effort. It can lead to a more effective, more satisfied, more secure, more confident you. This is the kind of person others will want to follow.

RELATING TO OTHERS

One of the ways leaders differ is in their approach in relating to others. This is not their leadership style, which will be discussed in the next chapter, but the ways in which they choose to interact with those with whom they have a relationship. This section consists of two major parts. The first part presents a model that can be used for diagnosing a relationship with another person in terms of where it is and which direction it is going. The second part prescribes some effective techniques for dealing with others and yourself.

Approaches to Interpersonal Relations

The diagnostic model looks at five different levels of approaches to human relations.* The model is normative in that it suggests a direction for improved relations.

The first approach, and most basic level of human relations, is known as the *mystery-mastery* approach. The underlying assumption of this first approach to dealing with others is that information and knowledge are sources of power, and that if you can control those and keep them from others, you can dominate and manipulate situations.

For the person using this approach, when someone wants to know why a thing is or is not working, typical responses might be:

> "You wouldn't understand."
> "It's too technical."
> "I don't have time to explain it to you."
> "Just take my word for it."
> "The computer is down."
> "The system is off-line."
> "Because I said so."
> "The reciprocal function has become discombobulated."

This approach might be appropriate to a person who assumes others are inferior, slow-witted, and irresponsible. However, the result of relating to others this way is usually a response on their part of frustration, anger, counterattack, and reciprocal game playing. Unfortunately, in a busy, complex, specialist-filled world, this approach is all too common.

The second human relations approach is the *structural approach*. This means a person's power base and interpersonal style are derived from the person's position on the organizational chart. This is an improvement over the previous approach, in that information might be readily shared, but the person relates to others on the basis of differential status, role playing, titles, and one-upmanship. Typical gambits include:

> "I, the doctor . . ."
> "As the person in charge . . ."
> "Since I am your supervisor . . ."
> "We parents . . ."
> "As one who speaks for God . . ."
> "Having completed college . . ."
> "With my many years of experience . . ."
> "You wo/men wouldn't understand . . ."

*I am indebted to Bill Torbert, then a professor at the Harvard Graduate School of Education, for ideas that led to the creation of this theory.

144

This approach emphasizes differences rather than common problems and a shared humanity. It creates "we-they" dichotomies. It leads to comparing oneself with others, which is always destructive because the outcome is inevitably false pride or self-depreciation.

The third approach is the *sympathy-supportive* approach. This approach improves on the last because the goal is to be supportive and helpful and can in fact lead to doing much good for others. The problem with sympathy is that it is always "top-down" and unilateral.

FIGURE 50. Sympathy *for* others (unilateral)

The basic message conveyed to the other is, "You poor slob, I'm glad I'm not messed up like you" or, as someone humorously said, "I'm okay, you're a jerk!" No one feels good about being patronized, and responses vary from rejection of the person offering help to defeatism and retreat. This approach also emphasizes differences, although they are softened from the previous approach. In other words, the assumption of the person offering the help is that the other is inept, lazy, or limited in ability to figure things out. Acting sympathetically toward another provides only temporary "relief," does nothing to strengthen that person's ability to cope, may create dependence, and continues to treat the circumstance as a given. This is a start, but it is improved upon in the following approach.

The fourth approach is the *empathy-collaborative* approach. Whereas sympathy is feeling *for*, empathy is feeling *with*. It is the ability to put yourself in the other person's place, to walk in their shoes. The collaborative part of the title emphasizes "We're all in this thing together, so let's help each other along the road." These two terms emphasize a relationship of equality, mutuality, and sharing.

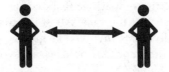

FIGURE 51. Empathy *with* others (shared)

There are several challenges in trying to use this approach to human relations. The first has to do with the difficulty of being empathetic. It is not easy to put yourself in the other person's place; in fact, often it is impossible. (I remind myself with the cartoon on my wall showing an eight-months-pregnant woman struggling to pull her coat on in the doctor's office. The sixty-year-old, gray-haired, male M.D. is saying "There, there, Mrs. Walker, I know exactly how you feel.") We damage relationships when we utter obviously false statements such as "I know exactly how you feel," or "I know what you're going to say." We never know. Better to respond, "My father died also, and I remember how pained I was, so I have some sense of what you're going through." Or "I can understand your frustration at not being able to locate the correct office to help you. Even though I'm a federal employee, I have the same problem when I call another agency. Let me see if I can get it for you." This type of response provides an assurance that a human being is on the line, not a machine, and that help will be forthcoming. It builds positive relationships.

A second major challenge with the empathy-collaborative approach is that it requires the giver to share some of himself or herself. Openness always involves risk, but pays great dividends. I took over as a director of a major office from a man whose style was to be totally in control and invincible. I felt I couldn't help the staff if I didn't know what their problems were, but they were not about to share with one who "never makes a mistake." I began the practice of starting the weekly staff meeting by disclosing my two dumbest mistakes of the previous week. At first there was shock, but then people began to share, and I was able to resolve a lot of things that would have been swept under the rug. When I've told this story at management development conferences, I've had some weak-egoed managers confront me with the question of whether this practice didn't diminish the staff's respect for me. On the contrary, they respected my humanness, open communication, and willingness to work with them to solve problems. If any of you really believe those who work closest with you don't know your weaknesses and failures, you're kidding yourselves.

A third challenge is the actual process of collaboration. Never mind the question of large groups—two individuals have difficulty in developing a united, integrated approach (as any married person knows). Problems are often encountered with differing goals, and/or beliefs, and/or values, and/or techniques. Differences in ideas and techniques are usually more readily resolved, but differences in fundamental goals or values may run so deep as to be axiomatic and irresolvable. In such cases the two may have to seek a third party to help facilitate the empathy and collaboration.

It would seem that the empathy-collaborative approach would be the final approach, but such is not the case. All of the first four approaches take the situation and the individuals involved as givens. In other words, "Given this company, and this office, and our policies, and you and I as we are, what can we do about this problem?"

The final approach is called the *mutual-confrontive* approach. This approach assumes all the empathy, support, and collaboration of the previous one (as implied by the word *mutual*), but the emphasis is on confronting: the system, the rules, the climate, the task, and you and me. The emphasis is on change and growth. The key questions are:

"Why are things as they are?"
"How should they be?"
"How could we change them?"

The challenges and techniques of change required here are discussed in Leadership Technique Section 8.

Here is a graphic representation of the model as a whole:

FIGURE 52. Approaches to interpersonal relations

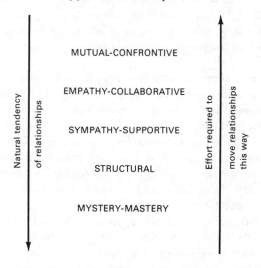

Once an individual has the five levels in perspective, it is possible to identify immediately at what level you are relating as you interact with someone else. In terms of movement, it seems to be the "natural" tendency for relationships to deteriorate (move toward mystery-mastery) unless at least one, but probably both, of the parties creates energy and concentrated effort to have the relationship improve (move toward mutual-confrontive). For example, you could make a request of a clerk in your organization. The person might respond, "Look, I'm the deputy processor for this whole section. I don't have time to stop and look that up" (structural approach). You could retort, "Hey, I'm a branch manager from upstairs and I'm telling you to do it right now" (structural approach). To which the clerk might counter, "I'm sorry, but I don't know where that information has been filed. You'll have to check back tomorrow." (The interaction has now degenerated to the mystery-mastery level.) Instead, you could have responded, "I know it must be frustrating to have people interrupt your work all day with requests for information. My job is somewhat like yours, and I have a sense of what that feels like. If you could give me the catalog maybe I could help you." This is an empathy-collaborative approach to the situation and holds the possibility of elevating the level of the relationship.

Keep the picture of the five levels in mind in your relationships with others and always work toward the highest level.

Effective Human Relations Techniques

The second part of this section is entitled Effective Human Relations Techniques, or "How to keep your head when all about you are losing theirs and blaming it on you." While the focus of this section is on looking at ways of relating to others, these practices, if conscientiously followed, also provide some great coping skills. At this time, when everyone is into stress management, these might be thought of as some commonsense approaches for avoiding or minimizing stress.

First, realize that communication between two people that results in understanding is a rare and unique experience. There is nothing natural about good communication. It requires learning effective techniques and a great deal of hard work. Several principles have been discussed throughout this book, including avoiding making assumptions (especially the assumption that you are speaking the same language) and treating them as if they were facts; considering the importance of open and honest feedback; listening; avoiding jargon; not interrupting or filibustering; being clear about the purpose for the communication; and being helpful.

Second, one quality that will make you stand out from the crowd is that of integrity. People with integrity are ones who have integrated their walk and their talk. They practice what they preach; they put their theory into practice; they avoid hypocrisy and double-dealing; they come on straight; they can be counted on.

Robert Townsend in his *Up the Organization* (New York: Fawcett Crest, 1970, p. 211, has spoken of integrity:

> (This) brings us to the most misunderstood part of all: *you don't have to abandon or compromise your principles in order to succeed in organizations.* The reason for this is that everybody else is so busy selling out, or has sold out so often, that when *you* come along and *don't* sell out or compromise, you stand out immediately.

Third, you need to develop the ability to relax under pressure. Participants in my seminars tell me with escalating voices, "I am a very calm person! The only time I get rattled is when everything goes wrong!" Of course! We're all calm when the lights are low and the music is soft. The victory comes in carrying over the feeling of calmness during the time when the zoo you work in (and/or live in) erupts. That's when cool heads are needed.

Coping with stress is one of the most topical concerns today. The ability to do it is not to be taken lightly as a key leadership ability and trait. I believe that the key to not letting stress become distress is the ability to gain perspective. How do you gain perspective in a complex, noisy world where the "trees" are closing in on you? A fair question. I think that one of the answers is that *at least* once a month you give yourself a one-half-day block of alone time. What do I mean by alone time? I mean four hours away from any living soul and any technological objects (yes! no car, no radio, no TV). Where do you find such a place? On a mountaintop or in the middle of a desert, or a lake, or an ocean. You cannot lie for four hours in a field of wild flowers on a hillside, watching cumulus clouds float overhead, and still feel the same way about the phone bill, or the person who was just promoted over you. Try it . . . repeatedly!

Fourth, you must own your own life. You must believe and act as if you know that your perceptions, your feelings, and your actions are really yours. No one causes you to do anything. No event influences you. People and events just are; you select the reaction. That is the measure of you as a person. You must come to act and not to be acted upon.

This concept was developed in the writings of columnist Sydney Harris. He shared the story of a friend who was treated very gruffly by a vendor with whom he had been most cordial. Harris expressed surprise at his friend's pleasant response when treated with such rudeness. The friend replied kindly, "Why should I let his actions determine my behavior?" This man would undoubtedly live a long, relatively stress-free life, because he had placed the locus of control directly inside himself, instead of reacting as if others and external events caused him to think, feel, and act in certain ways.

You must learn to be an actor, not a reactor. You must come to own your own feelings and behavior. This does not mean that you have to become an emotionless robot. You can respond to a situation with any emotions that you choose. What you must be clear about is that *you choose the response* and therefore *you are responsible for the consequences of that response.* You cannot escape responsibility by projecting the blame for the way you act or feel on someone, or something, else. When you begin to own and control your own life, you will develop an inner power that is obvious to others and attracts them to you as followers.

Fifth, relations with others and your own mental health are greatly aided by a sense of humor. Not all of us possess a sense of humor to the same degree. But whatever amount of humor you possess can be developed. You must learn to see the ridiculous in the world around you and especially develop the ability to laugh at yourself. This is not always easy to do, but here is a formula that might help:

$$Crisis + Perspective = Humor$$

Is there any way to accelerate the perspective? I think so. I suggest the following: 1) Escape the scene of the chaos, 2) lock yourself in a bathroom (most nemeses will not follow you there), 3) take a deep breath (maybe two), and 4) ask yourself "What would the writers of the *Mary Tyler Moore Show* or *WKRP in Cincinnati* do with the current situation?" Get the point! When you see Ted Baxter's pompous posturing in front of Mary Richards or the way Jennifer leads Mr. Carlson around by the nose, that's funny. What you must see is that your situation is just as ridiculous! The only difference is that you're one of the characters.

Let me give you an example of the kind of ridiculous situations you can get into as it applies to myself. I had just been hired as a faculty member at Whittier College. As a new associate professor, I was concerned with making a good impression on my new colleagues. It was the day of our first departmental faculty meeting.

It had just stopped raining as I left for my meeting with about ten minutes to spare. I had dressed in my best three-piece gray pin-striped suit. As I walked out the back door I passed an overloaded trash can that the kids had set out. I felt it looked rather messy to our new neighbors and decided to take a minute to make it neater. Briefcase in hand, I climbed up on the trash can and began jumping with my entire two-hundred pound frame. On the third jump I hit the can on an angle and my feet flew into the air. The can went over and I came down, bouncing off the house and the can. I ended up in a mud puddle on the walk, covered with garbage, my hand bleeding, unable to move a sprained arm. A lesser man would skip the meeting, right? Not me! I returned to the house and wiped the mud and garbage off my suit with a bath towel. I wrapped my bleeding hand in a paper towel, and cradling my immobilized arm, hiked off to the meeting, arriving twenty minutes late. Thus were my colleagues to get their first impression of their distinguished new associate.

Needless to say, this event was not side-splittingly humorous to me at the time. But now it is one of my favorite stories on myself as an example of the ridiculous human animal.

The sixth technique of human relations is common sense, which I feel is more appropriately named "uncommon sense." Do you find the tendency toward using good sense to be commonly distributed throughout humanity? Good sense, wisdom, the correct application of thinking or knowledge is rare. That is why those who possess it have no trouble in getting others to follow them. What is the obvious thing to do? Why? Have you considered it for thirty seconds (more thinking than most situations are ever given)? Do it. The reverse is also true: If it seems too good to be true, it probably isn't. I believe this slogan has been adopted by the Boston Consumer Protection agency. (Common sense works everywhere except in Boston. To survive in Boston you must employ Bothwell's Rational-Irrational Rule: Think of the common-sense, logical way to do something and then turn it around 180 degrees. That is what will work . . . in Boston.)

The seventh principle was analyzed previously, and that is the importance of empathy. The Golden Rule says "Do unto others as you would have others do unto you." As Harvard's Lawrence Kohlberg has shown us, the interpretation and application you give to this rule says much about your moral maturity. Kohlberg uses this principle to test a person's stage of moral development. Interpretations range from doing things for others with no expectation that they will do anything for you (though believing that the thing that you "send out" will return in kind from somewhere in the universe), to the interpretation "Do it to them before they can do it to you" (a slogan cynically found on many T-shirts today.)

The eighth principle has to do with the social processes in which we continually find ourselves. In any situation there are the following outcomes (this is a two-person model, but it could be two offers, two corporations, or two countries):

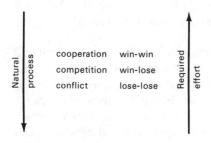

FIGURE 53. Outcomes of interaction

As discussed in the previous model of the five approaches to human relations, the natural order of things is to degenerate in the direction of conflict. Real effort and shared goals and values are necessary for relations to move to cooperation. For continued cooperation to exist, the following steps must be taken. First, both parties must believe that everyone can win. If this belief is mutually held, it's almost always correct. If one or both do not believe they both can win, the relationship will quickly degenerate into competition, then into conflict. Second, the approach taken to mutual winning must not be compromise (which is usually lose-lose, in that we both give up something that we want), but integrated decision making (IDM). Simply stated, this is a problem-solving approach that says, "What do I want and need?" "How can we both obtain it?" Quick, what assumption are you making right now? That this is usually impossible? If you believe that, you're right. But you're wrong!

Here is an example of how integrated decision making can work. A husband loved to go into the wilds and rough it on vacation. His wife liked to sleep in silk sheets after a hot shower, couldn't miss Johnny Carson, and loved to go shopping and dancing on vacation. In the past they had compromised (lose-lose)—first, by doing what each wanted to do in alternate years (during which time the other was always miserable); secondly, by doing a third thing that neither of them really wanted to do. Then they tried IDM. He identified what he really wanted in a vacation, and so did she. They problem solved it and came up with a win-win solution. They bought a large mobile home complete with bed, silk sheets, shower, and color TV. They went on vacation to an area where a resort with shopping and dancing is close to rugged wilderness country. They could spend part or all of the day in the town and then head for the wilds. While she reclines in comfort, he, outside, huddles over his campfire and climbs into his sleeping bag for a good night's sleep before the early morning fishing.

It will work more often than you may think. But you must believe and act as if it will work.

The ninth principle is humility. To be humble is to be teachable, to realize that you have something to learn from every person and every situation. To be humble is to have awe and respect in the presence of the least of God's creatures, not the greatest. As C. S. Lewis points out in the *The Weight of Glory* (Grand Rapids, Mich.: W.B. Erdmans Publishing Co., 1965), to be humble is *not* to know that you are humble.

The final principle is love, a much-maligned word today. Paul called it charity, another modern misuse. True love is based on concern for and service to others, with no consideration of "What's in it for me?" It is a most powerful force and the secret to all true success in our relations with others.

Love will be discussed later, using other words, as the basis for charisma. It can be seen that it is a basis for many of the principles discussed in this section. It is a basis for sensitive, trusting, other-focused communication. It is a basis for composure, steadiness, self-control, and direction. It leads one often to act with uncommon sense. It is certainly the basis for acting with empathy toward others. It creates the energy and patience to try and work out win-win solutions to conflicts. It is a basis for humility, because the focus is on others, not on self.

Love, as a principle and as a source of power, runs counter to much of what is happening in the world today. But then one need only look at the condition of the world today to see the result of loveless relationships and policies. If you would have others follow you, employ this gift frequently and freely. It will come back to you manyfold.

There you have the ten basic principles of effective human relations:

1. True communication
2. Integrity
3. Composure and steadiness
4. Self-control and action
5. A sense of humor
6. Uncommon sense and wisdom
7. Empathy
8. A win-win approach (integrated decision making)
9. Humility
10. Selfless love

These ten qualities and practices can not all be acquired instantly. It is a life work. You must tackle them one at a time and apply them until they become habit, then part of your character. Benjamin Franklin demonstrated the difficulty of becoming perfect by creating and attempting to integrate into his life just such lists. He said that he found that when he had mastered all of the other traits he lost his humility. But it is worth the quest. Through applying these principles you will have a great influence for good, and others will want to follow you.

POWER:
A KEY LEADERSHIP TOOL

Leadership, perhaps more than anything else, involves the use of power. Leaders must understand what power is, where it comes from, and how it is used or abused. For to lead is to exercise power, whether you understand what you're doing or not.

Power comes from the Greek word *potere*, which means "to be able to." When I ask leaders "to be able to do what?" they respond with:

> *To be able to:*
> make things happen
> influence people
> influence events
> create change
> produce results

Without power things do not happen. If nothing happens there is no leadership, no personal success, and no progress. To be effectively powerful, then, is a critical concern of the successful leader.

This section examines in depth the sources from which power comes to the individual. The importance of this analysis is directly related to the subsequent discussion of the basic principles of power.

Sources of Interpersonal Power

For many years the seminal article on sources of power has been John R. P. French, Jr., and Bertram Raven's "The Basis of Social Power," in *Studies in Social Power*, D. Cartwright, ed. (Ann Arbor, Michigan: Institute for Social Research, 1959). I will begin by examining their treatment of the sources, then expand the list significantly. Raven and French list five sources of power: legitimate, reward, coercive, referent, and expertise.

Legitimate power is sometimes called charter power, position power, or authority. Authority is power that people derive from their position in the organization. Where does the position derive the power from? The power comes from the charter of the organization; it is delegated to the position holder by the members of the organization—hence, it is legitimate.

153

Here are two examples. If you fire someone from their job, who empowered you to do that? They did; at least they are one of the members of the organization who authorized the person holding your position to fire those working under him or her. If you fail a student in a class, who authorized you to do that? Again, they did. Now the charter can be changed; they and other members can take away your power to fire and fail. In fact, there were many movements in this direction during the 1960s. But your power as a positional leader is derived from the consent of the governed.

Legitimate power, or authority, is a very important source of power, but it is not the only source. Unfortunately, many leaders in formal positions treat it as if it were. Leaders, when asked about their power, often respond in terms of the bounds of their formal position. If that position has few powers assigned to it under the organizational charter, then the occupant feels powerless. If you feel powerless, you tap none of the other sources of power, and therefore act powerless; you are powerless. But only because you have chosen to be powerless.

Reward power is often associated with authority and one's formal position. This is true, but it is only half the story. There are two types of rewards, formal and informal. Formal rewards are chartered to the position. They include dispensing raises, bonuses, promotions, transfers, high grades, privileges, and so on. These are important in influencing people, because many are strongly moved by them. But they do not lead to motivated followers. Motivation is an internal quality, where the motive and the action must come from the needs of the individual.

Perhaps the following dialogue, repeated many times at training programs for new supervisors, will make the point.

"How can you reward your subordinates for doing good work?"

"We're not allowed to give raises."

"Okay, what can you do to reward good work?"

"We're not allowed to give bonuses, either."

"Okay, what can you do?"

"They won't let us promote people, either."

"You're very good at brainstorming lists of things you *can't* do, now let's list some things you *can* do! (Silence)

"Let me see if I can help; could you say to a subordinate, 'Thanks, ya done good!'?"

(Silence, then several hands raised)

"Yes?"

"Why should you thank subordinates for doing the job they get paid to do?"

(Several affirmative nods)

"Now we've identified why your people lack motivation!"

Informal rewards include thanks, praise, recognition, encouragement, smiles, notes of commendation, flowers, and so forth. These forms of reward pay big dividends. If you had to choose between a ten-dollar raise or a note lauding your performance, which would you choose? I can remember very few of the raises in my career, but I can remember every positive note written about me since high school. I've had employees ask if they could make photocopies of commendation notes I have written to them, to send to family and friends.

These powerful informal rewards are used most often by the informal leader and the peers. This is unfortunate, because they are all available to the formal leader along with all the formal rewards. The two types are not mutually exclusive. Use them frequently and you will have followers who will charge into the fires of hell for you.

Coercive power has to do with the leader's ability to punish. There are also two levels of punishment, formal and informal. Again, the formal flows from the authorized position. Formal use of coercive power include firing, failing, fining, demoting, imprisoning, expelling, and putting to death (irreversible expulsion). We would like to believe that these sources of power are never used. In fact, they are used all the time. By inflicting pain on subordinates you can get them to move around a lot. But you do not get motivated followers.

A classic story on the use of formal sanctions has to do with a corporation that decides to change its employee benefit program. The old contract requires 100 percent agreement of all employees to create such a change. After an elaborate two-hour presentation by the personnel department, agreement for the change is obtained from every employee but one.

Old Charley is visited by the head of personnel, who spends another two hours explaining all the advantages of the new program. Charley still won't budge. In desperation, the personnel director goes to the president of the corporation and explains the dilemma. The president says, "Send Charley up; maybe I can reason with him."

Charley reports to the president's desk and says, "You wanted to see me?"

The president slides the consent slip across the desk and says, "Sign that or you're fired."

Charley signs and on the way out bumps into the personnel director, who is pacing nervously outside the president's door.

"What happened in there?" he asks, anticipating another failure.

"What do you mean, what happened? I signed that paper you were waving at me the other day," replied Charley.

"You signed it? But you were only in there thirty seconds—we talked to you for four hours! Why did you sign it for him when you wouldn't sign for us?"

"I don't know," answered Charley. "I guess no one ever explained it to me that clearly before!"

The informal punishments may be used by leader, peer, or subordinate, and include frowning, gossiping about, criticizing, ignoring or ostracizing (a very painful and effective form), threatening, implying a threat (a very subtle form, the response to which is often confused with motivation), depriving, withholding (information, love, etc.), tone of voice, and so on. All of these are used much too frequently, and while they may produce instant, short-term response, in the long run they lead to frustration, resentment, resignation, counterattack, retrenchment, immaturity, and sabotage.

Looking at the last four sources of power: formal reward, informal reward, formal punishment, and informal punishment, research has shown that formal punishment is most often used and least effective, and informal reward least often used and most effective. *Do you want to be an effective leader?*

Referent power is power you possess when others refer to you, look up to you, wish to copy or emulate you. This is power that is given to you by the followers, and usually has nothing to do with your position.

Ask people, "Who were four of the most powerful people in the world from 1960 to 1970?" Answer: The Beatles. Did their power come from position, reward, or punishment? No. And yet, if they shaved their heads, 100 million adolescents around the world would have shaved their heads. That's power. What is its source? Followers who use those individuals as a reference group and wish to be like them. Referent power is one I'm not sure you can "do." (Ask the three thousand other groups who tried to do it like the Beatles, or JFK, or FDR, or . . . etc.).

Expertise as a source of power comes from one's ability to do something extremely well. Since most people do not have the native ability, desire, experience, and practice to do a thing extremely well, those who do are seen as powerful, and people follow them (even if "following" only consists of watching them on the tube). The story is told of the woman who went up to a concert pianist after a recital and said, "That was marvelous. I'd give half of my life to be able to play the piano that well." The pianist's response: "Madam, that's exactly what I gave."

So far the original Raven and French sources of power have been extended from five to seven, by dividing reward and punishment into formal and informal groupings. Additional sources can now be considered.

First, there are three additional sources related to the source called referent power. Each of these could be thought of as extensions of referent power, but there are important differences.

Source number eight you might call power based on *respect*. If others hold you in high esteem, if what you do is held in high regard, you have a source of power. This is not identical to referent power, because a follower may wish to be like (have the power of) a leader without respecting him or her. A person may also respect a leader, like the President of the United States, without wishing to be President (with the attendant publicity and pressures).

Is respect only based on positive performances or those that serve good ends? Unfortunately, not so. Throughout history, men have respected dictators, gunfighters, war heroes, and in today's media, even anti-heroes. This is not to say that what they did was good, only that it was highly regarded. Followers may also respect the right person for the wrong reason, or the wrong person for inappropriate reasons.

The ninth source of power is *liking*. If people like you, if they care for you (for whatever reason), this is a source of power. Teenage boys have known this for centuries, as they have used variations of the line: "If you really loved me, you would..." I'm surprised that more females haven't responded, "If you really loved me, you wouldn't ask." It is true, as all too many have found out, that in relationships based on liking the person who cares least, controls.

Let's take a more positive approach. How do you empower yourself by getting others to like you? This is accomplished by helping others meet their needs. As they see you as a source of assistance in attaining things that make them happy, their liking for you may increase. Notice that you can use this power not only with followers, but with your peers, your boss, your spouse, and with strangers. In other words, I like and am influenced by strangers who are helpful to me (in meeting my needs). If you want others to follow you, help them meet their needs in the process. This is another act of leadership.

The tenth source of power is *charisma*. At one time I didn't believe in charisma. I often heard the term applied to JFK, and yet I "knew" he had won the debates with Nixon and the election through better makeup, wardrobe, and speech training. I concluded that charisma was Madison Avenue hype.

My attitude toward charisma changed dramatically through an experience I had in 1970. I had a brief encounter with a nationally known political figure. This was a man whose political views could not have been more opposite from my own. Our encounter lasted no more than a couple of minutes, but in his expression of concern for me and my associate, as strangers in his state, I was struck by a personal magnetism that drew me to him. I cannot say that it was the firmness of his handshake, the eye contact, or the tone of voice, but I know I felt drawn to him. His aides had said of him that if he could shake hands with every voter in the United States he would be the next President of the United States.

Several years passed, and one day I heard on the radio an announcement of a tragedy that had struck this man. It hit me in the pit of the stomach and I felt as if this had occurred to a personal friend. I pondered about how this could be possible with someone I had only met for a brief moment. The man had something, a powerful personal quality, and it was *not* Madison Avenue hype.

Since that time I have met a few others who have power based on charisma. I am not sure that charisma can be taught or given to someone in a course or a book. But it is not a quality that some of us have and others have none of. Each of us possesses it to a greater or lesser degree, and it can be expanded within us. Some of its elements are sincerely caring for others, being able to communicate that caring, doing something about it, having success in what you do, having the power of your convictions, and basing those convictions on true principles. Tall order, but possible for every one of us.

Raven and French's final source of power was expertise. This also has three extensions, which will continue to broaden our choice of options in employing sources of power.

The eleventh source of power is the *possession of knowledge*. The old maxim says, "knowledge is power." This is not true. Knowledge is knowledge. In and of itself it is nothing. But the possession of that knowledge provides one with at least the power of understanding and reason. Further, the possession of knowledge provides one with a potential for effective action, which, if repeated over time, as I have said, leads to expertise.

As a cadet at the United States Air Force Academy, three times a day for four years I marched to meals past the Eagle and Fledglings statue, with its inscription, "Man's flight through life is sustained by the power of his knowledge." And surely the possession of knowledge—especially knowledge of true principles and laws—is one of the sustaining powers of life. And as we have repeatedly seen, those who possess significant amounts of knowledge will never lack for followers.

A related dimension here is the leader's ability to properly apply the knowledge she or he possesses. This ability is often referred to as wisdom. Each of us has known people who possessed great knowledge, but were not necessarily wise—in other words, they were often not able to apply what they knew appropriately or effectively. Additionally, once one knows how to properly apply knowledge, it takes repeated application before one develops what could be called skill or expertise. Here, then, are levels of this great power source, but the process is seen to commence with the acquisition of knowledge. (This may be an interesting response to the person who rejects knowledge for knowledge's sake and wants to know "Practically speaking, what can learning do for me?" My answer, "It can empower you!")

The twelfth source of power is related to knowledge, but is more than its mere possession. This is the ability to *communicate one's knowledge,* which could include teaching, writing, philosophizing, public speaking, and selling. Again, one could say the ability to communicate is power. But this is only a half-truth. There must be something of substance to communicate if you are to be lastingly powerful, hence, the assumption of the possession of knowledge.

Once you possess substantial knowledge, the ability to transmit it effectively becomes a key to power and to the attraction of followers. Some of the great leaders in history have been known for their ability to persuade, sell, speak, write, and philosophize. Founders and leaders of great religious movements that have attracted and influenced millions have often been referred to as great teachers.

If you have the ability to share what you know, to analyze and explain an idea so the simplest person can understand it, to persuade others to your point of view, to present a vision, to expand another's view, then you will find many who will follow you and respond to your power.

The thirteenth source of power is related to those just discussed, but less directly. The reason for this is that the person possessing and using this source of power may lack expertise, knowledge, wisdom, or communication skills. This source of power is known as the *control and dissemination of information.*

The classic character who epitomizes this source is ex-PFC Wintergreen in Joseph Heller's *Catch-22* (New York: Simon and Schuster, 1961). Wintergreen is controlling WWII military operations in the Mediterranean theater through his role as radio operator between the field headquarters and the high command. He is running the war. Life and death flow from information that he passes on or withholds.

Do you really believe there is not an ex-PFC Wintergreen in your office (or church, or home)? If these people choose to play the mystery-mastery game discussed previously, then they maintain their power by withholding or selectively leaking valuable (sometimes vital) information. You have experienced this approach from doctors to receptionists, from presidents to cabdrivers. It is frustrating and it works in a very self-defeating way.

The alternative option is to follow principle number seven and to disperse as widely and as freely as you can all of the important information you possess. In this way everyone is more empowered. And do you ever really lose by sharing information with others? Never, in my experience. If you think otherwise, think about it some more.

It is helpful now to look at the thirteen sources of power that have been discussed in a summary table. The original five sources have been expanded extensively. This can enable you to read, understand, and apply—to increase your power, while also empowering those around you.

FIGURE 54. Thirteen sources of interpersonal power

(Those in the left-hand column are the original Raven and French five. The thirteen on the right are the expanded list by Bothwell and are numbered as they were presented in the section.)

LEGITIMATE	(1)	Chartered, Authority
REWARD	(2)	Formal
	(3)	Informal
COERCIVE	(4)	Formal Negative Sanctions
	(5)	Informal Negative Sanctions
REFERENT	(6)	
	(8)	Respect
	(9)	Liking
	(10)	Charisma
EXPERTISE	(7)	
	(11)	Possession of Knowledge
	(12)	Ability to Communicate What You Know
	(13)	Control and Dissemination of Information

Other possible sources of interpersonal power include seniority, how many others have preceded you in the position, who you are related to, friendship ties, location of your office, how you dress, your physical appearance, your talents, your wealth, your sexuality, strength, your birth sign, the number of followers you have, your involvement in some crisis event, prayer, faith, love.

This analysis of the sources of power concludes by briefly describing some other sources. As the table has shown, the list of thirteen sources could be expanded. Some additional sources bear considerable examination, while others are of dubious value. Rosabeth Kanter, in "Power Failure in Management Circuits," *Harvard Business Review,* July/August 1979, has provided some refreshing new insights into power in organizations that is worth reading. Analysis has also been made by Michael Korda in *Power: How to Get It and How to Use It* (New York: Simon and Schuster, 1977) of power positions in terms of where one's office is located, where one's desk is situated, and where one chooses to sit at meetings. John T. Molloy in *Dress for Success* (New York: Warner Books, 1975), has conducted research into the power of being properly dressed. Others have analyzed power in terms of who you know or are related to, the riches you possess, your sexuality, your physical appearance and/or strength, and even your birth sign. While all of these have elements of truth, they are fleeting and peripheral compared to those discussed in depth in this section.

To the extent that any of the sources discussed in this section, having to do with human relationships and acquisition and use of knowledge, are based on true principles, they will be valid and lasting. More profound and powerful than any of these discussed may be the power drawn from nonempirical sources, such as prayer, faith, and pure love. The tenets of many religious faiths speak eloquently to the power in this triad of elements.

Principles of Power

This final section has to do with basic concepts related to the uses of power. The first principle has to do with the ends to which power is applied. Obviously, power can be used for good or ill. Power tends to have a negative connotation both because of the many awful ends to which it has been applied, and because of what it does to the possessor. "Power corrupts. Absolute power corrupts absolutely," said Lord Acton. This is another incomplete truth. More truthfully we might say that power brings out the worst in the corrupt. In the righteous individual, the one whose heart has been changed, great power is a means of doing great good. Many religious people believe in a God who is all good and omnipotent—all-powerful. Power is neither good nor bad. Power simply is.

The second principle relates to the basic theme of this book. Power, to be used appropriately and effectively, must fit with the style of the leader's leaders, the goals of the effort, the norms of the organization, the characteristics of the subordinates, and the preferences of the leader. In this respect power may certainly be misused.

The third principle has to do with understanding the list of sources of power just discussed. The more of these sources a leader is able to employ in his or her cause, the more the chances of producing results and achieving success.

The fourth principle has also to do with the list of sources. As with any list related to any principle, the following is true: The number of perceived alternatives that people possess is directly related to their degree of freedom. If a person can only conceive of one thing to do, that person has no freedom—for his or her action is determined. A person perceiving thirteen alternatives has more freedom than a person perceiving two. Notice that the key word is *perceived*. A situation might feature one hundred alternatives in reality, but only perceived alternatives are available to the field of action. By understanding the thirteen sources enumerated, your freedom in choices of power sources is enhanced. (The bad news, of course, is that the more alternatives you perceive, the harder it is to decide on one course of action.)

The fifth principle is an extension of the fourth—looking at the idea from the other side. This principle states that if a person feels powerless and utilizes none of the sources enumerated above, then that person is in fact powerless. Little impact will be made by a person who sees himself or herself as unable to influence people and events.

The sixth principle of power is very important and underlies much of the previous discussion of the uses of power. This principle states that power is not a fixed quantity. In other words, if each individual in a situation is aware of the sources of power and expanded his or her uses of them, then every individual can be more powerful. In this regard, power is like love: There can be infinitely more for everyone. But people must believe this so they can spend their energies in expanding the pie rather than fighting over the current pieces.

The seventh principle is that power is in fact action, not just rhetoric. Power is not just the words of power, it is actually doing something. It is putting potential into practice. Leaders are doers.

The final principle of power states that an individual who is able to tap several of these sources of power and influence others and events in such a way as to produce results and achieve success will find that others will want to follow . . . which is the essence of leadership!

WHO'S IN THE BATTER'S BOX?: THE CHALLENGE OF LEADERSHIP SUCCESSION

The loss and replacement of a leader is a critical challenge for any group or organization. The time of leadership change is when countries fall, businesses go bankrupt, teams lose, and families dissolve. These problems often occur despite the talent and best efforts of the new leader. The former leader must bear a major share of the responsibility for subsequent problems.

It is for this reason that the final section of this chapter on you, the leader, will focus on your concern with the issues of leadership succession. Your initial concern might be with establishing an organizational policy as to whether key replacements are insiders or outsiders. Promotion from within rewards loyalty, creates esprit de corps, and has the advantage of turning the reins over to someone familiar with the organization. On the other hand, insiders can perpetuate current organizational weaknesses (they may already have polarized opposition) and they may have few new ideas. Bringing in an outsider can lead to changes, a new approach, and new energy. But the addition of an outsider might also lead to resentment, confusion, and opposition. The decision of who succeeds you may be out of your control, but you can now influence how that important decision might be made.

Another consideration has to do with the history of the organization. The choice of who is best to fill the leadership role can be influenced by whether the organization is old or new, large or small, simple or complex, status quo or rapidly changing, modern or traditional, formal or informal. The choice can be influenced by how much leadership turnover there has been and how long the current leader has been in power. Amount of turnover and length of tenure can influence whether or not others will really want the job and the likelihood of their success if they do.

Certain leadership precedents will be established by the incumbent leader. The person's age, sex, education, experience, and personality will all create a pattern that a new leader will have to deal with. There are many leadership styles. Whichever style the followers are familiar with will influence how they respond to a new and different style.

Another consideration has to do with how the organization or group was performing under the former leader. A successful organization will require and expect a successful new leader. An unsuccessful organization may require an even more successful new leader.

Final consideration might be given to what the process of transition is likely to be. Leadership transition can be peaceful, chartered, bureaucratic, or revolutionary. The new leader can be selected by a search committee or handpicked by the outgoing leader.

If you are the outgoing leader, you can assist an insider or outsider in obtaining the position. Be cautious about picking a successor too early, as you may be painting a bull's-eye on that person. With your concern for the organization you should be actively selecting, training, delegating, informing, assisting, and acting as mentor to one or more potential successor. The quality of a great leader is often measured by the quantity of leadership talent left behind. This could be your greatest legacy to the organization.

Leadership Technique #8
IT'S OBVIOUS
WHAT THE PROBLEM ISN'T:
PROBLEM IDENTIFICATION
AND SOLVING

The world of leaders and managers is filled to a large measure with confronting and solving problems. If you wish to be successful in the office, the factory, or the home, your ability to solve problems creatively becomes absolutely essential. As discussed in the career-development leadership section to follow, problem-solving skill is essential to an individual's advancement up the hierarchy of an organization. There are three levels of problem-solving skill to be examined. After discussing each, the focus will be on the second level of skill: Creative Problem Solving.

It is ironic, but true, that many individuals have problems they are not aware of. Many organizations have problems they either are not aware of or choose to ignore. Therefore, the beginning of wisdom is the ability to recognize a problem when it exists. Test yourself by looking at the following diagram. Do you recognize this as a problem? Can you label the component parts?

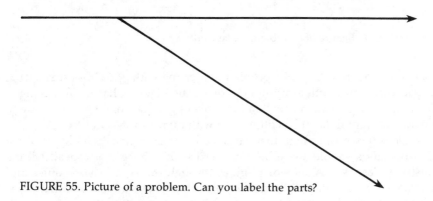

FIGURE 55. Picture of a problem. Can you label the parts?

On the next page is the same diagram with the component parts labeled. When you are confronted with a problem, draw the diagram in the form shown above and label each of the parts by answering as specifically as possible:

1. What is my *goal* in this situation?
2. Where am I now?
3. What has *caused* me to deviate from the goal? Is the *cause* worth investigating and correcting? Is this *cause* likely to be repeated?
4. What is the *magnitude* of the problem? How far am I off course?
5. What action could be taken to get back on course (the *solution*)? Would there be any advantage in *changing* the *goal*?

Some parts of this diagram warrant further comment.

THE CAUSE.   Many problem-solving texts and programs teach that to solve a problem you must identify and deal with the cause of the problem. This is not true. Again we see some of the Freudian influence in our thinking about dealing with problems. Freud taught that in order to solve a problem you needed to gain insight into the cause, or source, of the problem. The reality therapist will tell you that insight and a quarter will buy you a cup of coffee.*

*For more information on this interesting view of life, read William Glasser, *Reality Therapy* (New York: Harper & Row, 1965).

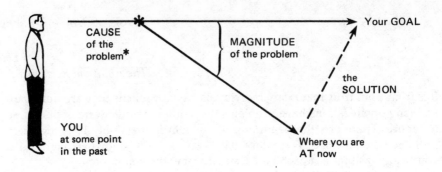

FIGURE 56. Picture of a problem . . . labeled

Having discovered that your problem in dealing with your boss stems from the fact that your mother improperly toilet trained you, what are you going to do about that? Solving a problem is the act of getting from where you are to where you want to be. It has little to do with causes of the problem.

Does this mean, then, that causes are not important? Not at all. What kind of causes should there be a concern with? Those that repeat! Let me illustrate. Case #1: A meteor plunges through the roof of your office and plants your boss in the subbasement. The astronomers inform you that this is a freak occurrence that won't be repeated again in a billion years. How much energy should you put into early meteor detection systems and deflection screens? What are the problems here? There is a hole in the floor and the boss needs to be replaced. Case #2: Every afternoon this week the man who delivers the soft drinks to your office has arrived at 3:00, parked his truck in the lot, and come into the building. Each afternoon, for four days in a row, at 3:05 the truck has rolled down the hill, crashed through the wall of the boss's office, and planted the boss in the subbasement. Today is the fifth day of the week and you have just been made the new boss. Does it not seem likely that you might want to determine why the truck keeps rolling down the hill and through the wall?

Now the quick-thinking reader will protest, "But how can you know for sure whether or not the cause is likely to be repeated unless you examine it?" This is a valid point. But keep two things in mind: First, the cause of the problem may be expensive to look into, difficult to find, impossible to determine, a result of multiple causation, or it may be *you*! Second, the problem can be solved without dealing with the cause. Identifying and eliminating the cause is another problem-solving operation.

THE MAGNITUDE.   Not all problems are of equal size or importance. You

*Most business schools would convince you that this should be labeled a decision point based on their belief that all problems are caused by bad decisions. We know that life is more complex than that. Don't we?

164

can illustrate this to yourself by drawing your perception of the size of the problem. For example:

FIGURE 57.

In this case, you have what you might consider a "nonproblem." You might note it, but simply continue with your activities.

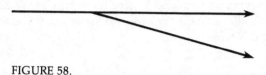

FIGURE 58.

In this case you have a problem that is worthy of examination and problem-solving effort.

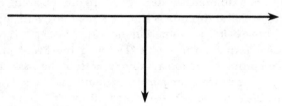

FIGURE 59.

In this case you have a serious problem that requires immediate attention.

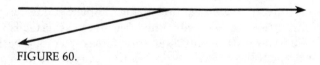

FIGURE 60.

In this case you have clearly identified yourself as the mayor of New York, the CEO of Chrysler Corporation, or the President's inflation fighter.

Level Two: Creative Problem Solving

This is the concept that will be discussed in depth in this skills section.

Level Three: Foreseeing and Preventing Problems
Before They Occur

It is almost always less expensive to prevent a problem than to correct it. However, it is more difficult to prevent it because that requires you to foresee the problem prior to its occurrence and take steps to avert it. At best, this requires superior planning skills. More often it would require—literally—

prophetic vision. If you have the ability to see the future, your wealth and success are assured and you needn't read further in this book. If you lack that ability, careful planning, common sense, and reading the signs of the times are the best you can hope for.

A final word: Some time ago I worked as a teller in a savings and loan. Our head teller would say, whenever a problem was discovered, "The important thing here is not to correct the problem, but to find someone to blame it on." He was jesting, of course, but all too often in the work place and the home we put more energy into placing blame than in solving problems and moving on with life. Motivation by guilt is seldom productive. Unless you are a sadist, *attack the problem, not the person.* If you are a sadist, why are you reading this book?

Creative Problem Solving

This section presents you with one model for solving the problems you confront in life. It cannot be called *the* problem-solving model, because someone can always point out a different model. There are others. Some of them may even be better for you. But this one is simple, straightforward, and it works!

Refer to Figure 61. It is presented in the form of a cycle. It could also be presented in linear form, starting with "Defining the Problem." But users facing an unsolved problem are too apt to retreat from the sixth step to one of the previous steps. The process can fail at any point, and the only way you can know for sure where you blew it is to return to the "beginning." The cycle leads you to this automatically.

The smaller dashed cycle the reader will recognize as the management cycle discussed in Chapter 2. That is why the step at the bottom of the diagram is referred to as the "Proactive Start." If you are beginning an enterprise, the process is one of planning, organizing, implementing, and controlling (by asking, "Are we achieving the objectives we established in the plan?"). If the answer to the control question is yes, you loop back into the management cycle. If the answer to the control question is no, you expand into the larger problem-solving cycle.

Step One: Defining the Problem

The *first step* in the problem-solving process is defining (or recognizing, to use my previous terminology) the problem. The *most important step* in the problem-solving process is defining the problem. The *most neglected step* in the problem-solving process is defining the problem. Consider these assertions one at a time.

Obviously, this is the first step in the process. If you do not recognize that you have a problem, you are not about to solve it. There are several reasons why this step is the most important. That which is defined as the problem becomes, in fact, the problem (by definition). If you have one problem and define your problem as something else, you now have two

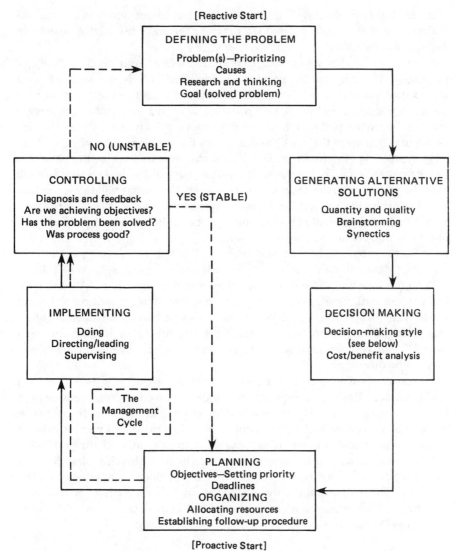

DEFINING THE PROBLEM

Problem(s)—Prioritizing
Causes
Research and thinking
Goal (solved problem)

NO (UNSTABLE)

CONTROLLING

Diagnosis and feedback
Are we achieving objectives?
Has the problem been solved?
Was process good?

YES (STABLE)

**GENERATING ALTERNATIVE
SOLUTIONS**

Quantity and quality
Brainstorming
Synectics

IMPLEMENTING

Doing
Directing/leading
Supervising

DECISION MAKING

Decision-making style
(see below)
Cost/benefit analysis

The
Management
Cycle

PLANNING
Objectives—Setting priority
Deadlines
ORGANIZING
Allocating resources
Establishing follow-up procedure

[Proactive Start]

FIGURE 61. The problem solving/decision making cycle

problems. Is the defined problem a real one? It is if you treat it as one and allocate time and money to deal with it. Many people and organizations go through life creating problems for themselves in the supposed act of solving them.

Another reason why the definition step is so important is that in most cases you will discover that you have not *a* problem, but problems. When multiple problems are discovered, they must be prioritized and the most important one worked on first. Otherwise you become a deck-chair straightener on a sinking *Titanic.* There are two problems here: The deck chairs are sliding and the ship is going down. If you are not clear about which is critical and which is irrelevant, you're dead! Do people ever make the *Titanic* mistake in real life? Consistently!

This is the step where the causes are isolated and dealt with, if appropriate, according to the previous guidelines. This is the step where a solved problem is defined. Here is an example of what this means. Your boss comes to you and says "We have a problem. Our tardiness rate is ten percent and that is unacceptable. Do something about it." The first thing you are aware of is that what the boss has defined as the problem is not the problem; it is a symptom of the problem. If you treat the fever by packing the patient in ice, the patient will die. If you eliminate the cause of the fever, the fever will subside. In this case, the tardiness is the fever. Now what will this symptom look like when the problem is solved? Suppose you set a goal of zero tardiness. You have just created an insoluble problem. People ask if there are any problems that cannot be solved. The answer is yes and no. Any problem can be solved if properly defined and attacked. But you can define problems in ways that defy solution. Zero percent tardiness is an example. Which leads back to the question, "What does a solved problem look like?" Would it be five percent tardiness? two percent tardiness? one percent tardiness? I don't know. That is up to you and your boss. But you had better decide before proceeding. If you do not, when you ask the question "Has the problem been solved?" and you see that the tardiness rate is three percent, how will you answer the question?

You can see why this step is so important. Now, why is it the most neglected step? Because it requires the people involved to do something they abhor—*thinking*! To avoid that, some idiot in your group will always say at this point, "It is obvious that the problem is . . ." At this point you must jump up on the table and scream *"Horse pucky!"* at the top of your lungs. Having obtained the group's attention, you quote them Bothwell's First Rule of Problem Solving: "That which is obviously the problem is obviously *not* the problem." This will momentarily silence the idiot. Then the hard work starts. You must ask some questions, you must gather some data, you must do some cogitating. Don't avoid it—*do it!*

Step Two: Generating Alternative Solutions

After the problem has been identified, you need a range of alternative solutions. Once this is suggested, the group idiot will again speak up and say, "It's obvious that the solution is . . ." Again, leap to the table and scream *"Horse pucky!"* Then quote Bothwell's Second Rule of Problem Solving: "That which is obviously the solution is obviously *not* the solution." Solutions suggested early on will be conservative, noncreative, and likely will not solve the problem.

What you are working against here is something called the Zagorskie effect. This quality of human beings was discovered and identified by a humble man named . . . Zagorskie. It is in effect our attempt to put everything into neat little boxes. You don't have this problem, you say? Let's see. Look at the nine dots below. Here is your problem: Connect the nine dots with four straight lines, without lifting the pencil from the paper or retracing.

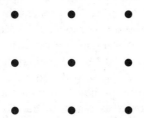

FIGURE 62. Connect the dots with four straight lines

Before you turn the page for the solution, I shall tell you that this problem has not one solution, but *several.* There now, don't you feel better? No?!

This is a good problem because it demonstrates the Zagorskie effect so simply and dramatically, and because the solution always produces a pronounced "Aha!" reaction at the moment of insight.

People always say "But you went outside the box (or square)!" To which I respond, "What box? I never said to solve the problem within a box or square. That is a limitation you (your Zagorskie effect) placed on yourself. And in doing that you created for yourself an insoluble problem." Now that you know you can "go outside the box" you can see several solutions to the problem. One of the highest-paid consultants in the U.S. was asked what he did that was so wonderful that he could be paid so well. His answer: "I ask my clients the questions they can and should be asking themselves." He went on to say that when the client says one day, "Hey, we could be asking these same questions ourselves," he knows that he is ready to collect his check and move on.

I have had this same experience. I ask clients what their problem is and they identify it. I ask what is the best solution to the problem and they identify it. I then ask why they haven't implemented the solution, and the discussion proceeds like this:

"They won't let us."

"Who won't let you?"

"Those people up there?"

"Which people? Name them."

"The system doesn't allow this?"

"What system? Who is in charge of it?"

"They are."

"Have you talked to 'them?' "

"No. I just know they wouldn't let us do it."

When we finally talk to "them" there is often no such restriction. We always place more restrictions on ourselves than the system does. How do we overcome this Zagorskie effect? There are several ways.

One of the oldest and most useful is the brainstorming technique developed in the 1950s by Alex Osborn. Osborn, in his book *Applied Imagination* (New York: Charles Scribners, 1953), introduced the brainstorming concept. The norm to be agreed to in brainstorming is that no evaluation will be made of anyone's suggested solution, no matter how absurd it may seem when suggested. Evaluation and criticism kill creative solutions fast. Set a goal for, say, twenty solutions. If in the process the well runs dry, walk away from it for a while. Refresh your perspective, then try again. Be imaginative! Practiced over time, brainstorming is a powerful technique for creating a wide range of creative solutions. You can do brainstorming, or an approximation thereof, by yourself, but it is really designed as a group technique. The sharing of the several unique perspectives is what sparks the creativity. The most fascinating new approach is synectics. See George Prince, *The Practice of Creativity* (Harper & Row, 1970) or William Gordon, *Synectics* (Collier-MacMillan, 1961), both listed in the Bibliography.

Here is one solution to the problem. Now, why didn't you do that?

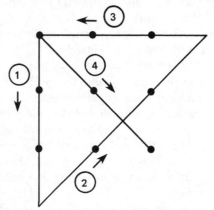

FIGURE 63. The nine dots connected

Step Three: Deciding on a Solution

It is frustrating to some to feel that energy has been expended in creating a list of innovative solutions to the problem and that now they are asked to discard all but one. This, however, is usually necessary. First, as the list of alternative solutions is examined it will be obvious that several of them are mutually exclusive; to do one of them precludes doing some other. Secondly, the fact of limited resources usually makes it impossible to implement more than one or two solutions. Finally, it will be seen that some of the solutions are clearly just not do-able.

After eliminating those that are not likely to work (be sure), the remaining solution should be analyzed using an informal cost/benefit analysis. The ideal solution would be one with maximum benefits and minimum cost. Unfortunately, the world seldom works this way. More often maximum benefit is correlated with maximum cost and minimum cost with minimum benefit. Should this be the case with your solutions, you have to decide which factor, benefit, or cost you (or the system you work in) needs to control. If your president says, "Get a man on the moon by 1970, spare no expense," you go for the maximum-benefit solution. If your president says, "You must hold the costs down," you go for the minimum-cost solution. The problem with the latter approach, often found in the public sector, is that you can expend $1 million a year for ten years trying to solve a problem you felt you couldn't afford to spend $3 million on in one year.

Once the solutions are ranked, you (the individual and/or the group) must decide on a solution. The decision-making process is a major topic that follows in the next Leadership Technique section. That discussion would plug in at this point in the problem-solving process.

Step Four:
Planning the Implementation of the Solution

Once the solution has been decided upon, the planning of the implementation must take place. The vague goal of the solved problem formulated in the first step must now be rephrased in the form of specific objectives to be achieved. A deadline must be established for the problem to be solved. A follow-up and reporting must be devised. Resources must be allocated, a budget established. Once everything is in readiness, you proceed to the action step.

Step Five: Implementing the Solution

This is an important step. You are not to become a professional thinker or planner. Action must occur if the world is to move forward. But, as stated at the beginning, if the preceding steps have been carried out correctly, this step almost takes care of itself. If you have failed in the previous steps, this step cannot possibly succeed. That is why effectiveness (doing the right thing) is more important than efficiency (in this case doing the wrong thing, but doing it extremely well). Good implementation of a powerful solution to a problem you didn't have until you defined it as one is like taking a potent medicine to cure a disease you didn't have—it can kill you!

This is the step where the followers/subordinates do the doing and where you do the leading/directing/coordinating (the subject of all the rest of this book). Obviously, if they do not *do* well and/or you do not *lead* well, you can also blow it at this step in the process.

Step Six:
The Control Step—Checking for Success

In the regular management cycle, this is where the manager asks, "Are the planned objectives being achieved?" In the problem-solving cycle, this is where the leader asks, "Has the problem been solved?" If the answer is yes, then the situation is stable and you loop back into the regular management-activity cycle. If the answer is no, then there is instability and the cycle dictates that you return to the first step and ask "What is the problem here?" then proceed with the analysis.

Some Summary Thoughts

1. This problem-solving approach really works. You should use it with every problem (Did he say every problem? *Yes, every problem*) that you face, work and personal. Your head will tell you that it will be too time-consuming to use this with every problem, but with practice it goes very rapidly. How long does it take to think? To brainstorm? To decide? Skilled leaders go through the whole cycle rapidly and effectively. Remember the old adage, "If you don't have time to do it correctly now, when will you have time to do it over again?" Go to your nearest tattoo parlor, show them this diagram, and ask to have it tattooed on your left wrist. Then, every time you have a problem, look down and say, "Let's define the problem . . ."

2. I always wanted to grow up and become an adult so that I would not have any more problems. As I grew older the problems continued and often got worse. I was commiserating with a friend about this one day, and I was confronted with this profound question: "Have you ever considered that life is for the purpose of having and overcoming problems?" What a shock to my system. Could it be that problems/ challenges are the stuff that life is made of? If that is true, then I shouldn't be too anxious to get rid of them, for when that day arrives I'll be lying in the pine box with my friends saying, "Doesn't he look nice?" And if we reflect on Hamlet's soliloquy, it isn't clear whether the problems end there. No one's come back from the other side to say there ain't no challenges there to be confronted!

3. This insight led me to the next level of wisdom. I resigned myself to life being made up of problems, but then I wondered why I got all the hard ones. I confronted this feeling in two ways. First, I worked for two years in a college counseling center. I was surprised to see some of the campus leaders coming in for counseling and shocked to hear of the problems they faced that were not apparent to the casual observer. It reminded me of the old tale in which God collected all of mankind's problems and assembled them in one massive pile. He instructed all mankind to come forward and select the problems that looked best to them. Each person humbly selected his or her own. Then, someone gave me this great little quote, which I hung over my desk. It helped me to get through a lot of long Friday afternoons.

> Be thankful for the problems of your job. If they didn't exist you wouldn't be there, and if they were less difficult someone with less ability would be working in your place.

I realized that the organizational reward for becoming a more competent problem solver was to get more difficult problems to solve. Isn't it possible that it also works this way in life?

4. Finally, if you are sure that you now have the tools to solve all of your problems, keep this last bit of inscrutable wisdom tucked away in your gray matter: The solution to every problem contains the seeds of other problems!

Leadership Technique #9
APPROACHES TO
THE BASKIN-ROBBINS DILEMMA:
EFFECTIVE DECISION MAKING

Consider what a decision is and what it means to make it. A decision might be thought of as a choice between alternatives. There are two different types of alternatives. These might be classified as real and perceived alternatives.

Of the two, the more important are the perceived alternatives, because it is a lack of perceived alternatives that limits a person's behavior. In any given

172

situation twenty different choices might exist. But if people can only perceive five of these choices, their behavior is constricted and the decisions they can make are limited. If they can perceive only two choices, the decision-making process is more limited still. And if they can only perceive one choice, their behavior is, in fact, determined. That determined behavior, a situation of no perceived choice, can often destroy an individual.

Recently the news reported a fire in a large high-rise apartment building. During the course of this fire two of the occupants and their small poodle dog were killed when they jumped out of a fifth-story window to their death. The firemen later interviewed on the scene reported that this choice was extremely unfortunate for several reasons. First was that just after the couple jumped, a ladder truck arrived at the building with a ladder sufficiently high to reach their room. Secondly, the fireman pointed out that although the fire had been burning in the hallway and there was a great deal of smoke, the fire never at any time came into their apartment. If they had simply stayed in the apartment and remained calm, they would have been all right. In this situation there were at least three real choices that existed for the couple. They, however, could only perceive one choice, and that was to jump. And in this case the decision to jump cost them their lives.

Another way of looking at this concept of alternatives or choices might apply not so much to the individual as to the society. The number of alternatives or choices that exist within a society determines the amount of freedom that society offers to its citizens. For example, in the United States people can join voluntary organizations known as associations. Those who join these associations are individuals who have a common interest in anything from stamp collecting to medicine to firearms to exotic goldfish to bird watching. The book known as the *Directory of Associations in the United States* runs to several hundred pages, with thousands of entries. As a citizen of this free country you might ask yourself, "How many voluntary associations do you suppose exist for a person who lives behind the Iron Curtain? How many people in Russia, for example, have the option to join an association with those who are interested in the ownership and use of firearms?" When you consider the great number of choices that are possible for Americans, you begin to realize the tremendous blessing we have.

When talking about choices or alternatives, consideration needs to be given to another facet mentioned previously in another section of this book. That is, while your number of choices or alternatives increases, you experience a corresponding increase in your freedom, but you also find that you experience an increasing complexity and difficulty in making a decision. This is what I refer to as the Baskin-Robbins dilemma.

When I was a kid and went to the ice cream store, the decision making was not very complex. If you wanted to get an ice cream cone, you could get vanilla, chocolate, or strawberry. Today when a family goes to a Baskin-Robbins store with its thirty-one flavors and has to decide between the flavors—not to mention the choice of one, two, or three scoops, or sugar or cake cone—the permutations and combinations by which the four people, the three scoops, the choice of cones, and the thirty-one flavors can be combined is almost infinite. This is why some families can take an entire holiday weekend trying to get an ice cream cone at the store.

The second word in the title of the process is *making,* indicating that the decision has to be made, the alternative has to be picked, the choice has to be chosen. However, with so many real or perceived alternatives confronting a person, it is possible to be frozen into inaction. Still, the personal decision is relatively straightforward compared to group decisions. This section does not confront the question of how individuals make decisions. Instead, it examines the vastly more complex area of how decisions get made in groups.

I have seen the dilemmas faced by groups in decision making over and over again as I have put on management development programs involving what are called stranger groups. This is a program that involves many people coming in from a number of different offices or agencies, each of them strangers to the other. It is not uncommon for the group to get superficially acquainted during the morning session and then decide to go out to lunch together. I find that after I have erased the board in the training room, placed my materials in my briefcase and walked out the door, a group of six or seven of these people will be standing outside saying, "Oh, perhaps we can go and get ourselves some hamburgers and fries." Someone else might say, "No, we might want to consider getting a salad." I will often leave the training room, go down the elevator, eat lunch, read a chapter in a book, take a short walk along the waterfront, come back into the hotel, and arrive back at the training room to find the group standing by the door saying, "Or perhaps we could get some Chinese food."

Four different group decision-making techniques will be explored and looked at initially along two dimensions. Number one is the *speed* with which the decision can be made, and number two, the *level of commitment* the leader of the group is likely to get from the followers or subordinates in implementing the decision that is chosen.

The first question to confront is, What is the fastest way to make a decision in a group of people? The answer obviously is to make an autocratic decision. Regardless of how many people are involved in the group, if the leader of the group decides to make the decision unilaterally, it can be made very quickly. This is the advantage of autocratic decisions. The disadvantage is that it's very difficult to get commitment from the subordinates and to find any motivation on their part for carrying out the decision made, because the motive or reason for carrying out this action is not theirs.

FIGURE 64. Group decision-making options

Approach	SPEED with which decisions can be made	COMMITMENT of group to decision		QUALITY of the decision
1. Autocratic				
2. Committee				
3. Democratic				
A. Voting				
B. Consensus				

174

If most decisions made in the world are made autocratically, and if autocratic decisions do not elicit motivation and commitment from followers, then how does anything in the world get done? The answer is through the exercise of coercive power.

If you make an autocratic decision and ask a subordinate to implement it, if there is the slightest hesitation, you can pull out your .38 Smith and Wesson (defined in Chapter 3 as negative KITA). The subordinate will say, "No one ever explained it to me that clearly before," and you'll get movement. There are several problems with this autocratic approach to leadership based on coercive power, however. First of all, the gun may change hands. Pick up any newspaper to see that this happens every day. Secondly, the followers may have a bigger gun. Third, even if you can get compliance, when your back is turned, you can anticipate sabotage.

This is not to say that autocratic decisions are always bad. The discussion at the end of this section will come full circle and show some situations in which autocratic decisions are absolutely the best.

A second method for group decision making is to appoint or select a committee. A committee is a group that represents the larger group or the whole organization in the decision that is to be made. Committee decisions are moderate to slow, depending on how well-structured and effective the committee is. The amount of commitment they get is moderate to high, depending on several factors.

There are two key questions that must be answered in determining the effectiveness of a committee. The first of these is, How much does the committee really represent the members of the group as a whole? If you were going to make a decision in an office with thirty male and thirty female employees with a committee that consists of ten males and two females, it is unlikely that the female group is going to feel that they have been truly represented. They are very likely to try to find some way to sabotage whatever decisions are made. It is important, therefore, for those who are organizing a committee to consider carefully the qualities of the represented group and to make sure that those qualities are, in fact, reflected in the committee.

The second key item that has to be considered is the ability of the committee to bind the larger group on the decision that is made. If three committees are sent out representing three different offices and a decision is made that reflects exactly the feelings of one, somewhat the feelings of the second, and not at all the feelings of the third, it is very likely again that there will be rebellion or problems in the ranks.

If the decision cannot or should not be made autocratically, and if it is not proper or possible to constitute a committee to make the decision, the decision must be made democratically. But when everyone is involved in making a decision, an important question arises: How rapidly can that decision be made? The answer, with a capital S, is *Slowly*. On the other hand, if a whole group of people can reach a decision, you usually get a high level of commitment, since all of the people have been involved in the decision-making process.

Now look at the three major categories that have been considered so far: Autocratic decisions are seen to be fast but low in commitment; committee decisions are moderate in speed and commitment; and democratic decisions are slow, but with high commitment. This is another version of the double-edged sword of life. Some profound thinker centuries ago, confronting this very dilemma, said, "Isn't it too bad that we can't have a process that is fast but which involves all the people?" This is the person who invented the democratic process known as voting. Most of us have been so indoctrinated into the ideal that voting is the solution or the process by which all group decisions are made that when you give a group of people an opportunity to make a decision (knowing from the discussion so far that there are at least three different ways to proceed), inevitably someone will say, "Why don't we discuss it for a few minutes and then let's take a vote and the majority will rule?"

While the advantages of voting are obvious, there are three *disadvantages* of making decisions through a group vote that are not so obvious. The first disadvantage is that whenever a decision is made by taking a vote, unless that vote is unanimous (and I ask the reader, when was the last time you saw a unanimous vote?), the voting process is immediately going to create a majority-minority split. Now the assumption of a true democracy is that the majority, those who are in the position of power, are supposed to be considerate, kind, sensitive, and sympathetic to the needs of the minority and see that their needs are taken into consideration in all future decisions. More often, in fact, the majority treats the minority something like this: "What is the matter with you idiots; can't you see that you are in the wrong? If most of the people in the office (or the company or the state or the nation) want to do this, then you, the minority, must obviously be wrong. Now why don't you just admit that you've made a serious mistake, that you're on the wrong side of the issue, change your mind, and come along with the rest of us?" How do the minorities act when they're treated this way by the majority? The answer is that in many cases they would rather die than change their behavior and help to implement whatever solution has been decided upon. And suppose the minority is able to persuade enough votes over to their point of view so that they become the new majority. Having been downtrodden and oppressed for so long, they will treat the new minority with empathy, love, and concern. Right? Wrong! Their attitude is usually, "If you think they did a number on us, just wait until you see the pain we inflict on them." It has ever been thus.

The second disadvantage of voting in groups is that it tends to create vested interest. You should shudder every time you're sitting in a group where some person, thinking himself wise, makes the following statement, 'Why don't we take a tentative vote? This is not binding, you understand, but let's just get a feeling for where people are. All those in favor, raise your hands. Any opposed, raise your hands." And so the process goes. The problem here should be fairly obvious: Once people have placed their hands in the air and have identified with a particular position, they now find themselves forced to defend that position, to defend their ego and the rightness of their position, and no longer to consider a search for truth or the best solution to the problem. This process is usually counterproductive.

The third disadvantage is that decisions are made without resolving underlying conflicts. If you sit in a room and say "All those in favor say aye, any opposed say no. The ayes have it. Motion carried.... Meeting dismissed," it's true that a decision has been made and that all those who are on the winning side file out of the room happy. But I have yet to know an individual who has raised a hand in a losing cause and then said afterward, "Wow, I really feel great that I got to hold up my hand and lose; now I'm really committed to carrying out the decision made by the other side." More often the feeling is the same as mentioned previously with autocratic decisions; those in the minority inevitably set out to change the minds of the others or to say, "We're going to sabotage the implementation of this decision."

There is another democratic process that can be used to make decisions in groups. This is not the process of voting but rather the process of trying to reach a consensus. Consensual decision making is an extremely old process that has been found in many cultures and many churches for centuries. It also happens, however, to be a current fad approach in business programs around the country. To reach a consensual decision the group must first agree that there will be no voting, that there will be no identifying of positions or hardening of categories. All persons in the main body or group are allowed to express their opinions, to discuss openly whatever the issues are, to change sides, to change their minds, to explore all of the possibilities. Then the leader of the group or any member, if the group has been properly trained, can try to state a sense of the group, the position that the group has reached. Now everyone in that group may not feel that is the best thing for himself, but he certainly can see it's the best thing for the group under those circumstances, and he hasn't had to identify with a losing position.

You might get the impression that consensual decision making will get us right back to square one, that it is a slow process. Those, however, who are experts at this process maintain that this is not the case. Some contend that they can get a group of two thousand people in an auditorium and after two hours of their training can get the group to reach a consensual decision faster than they can a voted one. I'm skeptical of this claim, but I remain openminded, and perhaps consensual decision making is, in fact, the wave of the future.

Our value system leads us, when we think about decision making, to approach the word *democratic* with a cheer-hurrah and to approach the term *autocratic* with a boo-hiss. Coming full circle, it can be shown that there are some situations in which autocratic decision making has a very distinct advantage.

First of all, an autocratic decision is a good one if one person and only one person in the group has the skill or expertise to make the decision or to execute the implementation of the solution. Picture yourself on an airplane about to land at a large international airport when suddenly the speaker crackles and the pilot's voice comes over the phone and says, "Ladies and gentlemen, we have a very serious problem here. We have a red light on in the cockpit indicating that the gear on this plane will not go down and lock. Because this is a serious problem, with your lives in jeopardy, and because we the crew are here to serve you, we would like those of you in the back of the plane to talk about and consider the situation we're now facing. Discuss it among yourselves and make a decision as to what you would like us to do with the plane. We will be happy to implement whatever decision you make." How many of you would like to be engaged in a lively discussion with all of the manure salesmen in the back of the plane as to how the plane ought to be landed? I don't know about you, but at that point I would like the pilot to get very autocratic in the decisions that are to be made. If the pilot tells me to stand on my head and stick my fingers in my ears, I'm not going to go up front and say, "You didn't consult me." Would you like to have the surgeon wake you up on the operating table and announce that he's going to take a vote in the operating room as to how to deal with your internal hemorrhaging and he thinks you ought to be involved.

Does that mean that autocratic decisions made by a pilot or a surgeon are never wrong? The answer is, obviously, not at all! But again, you have to ask yourself when this decision must be made, who do you trust, the pilot with one hundred thousand hours of flying time or the manure salesmen?

The importance of this was wisely demonstrated to me in a training program I put on in New England. I had just made this observation when a member of the class raised his hand. He said, "I am in a group that goes out to repair broken high-voltage lines. I am not the supervisor of that group, but I am the expert on how to knock down and take care of a broken high-voltage line. When we get the phone call that indicates a power line has broken, the supervisor says, 'Okay, we'll take truck number three. Wear your yellow helmets. Put these tools in the truck, and Bill, you can drive.' When we get to the scene of the broken line, however, he turns to me and says, 'Take it, Mike,' and I'm in complete charge of the situation until that line has been repaired." I'd submit to you that Mike has a very wise and a very ego-secure supervisor. Picture instead the supervisor with a weak ego who gets to the scene and says, "Shut up, Mike. I'm in charge here. I'll tell people what to do. Okay, Bill, run over and grab that broken line." *ZAPPPPPPP!!!!!!!!*

Autocratic decision making is also necessary in an emergency. In such a case the motivation is built in. If you're walking with a group of people about to cross a street and you look up and see a large semitrailer truck hurtling toward you, this is not the time to say, "Ladies and gentlemen, it appears we have a problem here. Why don't we sit down and discuss this rationally and calmly and reach a consensual decision that we can all feel good about." At that point, if someone screams *"Jump!"* the members of that group are going to move pretty rapidly in response to that autocratic command.

Autocratic decisions are also preferable in any situation where a decision must be made, for whatever reason, and the group is unwilling or unable to make it. At that point, the leader needs to take command and say, "This is the course of action that we will follow," and then be prepared to deal with the reactions from the members of the group.

Another reason for autocratic decision making might arise from a situation in which the decision benefits everyone involved. But this is a weaker justification. If the boss walks in today and announces that everyone in the office has just been given a one-thousand-dollar raise, it is very likely that he or she will get away with the autocratic decision. But knowing human nature, there will always be two people in the office who will storm into the boss's office and say, "You didn't consult us before giving us this raise."

In summary, there are four different ways that decisions can be made in a group: autocratically, by committee, democratically by voting, and democratically by consensus. Each of these approaches has advantages; each of them has disadvantages.

FIGURE 65. The double-edged sword of group decision making

Approach	SPEED with which decision can be made	COMMITMENT of group to decision	QUALITY of the decision
1. Autocratic	FAST	LOW	IT DEPENDS
2. Committee	MODERATE	MODERATE	IT DEPENDS
3. Democratic	SLOW	HIGH	IT DEPENDS
A. Voting	(Problems: 1) creates majority/minority split, 2) creates vested interests, 3) makes decisions without resolving conflicts)		
B. Consensus	(Problems: 1) can be very slow, 2) takes training and practice, 3) how does consensus deal with non-consensus?)		

The final factor to be considered in group decision making is that of quality. The answer to the question, Which decision-making approach will yield the highest quality decision? has to be, *It depends.* It depends on the way you can constitute a committee. It depends on the love and trust and concern that the members of the group have for one another, of their ability to work together to reach a group decision. This is a decision that the leader must make, one that should be considered carefully because of the powerful impact it can have on the results.

Leadership Technique #10
HURRY! HURRY!
DING! DING!
THE MANAGEMENT OF TIME

One of the most common complaints of leaders is that there is never enough time to do all that needs to be done. Our reaction to always running behind is often in our conception of time, what it is, and what it means in our lives. Many try to conquer problems in this area by attending courses or reading books on the management of time. The beginning of wisdom in this area is the realization that time cannot be managed, saved, borrowed, made up, or used. What we need to learn how to manage better is ourselves. Time is a measure, a flow that passes over our lives and creates certain benchmarks that help us to identify events and memories.

Following is a checklist by which you can evaluate yourself in relation to twenty of the ways in which you manage the use of your time. Fill it out and assess yourself to see how you are doing in the effective use of your time. Each of these twenty principles can then be examined in turn to identify helpful techniques in the use of your time.

FIGURE 66. Form for time use analysis

6—This is absolutely true for me	2—This is seldom true for me
4—This is usually true for me	1—This is rarely true for me
3—This is somewhat true for me	0—This is not true for me

1. I can define the meaning of the term *time*.   _____
2. I believe that time can be managed.   _____
3. I know the meaning of "Work smarter, not harder!" and how to implement it.   _____
4. I know the difference between *effectiveness* and *efficiency* and, given a choice, which is more important.   _____
5. I approach all work by establishing goals and setting objectives.   _____
6. I make a daily, prioritized, "to do" list.   _____
7. I have a habit of doing the most important things first.   _____
8. I analyze my job to determine how I can combine or eliminate activities.   _____
9. I do creative work when my energy is at a peak and routine work when my energy is low.   _____
10. I do creative work in large blocks of time.   _____
11. I know my major time wasters and have some idea of how to overcome them.   _____
12. I handle each piece of paper only once.   _____
13. I delegate activities that can or should be done by others.   _____
14. I try to communicate clearly and work at giving and receiving good feedback.   _____
15. I take time with my people to train, understand, commit, encourage, appreciate, assist, involve, and promote.   _____
16. I know how to plan, conduct, and follow up effective meetings.   _____
17. I keep a record of how I spend my time and analyze it periodically to see where I can make improvements.   _____
18. I am prepared so that my time is never wasted.   _____
19. I know the value of rest, play, exercise, planning, alone time, perspective, and a balanced life in working efficiently and effectively.   _____
20. I have the courage to be effective and to say "NO."   _____

EVALUATION: TOTAL POINTS [   ]

100–75 Time Management Expert
74–50   Improvement Warranted
49–24   A Good Start
24–0   Need Lots of Help

Principles of Effective Time Use

Principles 1 and 2 have been discussed in the opening of this section. Principles 3 and 4 can be examined together. Working harder means putting in more hours and more effort, often in busywork tasks that have low payoff. "Working smarter" implies an understanding of how to be more effective and how to apply the 20–80 rule.

What is effectiveness and what is efficiency and which is more basic? Most people are unsure. *Effectiveness* is doing the right things. *Efficiency* is doing things right. Of the two, effectiveness is the most basic, the first step. One of the most frightening threats to our world is all the people who are ineffective but very efficient. In other words, they are doing the wrong things but doing them extremely well.

The master of time begins by determining what is right and the best thing to do, and does that first (Principle 7). Of most value in this undertaking is the concept known as Pareto's principle, or the 20–80 rule. Pareto observed that in any set of human activities 20 percent of the things to be done account for 80 percent of the results. The remaining 80 percent of the tasks will only provide a 20 percent payoff.

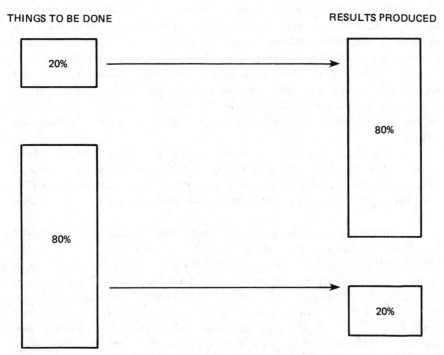

FIGURE 67. Pareto's principle

The effective leader identifies the 20 percent of his or her tasks that will produce the biggest payoff and puts time and energy there. The rest of the world wastes time fiddling around in the 80 percent busywork area, with little to show for it. Obviously, once you know what is most important to do, then you should develop the ability to do it as efficiently as possible.

Principle 5 follows the concepts just discussed in pointing out the importance of always working against goals and objectives. Leadership Technique Section #1 discussed the differences between goals and objectives and pointed out why both are important. In his book, Alan Lakein suggests brainstorming a list of all your goals and then arranging them according to:

A Goals—————Foremost Importance
B Goals—————Moderate Importance
C Goals—————Relative Unimportance

Following the 20–80 principle, I would suggest that you concentrate on doing the A Goals and B Goals and ignoring the "Jonathan Livingston. . . ."

This leads to Principles 6 and 7. Each day should begin with the preparation of a list of things to be done, rank-ordered. Start with the most important items first, not the other way around. Don't join the long list of people who congratulate themselves daily on having completed eight out of ten items on their list (can you guess which 80 percent?).

Principle 8 also flows from the 20–80 rule. See what parts of your job can be combined with others (yes, a kind of time-and-motion study) or eliminated altogether. This can be tied to Principle 13, identifying items that can be delegated down, laterally, or up.

Principles 9 and 10 have to do with providing an environment for creativity. Creative work takes energy and inspiration, both of which are reduced by fatigue. Creativity also takes two- to four-hour blocks of uninterrupted time. (Now you see why there's so little creativity in the workaday world.)

This leads to Principle 11, awareness of your major "time wasters." Based on the creativity concept just discussed, it should come as no surprise that 1 and 2 on the magic hit parade* are telephone interruptions and people who drop by. You need to develop creativity in dealing with these time wasters.

Here are two examples just to get your juices flowing. For the little old lady from Sun City who has nothing better to do than waste your time, or the bore from the next office who calls six times a day, try this: When all of your polite and rude attempts to get back to work have failed, say, "Have you been having the same problems with your phone that we . . ." then hang up. When they call back to say that they were cut off, say, "I know, the phone's been doing that all . . ." then hang up again. Once they discover that every time they call you there's a phone problem, they'll bother someone else whose phone works.

Have you had trouble with those people who drop by your desk with the opener, "Got a minute?" It may be work-related, or it may be pictures of the grandkids, but that minute never takes less than twenty. Entertain six of those a day, and you've lost two hours. So . . . make your desk and the area surrounding it as inhospitable as possible to "drop-bys." (Yes, the jar of jelly beans has to go. Sorry, R.R.!) If that doesn't dissuade them, have a busywork

*For a listing of the top twenty time wasters in fifteen countries, see R. Alec MacKenzie, *The Time Trap*, New York: AMACOM, 1972. Prepare your own list first and then compare.

drawer full of your C tasks. Respond, "Sure, I'd love to talk to you, but I have to get this column of figures added up first. Could you do it for me?" If they refuse, tell them you're too busy and turn your back. Eventually they'll learn to share their war stories with someone who doesn't put them to work.

You get the idea. Now try it with your other eighteen time wasters.

Two major time wasters are paper shuffling (Principle 12) and ineffective meetings (Principle 16). Don't be a paper restacker. Build up a small pile, then deal with the papers all at once. Don't let go of a paper until you've answered it, sent it to someone, made a note and filed it, or chucked it in the round file. Look at each paper and ask, "Is this an A, B, or C?"

How to Stop Retreating From Meetings

This is not to imply that meetings are always time wasters; they may be time savers. However, ineffective meetings definitely waste time. A few simple techniques can make a great difference in the quality of your meetings.

Before the meeting is held, perform the following steps:

A1. Determine the purpose of the meeting. Is it informational, planning, or problem solving?

FIGURE 68. Reprinted with permission from The Saturday Evening Post Company © The Curtis Publishing Company

THE SATURDAY EVENING POST

"What bothers me about these meetings is even though it's work, I have the nagging feeling I ought to leave and get back to work."

183

A2. Consider aspects of the physical setting. Can you make it free of interruptions? Will everyone be able to hear and see well? How comfortable is the room?*

A3. Diagnose the meeting. What are the objectives? What priority should be given to items on the agenda? What will the emotional climate be like? What questions will likely be asked? Will there be voting and how will it go? What deadlines and follow-up will need to be decided at the meeting?

A4. Develop a plan for the meeting. Create a shared agenda with inputs from all concerned. Will you or any others be working on any hidden agenda items?

A5. Notify all concerned about the meeting. Distribute the agenda well in advance, stating what the purpose is, when and where it will be held, who should attend, and what they should be prepared to do. The topics to be discussed and time allotted for each topic should be listed. Indicate whether or not it is okay for people to pop in on certain agenda topics without being there for the whole meeting. Allowing people to pop in saves time, but it only works if you stick to the time allocations for each agenda item.

A6. Prepare materials needed for the meeting, such as handouts, briefs, reports, audiovisual equipment, coffee breaks.

A7. Review your own frame of mind. Be confident and clear about what you wish to accomplish, how, and why.

During the meeting, the following steps are effective time savers:

B1. Always start on time. The norm is either you do or you don't. If you wait for stragglers, you will *always* wait for stragglers.

B2. Restate the purpose and objectives of the meeting.

B3. Stay on schedule. Be tough about this! If an item is not resolved, table it until the next meeting or set up a subcommittee to look at it. If tangential issues are brought up, have them scheduled again as agenda items for the next meeting. If you really do follow up on these and if you get inputs before the agenda is cast in concrete, people will let you get away with this and you can stay on schedule. See Cohen and March, *Leadership and Ambiguity* (New York: McGraw-Hill, 1974), for an interesting analysis of how people use the first agenda item as a garbage can to dump their concerns on.

B4. Follow a style that best fits you and the group. This style can be open discussion, with the airing of feelings and process observations appropriate, such as "How are we doing?" You may wish to follow parliamentary procedure and Robert's Rules of Order. Or you may wish to tightly control the flow yourself. Each approach has benefits and drawbacks.

B5. Try to avoid negative comments and sanctions of a personal nature. Don't respond to personal negative sanctions with personal negative sanctions. This does not preclude constructive criticism that is issue-oriented rather than person-oriented.

B6. You may wish to build in time for reflection or subgrouping, if this would aid the quality of thought or agreement.

B7. List areas of agreement. Review action items. Get commitments on specific assignments.

B8. Stop on time. This becomes another norm. Let them know that time is valuable by not letting anyone, including yourself, run over.

---

*This question of comfort has two aspects. For some meetings, such as a board of directors meeting, you obviously want to make people as comfortable as possible. However, if your staff meetings have been dragging on and on, try having stand-up meetings. Remove the table and chairs from the room, and any problem can be thoroughly discussed and resolved in fifteen minutes. Give everyone a comfortable chair around a nice table, an ash tray and a cup of coffee, and the most trivial issue can be discussed for two hours. Never mind the grumbling after the first stand-up meeting; when they see the time it saves, they will bless your name.

After the meeting has been held:

C1. Summarize in a set of minutes, with every effort to limit to one page. The minutes are not a transcript of the interaction (although you may wish to keep one); they are a record of issues confronted and their resolution, with additional informational announcements. The leader *should* do the minutes. The person who records the meeting and does the minutes will rule the kingdom.
C2. Share the minutes with concerned parties, possibly including nonattenders.
C3. Follow up on action items and commitments (theirs and yours).
C4. Begin the preparation for the next meeting (Go to A1 above).

Following this plan dramatically increases the effectiveness of your meetings and the people who attend them. Remember . . .

> It Takes a Darn Good Meeting
> To Beat
> No Meeting at All

Delegation (Principle 13), communication (Principle 14), and development of people (Principle 15) are of significant enough importance to have occupied major sections elsewhere in this book.

ILLUSTRATIVE CASE G

The Case of Lynn Wood

Lynn Wood was a very good attorney. One of the best, the law school had said. But nothing in three years of law training had prepared Lynn for running a law office. The key to having it all work, to providing quality service, seemed to be in the effective functioning of a receptionist, two secretaries, an administrative assistant, and a bookkeeper. But Lynn had decided that good ones were not to be found. Countless hours seemed to be spent in checking the appointment book, explaining what to type, making calls, signing checks—leaving little time for practicing law. Lynn had hired an expensive administrative assistant to solve all these office problems, and that had only made the problem worse. This person seemed to function in two modes: not at all and wrong. Oh, everyone worked very hard but never seemed to be able to do anything quite the way Lynn wanted. And lately, the fatigue, irritability, and tension had begun to rub off onto conversations with clients. And now the complaints were coming from home about Lynn's bringing work home every night. Something had to change and soon.

FUNCTIONAL TYPE   *Lynn Wood is an attorney operating a small professional office. This situation might represent that of a doctor, dentist, banker, or other professional.*

LEADERSHIP FACTORS   *The principles involved in this case include* time management, delegation, human relations, goal setting, *and* career planning.

QUESTIONS TO CONSIDER

1. *What are key challenges that starting professionals face for which graduate training has not properly prepared them?*
2. *What basic principles of good time management are being violated in this case?*
3. *What are the obstacles to good delegation that are all too obvious here?*
4. *What forms of goal setting, training, and performance appraisal would be helpful to this office?*
5. *How could Lynn benefit from an examination of career goals and plans?*

ANALYSIS   *Lynn Wood would benefit from many of the principles discussed in the time management section. Foremost among these might be a more appropriate form of delegation. As discussed in the time management section, if a person does not let go or has fears of subordinates always making mistakes, the delegation process is defeated and things are worse than if it had not been attempted.*

Professionals with businesses cannot escape the requirements of good management and sound human relations practices. Being involved in a service business that is very susceptible to repeat business and word-of-mouth promotion, the professional cannot afford employees who take their frustrations out on their clients. Goal setting, training, and staff meetings need to be held regularly and must be seen as an important part of getting the job done. Recognition systems that really reward outstanding work need to be developed.

As this case implies, professionals often have to make choices that involve the relative importance of practice versus family. This doesn't have to involve something as drastic as giving up the profession for the family. But it may involve, as more than one professional has done, leaving a lucrative practice in a large city and moving to a less demanding practice in a small town.

Professionals need to make regular reexaminations of their career goals in relation to where they are. It is helpful to go through a values clarification periodically, remembering what were the original motives for pursuing a particular profession. If service isn't an important part of that answer, problems can be predicted.

There are three approaches to effective time use: time scheduling, time budgeting, and time analysis. The first two are planning techniques; the third is done after the time is spent. The first two are usually taught and written about; the third is seldom mentioned. The first two don't work; the third is very successful. How can this be?

The leader of one time management program I attended passed out an eight-by-seventeen-inch chart that had the week divided into half-hour segments. I was asked to fill in each half-hour block with the pieces of my life. The problem with time schedules is that reality is not on the schedule. By 10 A.M. you're right on schedule when a person runs in and yells, "Fire!" You respond, "No, I don't have time for a fire now, but I could fit one in at two." You can run to every fire (and there are always fires to be put out), in which case the schedule is meaningless, or you can stick to the schedule and *burn.* Either way, the main result is *frustration!*

Time budgeting was designed to provide more flexibility. The idea was to allocate so much time to each activity of your life, for example, forty-nine hours a week for sleep, forty hours a week for work, and so on. The problem

186

with a time budget is the same as the problem with a money budget. You find that to meet the budget you cannot work on Saturday and must go to the bathroom for three hours instead. Same results: uselessness or frustration.

To gain the value of time analysis, do the following (please!):

1. List all the major categories of your life (I said *all*—don't forget travel). You can make these as broad (work) or as specific (on the phone, filling out forms) as you wish.
2. Each day at the same time, perhaps just before retiring to bed, sit down and fill in the time you spent in each category that day.
3. At the end of the week add categories across.

The first time you do this you will experience two major shocks. You'll find that there is one thing (like watching TV a "couple of hours a week") that is consuming a lot more time than you ever dreamed of, and some other area you claim to value (like writing that important book) that you spent little or no time on at all. Once you've had this realization, you can do either of two things.

4A. Change your life or your goals, or
4B. Just keep setting goals and analyzing your time.

(The reason 4B works is what I call "You, the Guided Missile," discussed elsewhere in this book.)

Principle 18 says don't ever let anybody or any unexpected thing waste your time. There are three solutions to the problem of unexpected time wasters: the big one, the little one, and the internal one. The big one for me is my omnipresent briefcase. (For a woman, a large bag or purse can accomplish the same purpose.) In it I carry letters to answer, bills to be paid, writing paper, typing paper, carbon paper, correcting tape, maps, addresses, stamps, paper clips, chalk, toothbrush, reading material, and so on. I have that briefcase with me anywhere someone else controls my time—at the bus stop, on the freeway, and in the doctor's examination room (ever read a *PDR*?).

There are some places (like a formal dance) where a briefcase would be seen as out of place. So you can place in your pocket a calendar or address book containing three-by-five-inch cards to write on, something to read (small, obviously), a folded check, and so forth. With just the three-by-five-inch cards you can send a note to a friend, make up a laundry list, or write a section for your next book. (Yes, you need to include a small pencil!) If you're ever caught (naked?) without your briefcase or pocket calendar, you simply adapt the attitude that every situation has something to teach you. An experience is an experience.

All of this must sound very automated and boring. The irony is that the effective time user not only produces many more significant results, but also has more time to relax and play. A balanced life (Principle 19) can significantly extend your life. Consider the Balanced Life Inventory on the following page. What is really most important to you? The Chinese, who take time to consider the lotus blossom over tea each day, live to be 112, while you will drop dead well-insured at 45. Who accomplishes more with life (and most enjoys the living)?

FIGURE 69. A form for analyzing how balanced your life is

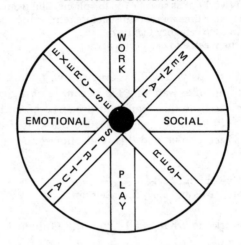

BALANCED LIFE INVENTORY

Take a look at the picture above and answer the following questions.

1. What percentage of your time do you spend in each area?

WORK _____ %	REST _____ %	EMOTIONAL _____ %
MENTAL _____ %	PLAY _____ %	EXERCISE _____ %
SOCIAL _____ %	SPIRITUAL _____ %	TOTAL _____ 100%

2. Is your life balanced? (Justify your answer)

3. What happens if the spokes of a wheel are of different lengths? Is it the same with the parts of your life? Why or why not?

4. Which people are more likely to get promoted, those who are balanced or those who put most of their time and energy into one or two areas? Why?

5. Which people are more likely to have "successful" lives?

6. What are the most important things in life? How are they gained?

Finally, Principle 20: Have the courage to say no. But managers ask, "Can you ever say no to your boss?" My response, "It all depends on whether *you're* really interested in *you and the boss* being effective and maximizing results." The choice and the consequences are yours.

Happy time!

Leadership Technique #11
A JOB IS WHAT
YOU DO WITH YOUR DAYS;
A CAREER IS WHAT
YOU DO WITH YOUR LIFE

The world has truly changed in our day. For millenia jobs were synonymous with days. You worked from predawn until bed time, then you slept until time to get up and do it again. Work and life have separated over the last century, as shown in Figure 70 on page 190.

Two phenomena have emerged with this change. The first has to do with the concept of spending your life engaged in a career that is challenging, fulfilling, and rewarding. Career development and life planning are preoccupations today for many.

The following set of exercises is designed to assist you in developing your career and planning your life.

I. Self-Assessment

A. Who Am I?

Describe yourself in terms of

Background—Where did I come from? What are my roots?
Characteristics—Trustworthy, loyal, helpful, friendly, courteous, etc.
Roles—Male, husband, father, Methodist, Democrat, etc.
Interests—Reading, travel, golf, stamp collecting, etc.
Values—Health, freedom, service, etc.

B. Who Am I Really?

Take the list of items from A and attempt to rank-order them. If you had to choose between being a manager or a wife, which would you choose? If you had to choose between being loyal or true to yourself, which would you choose?

Example: "This is really who I am . . .

1. A woman
2. Intelligent
3. Concerned about others
4. Catholic
   Etc.

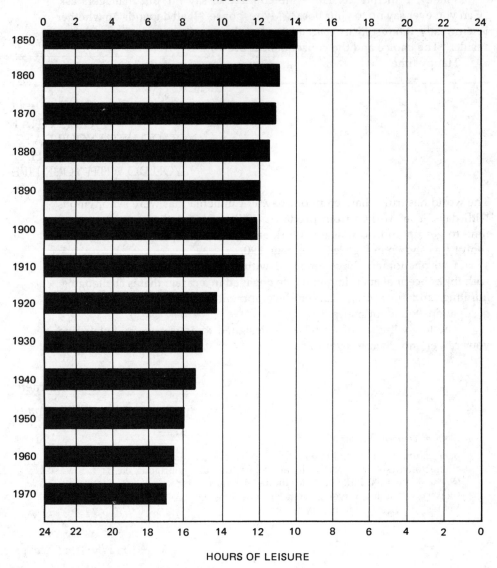

FIGURE 70. Changes in work and life-styles

C. Lifeline

    Draw a line that represents your life from birth to death. It might be straight, wavy, jagged, or circular, according to how your life appears to you. Mark where you are right now. What does the future look like? Why? How are you likely to get there?

D. Ideals

    Design for yourself an ideal job. Do not give it a name, but describe it in terms of characteristics such as: working indoors or out, with people or alone, etc.* Write a description of an ideal day. This may or may not include an ideal job. (If every day of the rest of your life were just like this, would it still be ideal? Hmmmmmmmmm!)

E. Goals

List the goals you have for your life in the areas of personal development, work, family, finances, health, career, social activity, service, achievement. Once the list is created, prioritize it. You now have a ranking of the goals for your life, from most important on down to trivial.

F. Reality and Reflection

Compare the list of goals to the time assessment of your life suggested in Leadership Technique #10. Is the way you are living your life related to your goals and values? If yes, congratulations; keep it up. If no, you have two options: You can change your behavior and/or your goals, or you can do nothing. Well, not exactly nothing. If you continue to refine your goals and to analyze how you use your time, change will occur without any conscious effort on your part because you are the world's greatest cybernetic machine.

You, The Guided Missile

What is a cybernetic machine or process?

It is one that is target-oriented and self-correcting. One example most people are familiar with is a guided missile. Study the figure below.

FIGURE 71. A cybernetic system: the guided missile

*Did you think to mention money? Isn't that interesting. Most people don't when fantasizing about the ideal job. I have volunteered, so far with no response, to man a fire-watch tower in Yellowstone Park with Loni Anderson. I have made it clear that money is no object in my taking the job.

The situation has four critical components. First, there has to be a target: the missile has to be programmed to "know" where it is going. Second, there has to be a map so the missile has a picture of the terrain it will traverse on the way to the target. Third, there has to be radar to monitor the ground being covered, to tell the missile whether it is on the right track or not. Finally, the built-in gyro makes adjustments in the course to make sure the target is reached. You are far more sophisticated than any guided missile that has ever been or ever will be built. The reason you are often not successful in reaching your target is that one or more of the parts of your system is missing. Look at the figure again.

FIGURE 72. Another cybernetic system: you the guided missile

If you do not have clear goals stating where you're going, how can you hope to get there? Do you have a specific plan for achieving the goal? Do you monitor how you use your time to see if your life is on track? You have to *do* the first three. If you do, the self-correcting gyro is built in—believe me. You cannot continue to confront yourself with the information that you are spending no time on your most important goal(s) without something changing. Remember, it's not always your behavior that changes: You may modify the goal. That's okay. It's your life; you program the missile!

II. What's Out There?

If you want to have a successful career it is necessary, but not sufficient, to know who you are. Unfortunately, the world goes on its merry way, regardless of your goals and needs. So it helps to know what's available to meet those needs.

The problem is tied up in something called the hidden job market. Do you know what it is and how it works? The concept is basically that a very large percentage of jobs are filled by insiders before they ever become public knowledge.

Let's look at how the world has changed in the last twenty years. Back then if you had an opening and you knew you wanted Helen, you hired Helen. That may not be fair, but it certainly is straightforward. Now, after twenty years of civil rights statutes, EEO regulations, and executive orders, what's changed? Everything and nothing. You have an opening; you know you want Helen. You advertise the position at great expense, and Helen applies along with 119 other hopefuls. You appoint a search committee (at more expense) to sift through 200 cover letters, 200 resumés, 200 applications, and 600 letters of recommendation. After weeks (months?) the choice is narrowed down to three: Dave, Sheila, . . . and Helen.

Dave comes in for the first interview and brings Congress, the World Council of Churches, and the CEO's of the Fortune 500 to speak for his selection. Sheila is next, singing in fourteen different languages accompanied by the Mormon Tabernacle Choir, dancing, and typing 120 words per minute. Finally, Helen comes in to have a cup of coffee with the committee and shows pictures of her latest fishing trip. The final deliberations are undertaken and, after what seems an endless wait, the white puff of smoke signifies the choice of the new office holder—Helen.

Since this is how it mostly works, you've got three choices:

1. Change it! That's what we've been trying to do for twenty years, remember?
2. Give it your best shot! Who knows, the position may be one of the few that really is competitive.
3. Be Helen!

What is required to be Helen? Simple—you have to know about the position before it is available to be known about. How do you do that? You have to use all your resources, and you have to look at every piece of information you receive with the question, "Where is there an opportunity in this for me?"

What are your resources? Only four will be considered here. First, your personal network of friends and associates. But be careful: Not all are helpful. Draw a table like Figure 73.

Now start putting the names of all the people you know into one of the four boxes.

Box #1. These are the people who don't know what's going on out there and wouldn't help you if they did.

Box #2. These people know the score, but won't help you.

Box #3. These are the most dangerous, because they want to be helpful, but they don't know what's going on. They can waste a lot of your valuable time.

Box #4. These are the wise elders of the tribe and willing to help. Seek them out and cultivate your relationship with them. (P.S. The only way you can pay these people back is by becoming like them and helping others.)

A second resource is the media, particularly the newspaper. But you have to know where to look. Avoid the "Help Wanted" ads like the plague unless you

	DON'T KNOW	KNOW
WON'T HELP	1	2
WILL HELP	3	4

FIGURE 73. Analysis form for associates as career resources

are a computer programmer, registered nurse, or short-order cook. Where do you look? The business page, the society page, the obituary page. You're looking for changes. What's going to be built? Who's getting married, moving, having a baby, retiring, dying? (Sounds macabre, but someone's going to do that job.)

The third resource is your local college. Enroll in a class. Then get to know the placement director and career center. These people are qualified but underutilized, and they love to be helpful. They keep an up-to-date "jobs available" board with new listings daily. They provide counseling, invite in recruiters for interviews, and have vast career guide resources. All for the price of a class!

Finally, there are the private placement agencies. There are three types: the good, the bad, and the ugly. If they ask for money first before they try to find you a job, that's ugly—run! If they find you a job and then you pay them, that's good news and bad news, but may be worth it. The best ones have their fees paid by the employers and concentrate on helping you. They're good; use them.

III. How Do I Get It?

Knowing who you are and what you want and need is the first step. Knowing what opportunities are available out there brings you two thirds of the way home. The final skills to be acquired have to do with how you get what you want.

Obtaining a new job, whether it is your first or a midcareer switch, requires mounting a job-hunting campaign. It's hard work, and the victory is not to the swift but to those who endure to the end. There are several elements in the campaign, and the most important points will be presented here.

Timing and Process

I found that with a Harvard doctorate and fifteen years of work experience I was getting active consideration from one out of every fifty positions I pursued. Your odds may be better . . . but then they may not. Could you sit down tonight and do fifty job applications? Hardly. Could you do one a week for the next year? Of course. And that's just about the lead time you need to secure a new position. I have college seniors come to me in May and say, "I've sent out five applications for jobs in the last month. How come I don't have a job?" I tell them they're forty-five applications short and eleven months too late. Keep in mind that *the best time to get a new job is when you already have one.* It's perverse but true: If you don't need to make a move, they're hot on your trail; but if you're hungry for work, you're the last one they want to talk to.

To correspond with fifty firms over a year requires that you be organized and have a good record-keeping system. Design your own, but make sure that it includes a record of the name, address, and phone number of every company, the name of your contact person, and a notation on every communication sent and/or received. Nothing will break your spirit more than to lose the job Phil calls to offer you because you respond, "Phil who?" Remember—in their eyes, they're the only one.

A final thought. It's not a bad idea to send every company who turns you down a polite (not sarcastic!) thank-you letter. You may be the *next* one they hire.

Selling Yourself on Paper

Your initial contact with an organization will usually be a cover letter and resumé or vita. Remember the importance of first impressions. Have both typed or printed clearly on attractive, not showy, paper. Remember the mistake discussed in Chapter 3 of the bright orange resumé that copied black . . . and don't! Keep the cover letter short and to the point. Concentrate on the organization's strengths and needs and what you can do for them.

You should have a resumé. You should keep it up to date. And you should do it right. The first two are up to you. Here are some thoughts on the third. Do not write your resumé in the old obituary format, listing the events of your life from birth in chronological order. The reader expects to find out in turning the page that you passed away in 1979. Do not put personal information (other than your name, address, and phone number) up front, as this simply gives the reader several reasons not to like you immediately. Do not describe your previous experience in terms of what your duties were. The prospective employer is not interested in your previous job description, but in what you accomplished (if anything).

FIGURE 74. The "Don't you really want a job or do you?"
approaches to resumé creation

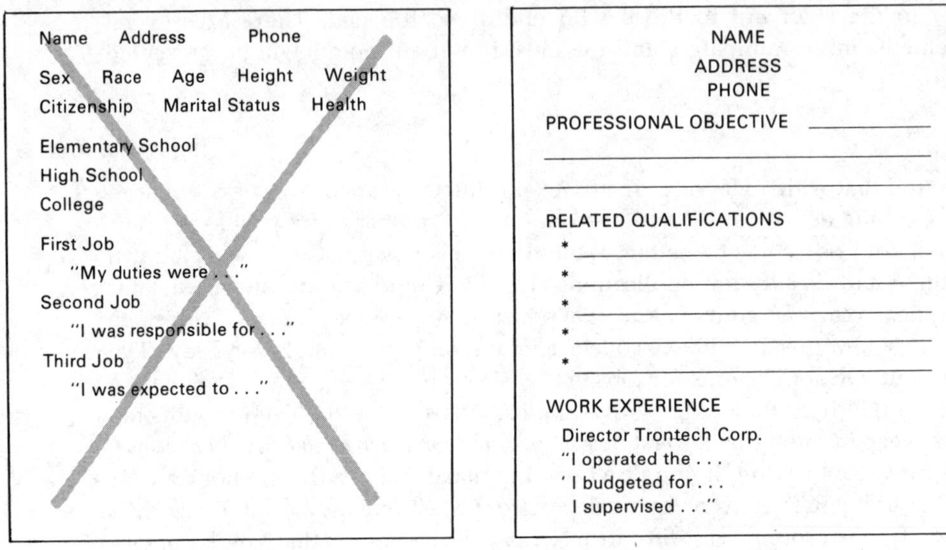

Name Address Phone
 	
Sex Race Age Height Weight
Citizenship Marital Status Health
 	
Elementary School
High School
College
 	
First Job
  "My duties were . . ."
Second Job
  "I was responsible for . . ."
Third Job
  "I was expected to . . ."
	NAME
	ADDRESS
	PHONE
	PROFESSIONAL OBJECTIVE _____
	_____
	_____
	
	RELATED QUALIFICATIONS
	  * _____
	  * _____
	  * _____
	  * _____
	  * _____
	
	WORK EXPERIENCE
	  Director Trontech Corp.
	  "I operated the . . .
	  ' I budgeted for . . .
	  I supervised . . ."

WRONG WAY "Obituary Format"	RIGHT WAY "Professional Achiever Format"

Now, how to do it right? Center your name, address, and telephone number at the top. (You'd be surprised how many of the new resumés, in wishing to avoid personal information, leave this off. This makes it very hard for an employer to let you know you got the job.) The next item is the shortest item on the resumé, but it is the most important. And it is the most difficult to write. You are going to write your Career Goal or Professional Objective in one, clear, intelligent, forceful sentence. Do not state, "I want to be a C.P.A." Write, "My goal is to obtain a managerial position in which my decision-making and budgeting skills can be fully utilized." Use action verbs. Show them you know what you're looking for.

The next item is the next most important item. List your qualifications related to your job objective. These can be phrases or sentences; just be consistent. Use action verbs. These abilities and skills do not have to come only from your paid jobs. They could be ones you've acquired as head of the PTA or in twenty years of running a home. Remember, this is not the place to impress people with your humility. Don't invent skills you don't have, obviously, but don't be modest and lose by default.

What should come next? Whatever is next most important about you—work, schooling, awards. Unless you're using a business-school format and trying to cram your fifty years of experience onto one page, the key is to get the reader to want to turn the page and read on. No one says you have to describe your life in chronological order. Start and end with most important things. Present yourself as a doer. While you should be concise, the length of the resumé is less important than how interesting and informative it is.

Should you include a section of personal information? The "experts" say no; I say yes. The "experts" say that this will allow some readers' biases to eliminate you early on. Exactly! You are who you are. And if they don't want someone like you, both parties save time and energy if they are clear about that from the start. This way you can go into the interview with confidence knowing they want you and that there are no hidden surprises. (With my name, I don't want the first comment in the interview room to be, "Good heavens, she's a man!")

A final word on the resumé. Once you have it designed the way you want it, have it printed on an attractive off-white paper. This will set it off from the other two hundred, and you're on your way to the finals. Resumés reproduced on a *good* copy machine are okay for short-term emergency opportunities. I've seen mimeographed resumés. One person even sent in a postcard! It's frustrating to prepare an intelligent, attractive resumé, complete with all the information the employer could ever need, and send it in only to receive in return the company's seven-page application form to fill out. This is maddening, but in this age of standardized everything, it is usually a requirement. My suggestion, if you can afford it, is to hire someone with an I.Q. above 30 and some typing skill. Supply this person with every piece of data on your life, including your blood type and highest rank in scouting, and let him or her fill out the blasted thing. Yes, check it before it's mailed off. You've come too far to blow it with a typo or misunderstanding (SEX: *Yes,* instead of SEX: *Male*).

Selling Yourself in Person

Congratulations, you've made it into the final three, and you're on your way to the interview. The moment of truth has arrived. If you fooled them on your resumé, here's where it will come back to haunt you.

Remember the importance of those first impressions. As you walk through the door, what will they notice about you first? Right, your sex, age, and race. There is nothing within reason you can do about any of these, so forget them. If they don't like forty-five-year-old black women, that's their problem, and your challenge.

The next thing they'll notice is how you dress. Dress for the job and the occasion. If the job is as a receptionist in a business office, don't come to the interview in jeans and a T-shirt (of course, people do it). If the interview is for a machinist, don't wear a three-piece suit. Be conservative, attractive, and clean.

The next thing they'll notice about you is how you present yourself. Neither the Caspar Milquetoast nor the bionic person approach is likely to get the job. Be confident and forthright. If you're nervous, say "I'm excited about obtaining this position, that makes me a little nervous." You know you're nervous, they know, you know they know—so state the obvious. They'll be impressed with your openness.

The sooner you can relax and be yourself, the better. Be honest and direct. If the answer to a question is, "I don't know," say so. Don't be flustered or rushed. Don't let them throw you. They often want to see how you react under pressure. (Professional recruiters at graduate business schools often like to use the inquisition approach on their subjects. They often hire only masochists.) If you need a moment to compose an answer, say so.

Do your homework before going to the interview. Be prepared to interview the interviewer. Be sharp. Be professional.

Having come this far, don't fall on the final water jump. When the subject turns to money, don't cave in and say you'll take anything. Know who you are. Know what you're worth and ask for it. Find out what the range of pay is in this industry and organization. Go for the top of the range. You must believe that if two equally qualified people are finalists for a position, the one who asks for more (within reason) will always be hired. Your instincts will tell you otherwise. Your instincts are wrong. Ask yourself, why would they want someone who comes cheap? Remember, you're a bargain at twice the price.

In conclusion, view your life and your career as synonymous. Always be looking for new opportunities and be prepared to capitalize on them immediately. (I always carry a current resumé on any plane trip.) Follow up; be grateful for consideration. Help others' careers whenever you can. Don't compare your life or career to anyone else's. Your only concern is with achieving your goals and thereby finding your happiness.

Moving Up
the Bureaucratic Ladder

FIGURE 75. How the requirements change as you move up the organization* (Illustration by the author based on the article by Robert L. Katz, "Skills of an Effective Administrator," *Harvard Business Review*, January–February 1955, pp. 33–42).

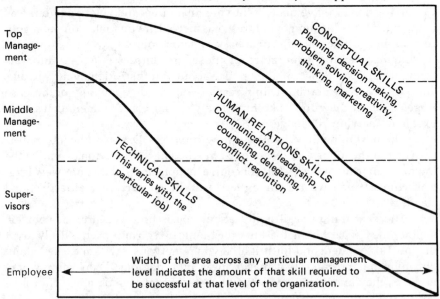

*NOTE: Katz article was only dealing with levels of administration/management in the organization. The extension to the level of the employees is the author's.

Study this picture carefully. It represents one view of how the required skills change as one moves up the career ladder in an organization. The four rectangles represent the four general levels in any organization. The diagonal lines create an area, the width of which shows the amount of a particular skill needed to be successful at that level of the organization.

At the basic employment level, talk is often of a "hired hand." They want your hands, not your heart or head. The interest is less in how well you get along or what ideas you have than in what you can do. Your advancement will depend on an increase in your technical skills (typing, drafting, driving, and so on).

At the level of the first-line supervision the skills required begin to change. (Many supervisors never grasp this and continue to try to be super technicians.) The organization is now more interested in your human relations skills: communication, counseling, empathy, conflict resolution, delegation, control, and so forth.

At the midmanagement levels the technical-skill needs often diminish, to be replaced by your conceptual skills: planning, thinking, problem solving, and decision making.

At the executive level, the requirements for technical skills and human relations skills largely vanish. No one really cares whether the president of World Wide Motors knows how a carburetor works or whether he or she is a nice person. The skills required at this level are decision making, forecasting, vision, and creativity. These are the skills for which the world pays top dollar. (This is true for all careers except professional athletes, movie stars, and prostitutes.)

Knowing this, one can acquire these skills and catapult right to the top, right? Wrong. It's not that easy. In fact, it's very complicated. To see this, consider how promotion decisions are made in large organizations. Picture a large paneled meeting room. Several WASP males wearing three-piece suits are sitting around an olive-shaped conference table. The room is thick with cigar smoke. Someone asks, "But can Smith make a decision?" The first thing you notice is that Smith is not in the room. Smith's supervisor, who has been waiting for this chance, responds, "The other day I asked Smith, 'Would you say indecision is your biggest weakness as a manager?' and Smith responded, 'I'm not sure, I can't make up my mind.' " A chuckle ripples through the room and Smith is probably dead as a candidate for the position. If the job goes to someone else, it is unlikely that Smith will ever even know the meeting took place.

So here is the mine field you've got to traverse. First, you've got to be aware that your skill base must change as you move up the organization. Second, you must acquire those new skills. Third, you must demonstrate them so they are visible to the higher-ups. But, and here's the catch 22, you must do this in a way that does not threaten your immediate supervisor, who can torpedo your career ship before it ever leaves the dock.

How do you do that? There is no easy answer. It helps to have a mentor above and away from your direct line of authority. It helps to assist your supervisor in the climb up the corporate mountain, especially if your supervisor has ample coattails. Sometimes you just have to move laterally to move up—maybe even laterally to another organization.

Good luck! And remember, the greatest mistake you can make is to assume you are working for someone else.

Career Postscript

Regardless of what others do to you or think about you, remember that it's your career and your life. You set your goals and *you* determine whether you succeed or fail. Here is an illustrative case study that happens to be me.

*Live in Fame
or Go Down in Flame*

I hold two academic world records. I set the first in 1964. That was the year I became the first senior ever to flunk out of the United States Air Force Academy.

The publicly stated mission of the Academy was to develop and educate officers for management and leadership roles. And I got along very well in courses that trained me for just such positions. The problem was, I did rather badly in engineering classes. And the curriculum (designed by West Point graduates) was 60 percent engineering.

Up until 1964 the Academy had been successful in "turning out" large numbers of freshmen, quite a few sophomores, and an occasional junior. But they absolutely never flunked out seniors. The thinking was that too many tax dollars had been spent on a cadet by that time.

But during my senior year a new commandant of cadets came in from the Strategic Air Command, the "shape up or ship out" branch of the Air Force. In the fall of that year I was among a select group of twenty-five seniors called into the commandant's office and informed that we were academically at the bottom of our class. Of course, this was not news to any of us, since USAFA had been grading us on a curve since the day we had walked through the door. Not only that, there are traditionally two positions of honor at any academy graduation: first in the class and last. We were the twenty-five vying for the latter honor.

The commandant said, "I know the policy in the past has been not to expel senior cadets, but I'm about to change all that. I would like to use one of you as an example to the wing that seniors can no longer slide through academically. So I'm giving each one of you my personal guarantee that if you fail a single class, I will see that you very quickly become a civilian." He was a man of his word, for I did and he did.

In January of 1964 the U.S. Air Force had certified me as a leadership reject, academically unfit for higher education. In June of 1977 I established the second of my world records. I became the first flunk-out from a United States military academy to go on to receive a doctorate from Harvard University. Ne Illegitimus Carborundum!

From this experience I gained several things. First, I determined to be successful at accomplishing my mission in life, even if the Academy failed at theirs. Secondly, I became obsessed with understanding more about the damage done to individuals by large bureaucratic organizations and began a quest for that understanding and a platform from which to share with others what I learned about bureaucratic survival skills. Finally, I was determined to experience leadership from many different perspectives. Having been a custodian, corporate president, coach, supervisor, church leader, salesman, dean, and parent, I have gained experience in the full range of experiences associated with leadership. That's why this is not a book of fairy tales. You *can* benefit from others' failure and success.

Leadership Technique #12
WHO AM I REALLY?:
PERSONAL LEADERSHIP ASSESSMENT

To begin a journey, you start from where you are. The process of leadership growth and development begins with an analysis of your current strengths and weaknesses. The strengths are what you build on to be successful; the weaknesses outline the objectives that guide your personal development. This section is designed to aid you in assessing your knowledge, attitude, and abilities.

The section is divided into three major areas of analysis: insights into self, relationships, and knowledge and skills. Each of the three areas contains a series of self-analysis forms to fill out. These forms will be more helpful to you if you do them slowly and thoughtfully. They will be most helpful if you ask those close to you to fill them out about you and then compare your view of yourself with theirs. If you gain the self-vision that can come from completing every assignment in this section, you will be way ahead of most people and will greatly strengthen yourself as a leader.

These exercises are tied closely to several of the chapters and leadership technique sections, which is why this section comes late in the book. It would be helpful to look again at some of the pertinent chapters and sections as you work on related exercises here.

Insights Into Self

This first set of exercises is designed to help you look at yourself, who you are, what you want, how badly you want it, what you're willing to do to get it, and whether or not you have already arrived. As you learned in "You, the Guided Missile" it doesn't matter what the target is out there or what the rewards are for hitting it if the ship is not ready to fly. You are the ship. This section is part of your preflight checklist.

These are the exercises that follow:

1. What are my goals and objectives?
2. What are my values?
3. What are my interests?

4. An inventory of my leadership traits: Am I ready to lead?
5. What is my motivation for success?
6. Round pegs in square holes: Does my current job fit?

Inventory of Goals and Objectives

You begin at the beginning. This is your target and the benchmarks along the journey. You may want to review your answers to the first few exercises in the Leadership Technique Section #11, or you may just want to start here. For each area of your life, write a major goal and supporting, specific objectives. The areas might include work, play, mental, spiritual, social, emotional, and health. (Use other sheets if necessary.)

1. Goal

   A. Objective

   B. Objective

2. Goal

   A. Objective

   B. Objective

3. Goal

   A. Objective

   B. Objective

4. Goal

   A. Objective

   B. Objective

Values Clarification Exercise

This exercise is designed to help you assess the relative importance of the things you value. Look at each one of the items and begin ranking them from most important to least important. Making an initial ranking of high, moderate, and low values may be a good way to start. (Place the letter for each value behind the number for your ranking.)

A. A comfortable life (security, creature comforts, satisfaction)
B. Equality (brotherhood, equal opportunity)
C. An exciting life (stimulating, active life)
D. Family Security (taking care of loved ones)
E. Freedom (independence, free choice)
F. Happiness (contentedness)
G. Inner harmony (freedom from inner conflict)
H. Mature love (sexual and spiritual intimacy)
I. National security (protection from attack and resource scarcity)
J. Pleasure (an enjoyable, leisurely life)
K. Salvation (deliverance from sin, eternal life)
L. Self-respect (self-esteem)
M. A sense of accomplishment (making a lasting contribution)
N. Good health (freedom from pain and disability)
O. A long life (ample time for many experiences)

P. Strong relationships (with family and close friends)
Q. Service (an opportunity to do things for others)
R. Wealth (sufficient resources for all your wants and needs)

1. _____   7. _____   13. _____
2. _____   8. _____   14. _____
3. _____   9. _____   15. _____
4. _____   10. _____   16. _____
5. _____   11. _____   17. _____
6. _____   12. _____   18. _____

Did you find this helpful, frustrating, or both? Was it easy or hard to decide? Did your values fall evenly into the three levels of ranking, or were most high or most low? What have you learned from this assessment?

Inventory of Interests

1. Brainstorm a list of all the things that interest you, things you like, things you'd like to know more about, things you'd like to see, do, or be.

2. Now take that list and prioritize it.

Inventory of Leadership Traits

Research on traits of leaders has identified over 1,400 separate traits. Below is a list of the ten traits most commonly mentioned as identified with leaders.
Rate yourself on each trait: 10 (high) to 0 (low)

1. Friendliness, ability to get close to people _____

2. Technical knowledge and skill _____

3. Ability to motivate others to accomplish task _____

4. Action in support of the group's task _____

5. Human relations skill, ability to get along with people _____

6. Need to be effective and to achieve _____

7. Emotional balance and control _____

8. Administrative ability _____

9. Intelligence, intellectual skill _____

10. Dominance, control, decisiveness _____

Note: If you don't rate particularly high on these ten, remember that there are 1,390 others that might describe you.

Motivation for Success

1. Do I remember significant others in my life who were outwardly interested in my success?
   Who?
   How Strongly?

2. How successful have I been so far? (my track record)
   In school
   In work
   In relationships
   In personal growth
   In service

3. How badly do I want to succeed? (elaborate)

4. What price am I willing to pay for success? (elaborate)

5. What rules will I play by to get what I want? (elaborate)

Round Pegs in Square Holes

1. What type of work are you doing right now? (Don't just name your work, describe it.)

2. What education led up to this work?

   What experience led up to this work?

3. Does what you're doing fit:
   Your goals and objectives? (elaborate)

   Your values? (elaborate)

   Your interests? (elaborate)

   Your self-image? (elaborate)

4. Describe what an ideal job would be like for you.

5. How well does this ideal job fit what you're doing right now?

6. What are you going to do about it?

Relationships

Your greatest assets in the pursuit of success are your friends, work groups, peers, and supervisors. One of the greatest barriers to your success can be problems you encounter in your interpersonal relationships. The exercises in this section are designed to help you think about the quality of those relationships. Remember that you are often blind to your own inadequacies and relationship problems. It would be a good area to ask the assistance of those you trust to help you better come to see how you function.

These are the exercises that follow:

1. What is my orientation toward my subordinates?
2. How do my subordinates view me as a leader?
3. How do I relate with others "over and up the organization"?
   A. Peers
   B. Superiors
4. What is my social style and how does that affect how I function?

A Leadership Style Analysis

Answer the following questions according to how you *actually act* as a leader. If you are not currently in a leadership situation, think of one you have occupied in the past and respond accordingly. If you have not held a leadership position, make a response in terms of how you honestly feel you would act.

TRUE	FALSE	
_____	_____	1. I allow subordinates complete freedom in how they do their work.
_____	_____	2. I make sure that the work is moving along at a consistently rapid pace.
_____	_____	3. I make frequent checks of each subordinate to see how the work is going.
_____	_____	4. My subordinates use their own judgment and make their own decisions in things that directly affect their work.
_____	_____	5. I create the plans for my people and tell them what will be expected of them during the next work period.
_____	_____	6. When my superiors want to know what is going on, I speak for my people.

_____ _____ 7. When conflicts occur, I let the "troops" resolve them among themselves.

_____ _____ 8. My people establish their own objectives and standards for their work.

_____ _____ 9. I try to have a problem solved as close to the source as possible.

_____ _____10. I keep careful track of tardiness, absenteeism, and attitude problems among my people.

Consider the following two descriptions of subordinates generally:

    I. People generally dislike working and will try to avoid it whenever they can. They tend to lack ambition and have to be prodded, threatened, or bribed to do what needs to be done. They are generally irresponsible, so a leader must watch everything they do very carefully. People's primary concern is for job security, so they will do what is necessary to stay employed. People would prefer to have the leaders at the top of the organization make plans and decisions and simply tell them what to do.

    II. People find work a very natural part of their lives and will often engage in strenuous activities off the job. People want to achieve and be successful and will work hard toward objectives that they set and to which they are committed. People will not only accept, but will often seek responsibility and can be trusted to do what is best. People are creative and would prefer to think for themselves, do their own planning, solve their own problems, and make the decisions that directly affect their work.

Think of the subordinates with whom you are currently involved or with whom you have previously been involved. If you thought of the two positions above as anchoring two ends of a continuum, where would you place your feelings toward your subordinates? Indicate that point with a *P*.

I _____ II

  0   1   2   3   4   5   6   7   8   9   10

Now grade the survey that you took on page 205 at the beginning of A Leadership Style Analysis. The scale is as follows. (For example, if you answered Statement 1 true, give yourself one point. If you answered it False, place a zero under points.) Note that the points reverse on some questions.

	TRUE	FALSE	YOUR POINTS		TRUE	FALSE	YOUR POINTS
1.	1	0	_____	6.	0	1	_____
2.	0	1	_____	7.	1	0	_____
3.	0	1	_____	8.	1	0	_____
4.	1	0	_____	9.	1	0	_____
5.	0	1	_____	10.	0	1	_____

Add up your TOTAL POINTS _____ (You will have scored between 1 and 10)

Locate this point on the continuum above and mark it with an *R*.

The *P* represents how you *perceive* your attitude toward those with whom you work. The *R* represents your *rated* behavior toward those subordinates. If a gap exists between your theory and practice, as hypothesized by Argyris and Schön, your continuum should look something like this:

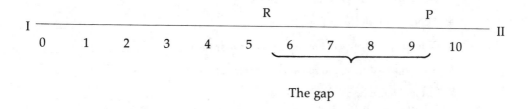

The gap

You should see graphically the gap between what you say you believe and how you actually act. Your behavior should be more Model I (Theory X) than your attitudes, if Argyris and Schön are correct. The width of the gap represents the amount on integration you lack between your "talk" and your "walk." And since the *R* only represents how you say you act, the theory would suggest that your actual behavior would fall something like this.

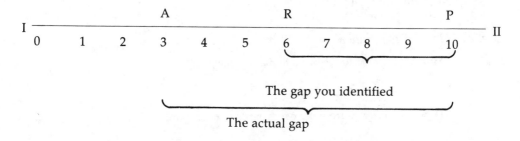

The gap you identified

The actual gap

If you didn't find these gaps, congratulations. Before you throw a party for yourself, however, have your subordinates rate you. (Oops!)

If you found the gaps as predicted and want to know what to do about them, I suggest you finish this book and then read and act on the 1974, 1976, and 1978 Argyris (and Schön) books in the Bibliography. Good luck on becoming "whole" again.

Leadership Rating

Listed below are a set of ten traits that should be found in an effective leader. Do you possess them? Have the members of your office, your team, or your family rate you on these ten traits. (Just to keep them honest, have them rate themselves on the same ten traits.)

Score each trait from 10 (high) to 1 (low).

	My Boss	Myself
1. Ability to communicate clearly	_____	_____
2. Ability to make effective decisions	_____	_____
3. Demonstrated interest in subordinates	_____	_____
4. Ability to motivate and inspire	_____	_____
5. Demonstrated respect for and trust in subordinates	_____	_____
6. A teaching attitude and patience with mistakes	_____	_____
7. Just and fair judgments	_____	_____
8. Loyalty to subordinates and toughness in their behalf	_____	_____
9. Humility and openness to new ideas and different opinions	_____	_____
10. A sense of humor and ability to relax	_____	_____
TOTAL POINTS		

What have you learned?

What will you do about it?

Over and Up the Organization

1. How am I similar to my peers in the organization?

   How am I different from my peers in the organization?

2. How well do I get along with my peers?

   Where could I improve?

3. How am I viewed by my peers? How do I know?

4. What is my relationship to those above me?

5. How do those above view me? How do I know?

6. What knowledge, attitude, and skills would I need to acquire to be more like those above me?

Social Style Inventory

The Wilson Learning Corporation has developed a most interesting theory of four social styles that all of us use in managing interpersonal relations (MIR). The MIR program helps people assess their individual styles, to look at how that style interacts with the style of their bosses, peers, subordinates, clients, spouses, and important others. Techniques are then taught for using this knowledge in leading, communicating, problem solving, selling, and servicing.

Because the program and materials are copyrighted and too extensive to reproduce here, if you are interested in more information contact Wilson Learning Corporation and see how you can gain access to these materials. This would be an important source of leadership assessment and leadership skill to add to those you currently possess.

Wilson Learning Corporation
6950 Washington Ave. So.
Eden Prairie, MN 55343
(612) 944-2880

Knowledge and Skills

This is an inventory of some of the key traits and techniques you bring to a leadership situation. An honest assessment of your strengths and weaknesses can show you what you can build on and where you need to improve. Remember that these paper-and-pencil tests only scratch the surface of who you really are.

These are the exercises that follow:

1. What is my learning style and how does it affect my view of the world?
2. What communication skills do I possess?
3. Do I use my time effectively to minimize the stresses of life?
4. Can I roll forward with a balanced life?
5. What are my problem-solving and decision-making skills?
6. How do I rate as a professional?
7. What is my unique gift that explains "Why I am here?"

Learning Style Inventory

Chapters 3 and 4 discussed Kolb's learning-style theory and briefly discussed the four styles. As Chapter 4 pointed out, one trait of a true leader is having learned how to learn, ever growing in knowledge and skill. In the book *Organizational Psychology* by Kolb et al. (2nd ed., Englewood Cliffs, N.J.: Prentice-Hall, Inc., 1974), an assessment instrument is presented that allows you to identify your learning style. Understanding your style and its built-in strengths and weaknesses should help you in developing your view of the world. Becoming sensitive to others' differing styles could improve your interpersonal relations.

What are you most likely to "see" with your learning style?

What are you most likely to miss with your learning style?

What could you do to strengthen your abilities to use different learning styles in which you are currently weak?

Communication Skills

Communication was discussed in detail in Chapter 2 and Learning Technique #4. You should review those parts of the book and consider your strengths and weaknesses in terms of:

1. What is my ability to recognize and overcome the barriers to good communication?
2. Do I think logically and clearly about my communications?
3. How clear are my powers of perception?
4. Can I give effective instructions?
   Can I give effective feedback?
5. Am I a good listener?
6. Do I recognize and act on nonverbal messages?
7. How well do I remember things?
8. Do I empathize before I chastise?
9. Can I write clearly and succinctly?
10. How am I as a public speaker?

(Can you see areas of needed improvement?)

Time Use and the Balanced Life

Leadership Technique Section #10 discussed how you manage yourself in the use of your time. In completing that section you should have filled out two assessment forms that would be good to review at this point: the Form for Time Use Analysis and A Form for Analyzing How Balanced Your Life Is. This is an area in which everyone can continually improve. One difference between a leader and a great leader is the mastery of time and knowing how to effectively multiply your hands.

CODE FOR PERSONAL ASSESSMENT: A—Always or Yes
U—Usually
S—Sometimes
R—Rarely or Not Yet

1. I have the ability to recognize problems

   A. In my personal life. _____

   B. In my organization. _____

2. I know when to deal with the cause of a problem and when to ignore it. _____

3. I can define what a solved problem would look like. _____

4. I know how to brainstorm a list of solutions. _____

5. I know how to do a cost/benefit analysis of my solutions. _____

6. I can identify several different types of decisions. _____

7. I can identify at least ten approaches to making decisions. _____

8. I understand the importance of alternatives to decision making. _____

9. I know the difference between actual alternatives and perceived alternatives and which is more important. _____

10. I know and can use at least four different group approaches to making decisions and know when each is important in terms of *speed, commitment,* and *quality.* _____

11. Once I have decided (alone or with my group) on a solution, I know how to plan its implementation. _____

12. I understand the process and value of setting deadlines in implementing solutions. _____

13. I know how to lead my subordinates in implementing a solution. _____

14. I know the key questions to ask in the control step. _____

15. I know what to do if the problem

    A. Has *not* been solved. _____

    B. *Has* been solved. _____

How Do You Rate as a Professional?

Rate yourself on the following sixteen characteristics, using the following rating scale:

> 5—This is me!
> 4—This is usually true of me.
> 3—I am sometimes this way.
> 2—I seldom display this trait.
> 1—I do not have this trait.

The professional:

1. Does not require close supervision. _____

2. Does not work by the hour (gets the job done). _____

3. Does not feel "I am an employee working for a boss." _____

4. Does not expect to be paid by the hour (does what's necessary). _____

5. Takes full responsibility for actions and decisions. _____

6. Continually seeks self-improvement. _____

7. Contributes to the profession. _____

8. Is loyal to fellow workers, both peers and management. _____

9. Avoids rumor, gossip, and hearsay. _____

10. Supports professional organizations. _____

11. Adjusts grievances through channels (avoids complaining, negativisim). _____

12. Meets obligations and commitments (honest, dependable). _____

13. Is sensitive to the problems of others, peers and management. _____

14. Does not advance at the expense of others (cooperative, all win). _____

15. Is proud of the profession. _____

16. Has a desire to serve others. _____

80–68 A true professional   Total ⬚
67–55 A Semipro, on the way
54–42 Gets the job done
41–29 Attitude and behavior below par
28–16 Lacks professionalism

Why Am I Here?

(In courses and classes I ask people in introducing themselves to tell the group something about themselves that makes them unique. Often I get a mumbled "Ain't nothin' special 'bout me!" I'm sorry, but I don't buy that. You are one of a kind and have some gift to give the world. It is your secret to success. Can you unlock it?)

1. What do I do really well?

2. What is/are my unique gift(s)?

3. How could I really make a contribution?

4. Have I started? If not, when will I start?

A good way to complete this set of exercises is by establishing objectives that require action for self-improvement now. Before you use the following Personal Plan of Action, you may want to make several copies, since each objective requires a separate sheet. Every question on the sheet is important to consider. If you normally skip over any of these considerations, you may see the fine line between disappointment and success. After studying the sheet, you may want to design one of your own. In either case, have at it . . . and *success!*

Personal Plan of Action

Objective #_____ What do I want to achieve?

Obstacles: Why have I not achieved my objective already?

    A.

    B.

    C.

Solutions: How could these obstacles be overcome?

    A.

        1.

        2.

        3.

    B.

        1.

        2.

        3.

    C.

        1.

        2.

        3.

Deadline: When do I want this objective accomplished?

Rewards: What will I gain by achieving this objective? (Be specific!)

    A.

    B.

    C.

Is it worth it to me?

    Yes—Do it now!

    No—Scratch the objective with a clear conscience, and move on to another.

5

How: The Appropriate Leadership Style

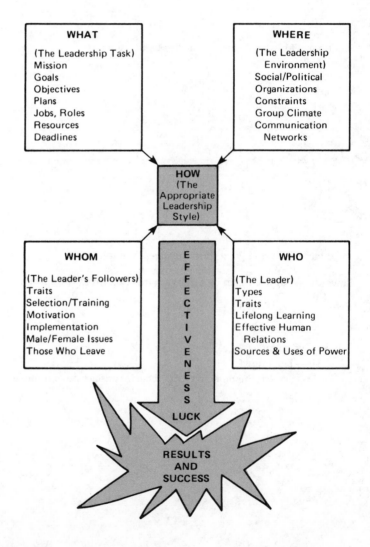

WHAT

(The Leadership Task)
Mission
Goals
Objectives
Plans
Jobs, Roles
Resources
Deadlines

WHERE

(The Leadership
 Environment)
Social/Political
Organizations
Constraints
Group Climate
Communication
 Networks

HOW
(The
Appropriate
Leadership
Style)

WHOM

(The Leader's Followers)
Traits
Selection/Training
Motivation
Implementation
Male/Female Issues
Those Who Leave

WHO

(The Leader)
Types
Traits
Lifelong Learning
Effective Human
 Relations
Sources & Uses of Power

E
F
F
E
C
T
I
V
E
N
E
S
S

LUCK

**RESULTS
AND
SUCCESS**

You have taken a theoretical journey in quest of appropriate leadership styles. In the last chapter you learned that many leaders' styles are simply extensions of their personalities. This book has provided you with an expanded view that shows the appropriate style being chosen after a consideration of four key variables. These add to the leader's personality the qualities and needs of the followers, the constraints and realities of the environment, and the goal to be accomplished.

To be successful as a leader you must (1) be aware of and consider the four independent variables, (2) be aware of the various leadership styles there are to choose from, and (3) select the style that most effectively fits the variables in that situation. The previous four chapters have prepared you for Step 1. This chapter covers Steps 2 and 3 and will present you with a menu of leadership styles to choose from and will analyze how to select the most effective style.

THE MENU OF LEADERSHIP STYLES

The chapter begins by discussing a number of leadership style theories. You will be presented with an ever-increasing set of perceived alternatives, beginning with two and building to eight. My own model of ten styles is then presented. Many of the theories mentioned here use the term *management style,* but the theories are sufficiently broad to apply also to leadership. A more in-depth understanding of the theories of the scholars mentioned can be obtained by studying their books and articles as listed in the Bibliography.

Two Styles of Leadership

The best-known theory of leadership styles was really not a leadership-style theory at all. Doug McGregor, in his book *The Human Side of Enterprise* (New York: McGraw-Hill, 1960), introduced a number of significant new management concepts. The one that gained most notoriety was his now-famous Theory X and Theory Y.

Theory X and Theory Y are often interpreted in books and seminars as two distinct leadership styles. What McGregor was referring to was not two styles for dealing with people, but two sets of assumptions we make about people. To paraphrase McGregor crudely, a Theory X person would view others as lazy, not very bright, and irresponsible. A Theory Y person would view others as responsible, motivated, creative, and desirous of control over his or her work and life.

McGregor had identified two sets of assumptions, or personal theories, the possession of which (along with other variables) would influence a leader's chosen style. Note that McGregor was not referring to what people are generally like, or even what *your* people *are* like; he was referring to how you, the leader, perceive your people.

There is no way of knowing where Doug McGregor would have taken this idea had he lived for another twenty years. After his untimely death, his ideas were followed up by several scholars. One who built on the McGregor theory was Chris Argyris of Harvard University. In his book *Management and Organizational Development: The Path From XA to YB*, Argyris extended McGregor's initial idea. He theorized that a specific leadership style would logically flow from the Theory X and Theory Y assumptions. Wanting to maintain the practice of using neutral labels, he named these two leadership patterns (styles) Pattern A and Pattern B. From the description of these two styles, you can see that Argyris could have labeled them autocratic (or authoritarian) and democratic (or participative). The value loading that would have accompanied these latter labels, had they been used, is evident.

Argyris's approach to the concepts became more normative than descriptive. As the subtitle of the book implies, to be more effective, a leader should take his or her assumptions and leadership style from XA to YB. This belief that YB is inherently a better approach to leadership than XA has become widespread. As discussed in Leadership Technique #9, both assumptions and styles can be effective if applied in the appropriate situation. (Sometimes your people really *are* lazy, stupid, and irresponsible.)

In a following book, *Theory in Practice: Increasing Professional Effectiveness,* Chris Argyris, with coauthor Don Schön, combined XA together into a single theory which they labeled Model I, and Theory Y and Pattern B combined to become Model II. They went on to show that our culture and institutions are permeated with Model I assumptions and practices. In part, this accounts for why it is so hard to learn and practice Model II. They demonstrated the gap between what we espouse (Model II) and what we do (Model I). We do not "walk our talk" and are usually blind to the gap between what we practice and what we preach. Even when you can become aware of this gap in yourself, the changing of assumptions and styles is very difficult.

The result of much of the Model II training that goes on today is simply to provide leaders and managers with new twists for applying Model I. Changing a Model I person or organization with Model II techniques is very difficult. The usually noneffective approach resembles the bumper sticker that reads "Support Mental Health or I'll Kill You!" Argyris in his 1976 book *Increasing Leadership Effectiveness,* and Argyris and Schön in their 1978 book *Organizational Learning: A Theory of Action Perspective,* address the ways that you and your organization can make these difficult but essential changes.

Three Styles of Leadership

In a classic early leadership study Kurt Lewin, Ronald Lippett, and Ralph K. White researched and wrote about three styles of leadership. They labeled the styles authoritarian, democratic, and laissez-faire. The authoritarian style is directive, impersonal, and allows no give-and-take with the followers. The democratic style encourages subordinates to communicate openly, to participate in decision making, and to work cooperatively. The laissez-faire leader gives followers complete autonomy and provides no structure or direction. (Would this be a nonleadership style?)

The studies looked at the relationship between the three styles and the group's morale, productivity, and quality of relationships. While inconclusive, the democratic style seemed to work best under the broadest set of circumstances. In any case, you have here three styles from which you can select as a leader.

Four Styles of Leadership

Rensis Likert, a leading researcher in human behavior at the University of Michigan, has proposed four styles or systems of management. He defines these as System 1—Exploitive Autocratic, System 2—Benevolent Autocratic, System 3—Participative, and System 4—Democratic. The strength of Likert's theoretical model is the linking of the independent variables (the four styles) with various intervening variables (such as motivation, employee attitudes, and loyalty) to dependent variables such as productivity or profitability. The theory deals with the subtle complexity of real world-leadership situations. The model is normative, implying—as shown earlier with Theory X/Theory Y—that System 1 is less desirable and System 4 is best. But as you have seen . . . it depends!

Five Styles of Leadership

Two theories fit into the category. The first is Robert Blake and Jane Mouton's managerial grid. The grid has two axes labeled "concern for people" and "concern for task." The five styles they identify are:

1,1 The Impoverished Style: This is really a nonleadership style representing neither a concern for people nor for the task. This approach would perhaps be found in a new leader or one who has burned out.
1,9 The Country Club Style: This type of leader goes overboard in a desire to make sure that the troops are happy. All of the subordinates' good feelings usually dissipate from a lack of achievement.
9,1 The Authority-Obedience Style: This leader is obsessed with getting the job done and views people as a means to an end. The result is usually frustration and often rebellion on the part of the subordinates.
5,5 The Organization Man Style: This could be a leader moving in the right direction, or an ambivalent compromiser, or one with a yo-yo style that vacillates from people pressures to task pressures.
9,9 The Team Style: This style is an ideal style. A balance between the needs of the people and the job to be done is certainly desirable, but hardly to be obtained. Usually a leader must choose, and the formal position tips the concerns in the task direction. An informal leader will usually take over the people concerns.

Victor H. Vroom and Philip Yetton have constructed an intriguing model of leadership decision making. The model attempts to move from being purely descriptive about group decision making to providing a normative guide for the leader. Three basic styles are identified for the leader: *A* for autocratic, *C* for consultative, and *G* for group. Each of these styles has several variants, but after much research, Vroom and Yetton settled for five.

AI Having all the information you need and not needing subordinate support to implement your decision, make the decision on your own.

AII Lacking information you need to make the decision, go to others to get the information you need. You are not interested in their opinions of what to do. You make your own decision.

CI Talk to your subordinates individually to get their information and suggestions. Consider their advice, then make your own decision.

CII Bring your subordinates together and have them present their opinions and ideas face to face. Consider their advice, then make your own decision.

GII Bring your subordinates together and make the decision as a group. The goal is to reach consensus with you being equal to the others in terms of influence.

The style that will be chosen is linked to three outcome variables:
1. The quality or rationality of the decision.
2. The acceptance or commitment on the part of subordinates to execute decisions effectively.
3. The amount of time required to make the decision.

The five styles are linked to the three outcomes through a decision tree that is well researched and designed. I commend this model to you as a guide to successful leadership decision making.

Six Styles of Leadership

I am not aware of any major theory of leadership that features exactly six styles.

Seven Styles of Leadership

One of the most widely presented models of leadership styles is Tannenbaum and Schmidt's. The theory first appeared in the *Harvard Business Review* in March–April 1958. It is now an "*HBR* Classic" and was reprinted with a retrospective commentary in May–June 1973.

The model presents a continuum of seven styles that go from a position in which the leader mostly controls to a style in which the group largely controls. Tannenbaum and Schmidt describe these styles as:

1. (Leader) makes decision and announces it.
2. (Leader) "sells" decision.
3. (Leader) presents ideas and invites questions.
4. (Leader) presents tentative decision, subject to change.
5. (Leader) presents problem, gets suggestions, makes decision.
6. (Leader) defines limits, asks group to make decision.
7. (Leader) permits subordinates to function (autonomously) within defined limits.

The value of this theory is in seeing seven options available to the leader as they relate to authority (power) and freedom (autonomy). While a leader can theoretically alter styles along the entire range of this continuum, it is my hypothesis, as discussed in the introduction to this chapter, that most leaders seldom vary more than one step up or down the continuum. The effective leader will work to develop ability with the broad range of styles.

Eight Styles of Leadership

The two theories with eight styles, that of William Reddin and that of Hersey and Blanchard, are very similar in appearance. Each model constructs a two-by-two table based on two variables, and then extends the table along a third dimension, one in an effective direction and one in an ineffective direction. Reddin labels his styles: (ineffective) deserter, missionary, compromiser, autocrat, and (effective) benevolent autocrat, bureaucrat, developer, and executive. Hersey and Blanchard label their ineffective styles as Q4, Q3, Q2, and Q1 and their effective styles as S1 (telling), S4 (delegating), S3 (participating), and S2 (selling).

WELL . . . HOW MANY LEADERSHIP STYLES ARE THERE?

A summary of the various theories of leadership styles is presented in Figure 76. That these theories end with eight styles does not mean that there are only eight leadership styles. It may show that if a theory is to be a guide to thought and action, more than eight options only lead to confusion and indecision. You might test that assumption as you look at my presentation of ten styles.

But, learning difficulties aside, how many leadership styles are there? When all the possible combinations of independent leadership variables are considered, the number is virtually infinite. This book will not present you with an infinite number of styles to choose from, but will expand your free-dom of choice with presentation of Bothwell's model of ten leadership styles. (See Figure 77 on page 221. Remember the double-edged sword of decision making: The more options, the more difficulty in deciding.)

On the left of the model you are in total control and are able to act uni-laterally. As you move toward the right, the group becomes increasingly involved in the problem solving and decision making. With the final two (nonleadership) styles you abdicate your role and the group takes control, with another member inevitably rising to fill the leadership vacuum.

Another way of conceptualizing the relationship between these ten styles and the four independent variables found in any leadership situation, as discussed in this book, is to look at the styles in the model of the leader-ship pentagon. (See Figure 78 on page 222.) This assists in the insight that most choices are not a continuum, but in fact things usually come full circle.

FIGURE 76. Styles of leadership as seen by various theorists.

TWO McGregor	THEORY X				THEORY Y*		
Argyris	PATTERN A MODEL I				PATTERN B* MODEL II*		
THREE Lewin Lippett White	AUTHORITARIAN		DEMOCRATIC*		LAISSEZ-FAIRE		
FOUR Likert	SYSTEM 1 EXPLOITATIVE AUTHORITATIVE	SYSTEM 2 BENEVOLENT AUTHORITATIVE	SYSTEM 3 CONSULTIVE		SYSTEM 4* PARTICIPATIVE		
FIVE Blake Morton	9–1 Authority-Obedience	5–5 Organization Man	9–9* Team		1–9 Country Club	1–1 Impoverished	
Vroom Yetton	A–I	A–II	C–I		C–II	G–II	
SIX							
SEVEN Tannenbaum Schmidt	MAKE AND TELL	MAKE AND SELL	MAKE AND ANSWER QUESTIONS	MAKE TENTATIVE	PRESENT PROBLEM, GET INPUTS, MAKE DECISION	JOINT DECISION	GROUP DECIDES WITHIN LIMITS
EIGHT Reddin	DESERTER	MISSIONARY	COMPROMISER	AUTOCRAT	BENEVOLENT AUTOCRAT	BUREAUCRAT	DEVELOPER	EXECUTIVE
Hersey and Blanchard	Q4	Q3	Q2	Q1	S1 TELLING	S4 DELEGATING	S3 PARTICIPATING	S2 SELLING

INEFFECTIVE ←———→ EFFECTIVE*

(*Indicates the style most widely accepted as effective.)

FIGURE 77. Bothwell's model of ten leadership styles

(1)	(2)	(3)	(4)	(5)	(6)
Decide yourself and order it done	Decide yourself and convince them to do it	Decide yourself, modify with suggestions, then have them do it	Decide tentatively; they can influence with persuasive argument	Consult individually, decide, then announce	Consult in a group, decide, then announce
AI	AII	I I	I II	C I	C II
A—Authoritarian		I—Influenced		C—Consultative	

(7)	(8)	(9)	(10)		
Explore and decide as a group while you retain the veto	Explore and decide as a group where all are equal	You define the constraints then let them decide without you	Withdraw completely; they decide and act alone		
P I	P II	W I	W II		
P—Participative		W—Withdrawal			

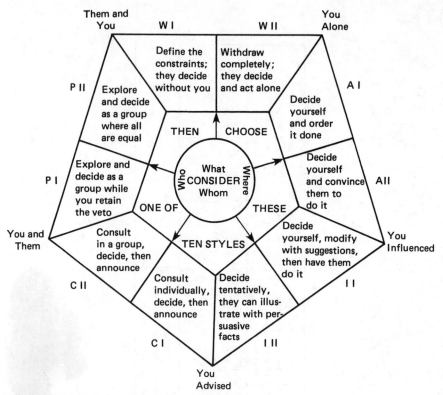

FIGURE 78. Application of the Bothwell ten-style model of leadership

LEADERSHIP EFFECTIVENESS:
THE CONSEQUENCES OF THE CHOSEN STYLE

To be successful as a leader, you must be effective. Being effective as a leader means selecting and applying the most appropriate style for a given situation. You have been presented with a menu of from two to ten different styles. You will be successful as a leader if after considering the four elements of the situation in combination you select the most appropriate style and properly implement it.

The question becomes, what is the best way to select the appropriate style? To the true social scientist, or the analytic, left-brain thinker, a scientific approach to answering this important question would be most appealing. A model for this "scientific approach" might look something like Figure 79.

The model weights each of the four independent variables along four multi-point continuums. You select the point where you perceive the situation to be on each continuum and record the weighted number on the right. This number is then multiplied by a weighting factor related to how important you view that independent variable to be. The four weighted totals are summed giving you a score that indicates the most effective style for that situation.

222

FIGURE 79. A "scientific" approach to selecting the appropriate leadership style

(1) Select from each of the four situational factors the position that best represents the situation. Write the corresponding number on the first line following the five boxes.

WHAT (The Task)

1	2	3	4	5
Deadline is urgent and/or scarce resources	Deadline is immediate and/or limited resources	Deadline is important and/or fair resources	Deadline is routine and/or good resources	Deadline is not important and/or plentiful resources

_____ × _____ = _____
        W.F.

(2) W.F. = Weighting Factor. Multiply the first points by a number up to "5" depending on how important this particular situational factor is.

WHERE (The Environment)

1	2	3	4	5
Environment mandates leader must have total control	Environment mandates leader must have most control	Environment allows leader to share control	Environment mandates leader must relinquish most control	Environment mandates leader must relinquish all control

_____ × _____ = _____
        W.F.

WHOM (The Followers)

1	2	3	4	5
Followers are incompetent and/or inexperienced	Followers have limited competence and/or experience	Followers have some competence and/or experience	Followers have great competence and/or experience	Followers are totally competent and experienced

_____ × _____ = _____
        W.F.

WHO (The Leader)

1	2	3	4	5
Leader decides alone	Leader decides with input	Leader has to consult to decide	Leader works with the team to decide	Leader gets out and the team decides alone

_____ × _____ = _____
        W.F.

TOTAL POINTS _____

(3) Add up total points and see which leadership style is indicated.

4 points A–I	15 points A–II	26 points I–I	37 points I–II	48 points C–I	59 points C–II	70 points P–I	81 points P–II	92 points W–I	103 points W–II

223

There are problems with this "scientific approach" to leadership style selection. As noted at the beginning of the book, the number of options within each of the four independent variables is large and therefore their combination is virtually infinite. To capture the complexity of an actual leadership situation in a two-dimensional model is impossible. Even putting the analysis into a computer program that accurately forecasts the appropriate style is unrealistic. In either case, the weighting of variables and decisions about their relative importance is entirely subjective, which brings you to the *art of leadership.*

Considering the selection of the appropriate leadership style to be more of an artform than a science would appeal more to the intuitive, right-brain leader. This approach would suggest that you consider each of the four independent variables thoughtfully and weigh them for their relative importance. If the goal to be accomplished requires immediate action, the authoritarian style will probably be most effective. If your subordinates have important data or skills, then you will want their influence. If the followers have information you need to make a good decision about a course of action, then you will want to consult them. If implementation by the followers is critical to the plan's success, then a participative approach will be most effective. And for their development and growth there may be times when you want them to do it alone.

There can be other overriding considerations. If the political or organizational environment dictates that you act in a certain way or be terminated, that may be the obvious way to go. Or you may have a strong feeling for doing it a certain way, and the confidence you gain from proceeding that way may be the deciding factor in selecting a style.

Real-life leadership situations are very complex, and the demands of the four variables are often conflicting or mutually exclusive. For example, an immediate deadline might demand unilateral leadership action, but the importance of followers properly implementing the plan might require group participation. If you plug that situation into the scientific analysis approach, with one variable weighted way to the left and the other way to the right, the style indicated by the sums could come out right in the middle, which might be a style totally inappropriate because it violates the demands of both variables. This is where the subjective, nonscientific approach, based on your gut-level feelings, reinforced by your reason and experience, can sometimes lead you to the best leadership style to apply. If you trust yourself and proceed with confidence, you can carry the day. You will have learned to properly apply the *art of leadership.*

THE FINAL INGREDIENT: LUCK

Because of life's complexity, it is never possible to entirely understand and predict every variable in a leadership situation. Having done all that has been discussed in this book, it cannot hurt your cause if you also have a little bit of luck. Luck, however, is not entirely a matter of chance or fate. You control your "luck" by your efforts and by watching the doors of opportunity that open before you. You will find that the harder and smarter you work, the luckier you get!

THE BOTTOM LINE: PRODUCING RESULTS AND ACHIEVING SUCCESS

You are interested in obtaining the rewards that come with success. But the world does not usually reward:

- good intentions
- best effort
- accomplishing something, but the wrong thing
- busywork
- creative excuses for failure

The world mostly rewards the leader (or group, organization, or country) that can produce the desired results. If your leadership effort has been effective, then the results produced will be seen as successful and the rewards will follow.

Rewards come as a consequence of results successfully produced. It does not work the other way around, as many wish. You can't say to the system, "You give me the rewards, then I'll use them to produce results." The misconception built into this reverse natural law is a factor in many of our current social ills, as I will discuss in the final chapter.

Remember that success is not a place to be arrived at; it is the journey. It consists of setting goals, developing plans, allocating resources, acting to produce results, and evaluating the fruits of those labors. Then you set a higher goal, and the cycle continues. Living is rowing up the entropy stream: It requires constant effort. If you discontinue the process you start drifting backward until you reach the waterfall, where the temporal process ends.

At this point you know more about the *art of leadership* than most of the leaders on this globe. Apply your understanding to one more case, then step back in the final chapter and take a look at the global challenges that confront leaders now and in the future.

ILLUSTRATIVE CASE H

The Case of Pat Dawson

Pat Dawson stared out of the office window at the river winding through the valley. The time to decide had arrived, but turning it over and over had not resolved the dilemma. Based on previous leadership training, Pat was a person who consciously chose a leadership style to appropriately fit the demands of a given situation. But this time the variables seemed to work against one another.

Pat thought out loud: "With two exceptions, my people are competent and responsible. They're used to having me consult them before making an important decision like this. And in terms of my own style preference I'd prefer to work democratically with them. But Len and Frieda don't work well with too much autonomy. Len needs to be led by the hand and Frieda assumes control in a power vacuum. The policy manual says I, and I alone, am responsible for these types of decisions. And that's the way they were always made by J. B., who preceded me. There is also the pressure of time. Everything points to moving unilaterally, but a decision of this magnitude should not be made quickly and without a lot of input from my people. What to do? What to do?"

The buzzer on the intercom sounded, and Pat knew it was time for the staff meeting to start.

FUNCTIONAL TYPE   *Pat Dawson is a new leader in an organization that has had a long line of leaders. Pat's problems are similar to those of any leader in a similar situation.*

LEADERSHIP FACTORS   *The principles involved in this case are those of* leadership styles *and* leadership succession.

QUESTIONS TO CONSIDER

1. *Does it matter how many leaders have held a job before a person takes over? Why?*
2. *Does it matter how one leader's style is similar to or different from that of a predecessor? In what way?*
3. *Should Pat involve the employees in making the decision of how decisions will be made? What are possible repercussions of involving them? Of not involving them?*
4. *How much should one's personal preferences play in a decision such as Pat faces?*
5. *If an incorrect style is chosen, can it easily be changed? Is it better to change the style or stick with the decision once made?*

ANALYSIS   *Pat Dawson could review all of the principles presented in Chapter 5 on selecting a leadership style, but this would probably not be of great help. The case indicates that Pat has done a great deal of this already.*

Probably more important would be the implementation of good decision-making principles. The point is that a decision has to be made on which style to use in this situation. A thoughtfully chosen style implemented with confidence has some chance of success. Believing in yourself and acting thoughtfully and effectively can carry the day, even though it will not win over every follower. But followers like winners and those who can produce results.

Select a style and get on with it.

This case presents the very real conflicts of leadership style that are found in complex organizational situations. That's why there is not a cookbook of solutions.

Postscript to the Cases

This book has presented eight cases and an analysis of each: Chris Laine, Terry and Dee Erdman, Lynn Wood, Brooke Gionelli, Dana Wallach, Adrian Kim, Fran McEwen, and Pat Dawson. Did you envision these eight hypothetical people as males or as females? Actually they could be either male or female. The names were carefully chosen so that they represent either sex. If you stereotyped them only in one way or the other you may want to reread the section on men and women in the world of work and examine your own hardened categories! (Don't think your categories are hardened? Look back at the Terry and Dee Erdman case in Chapter 1. Which is the father and which is the mother? See what I mean?)

Leadership Technique #13
CREATING ORGANIZATIONAL CHANGE, OR HOW DO YOU TURN THIS SHIP AROUND?

Changing organizations, like changing people, is a complex, risky undertaking. The more professional training a person has received in how to create change, the more the person is concerned with approaching the task carefully and doing it well. Even if a leader has limited training and skill in organizational change, the fact remains that change is often expected or required.

The following approach, developed by Dr. Kurt Lewin, while not guaranteeing success, does provide a thoughtful, planned change strategy. Kurt Lewin presented this concept for organizational analysis and change in his *Field Theory in Social Science* (New York: Harper and Bros., 1951). It was a pioneering effort and has influenced many of the more modern organizational development change strategies.

FIGURE 80. Outline form for Lewin's force field analysis

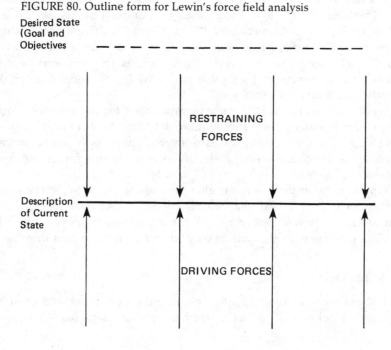

227

You begin this technique by drawing a diagram similar to Figure 80. The dotted line represents the goal for your change effort: what you would like your situation to look like after the change has occurred. The solid line represents the current situation. This you will describe as clearly and specifically as you can in terms of two sets of forces to be discussed. The current situation is relatively static because these forces are balanced.

The next step is to analyze the force field. The first set of forces to be identified and labeled are called driving forces. These are forces which, if not opposed by opposite forces, would press for change in the direction you desire. These are the forces working in your favor. They exist in every situation, and to ignore them is not to take advantage of pressures already working to create the change you desire.

The opposing forces are known as restraining forces. These must also be identified. There can be few or many, and they can be of varying magnitude. This process is less helpful if the forces are listed in general terms, such as, "The employees are resisting the new plan," and more helpful if stated in very specific terms, such as, "The accounting department is afraid that the new plan might eliminate their jobs," or "The sales department is angry because..." To make these forces this specific will require some digging, some questioning, and some thinking.

The analysis of these two sets of forces is part of the strength of this method of organizational change and is valuable even if no other steps are undertaken.

Once the current situation, change goal, driving forces, and restraining forces have been identified and labeled, three approaches to creating change can be considered. Option number one consists of increasing the driving forces. This is usually the first change strategy attempted and usually the least effective ("You eat that spinach or I'll spank you"—driving force, fear of punishment). The reason it is often ineffective is based on a basic law of physics which states that for every action there is an equal and opposite reaction. You push people; they push back (child is force-fed spinach, but promptly spits it up on your shoes).

Option number two is to remove restraining forces. This takes more creativity, but is usually more successful (child doesn't eat spinach because it tastes bad, so you offer child chocolate-covered spinach). If you do nothing but remove restraining forces, the already existing driving forces will create pressure for change.

Option number three is not to alter the existing forces but to reinterpret the situation in such a way that what were previously seen as restraining forces are now viewed (and work as) driving forces. (Popeye knows that spinach doesn't taste good, which is why when he eats it he gets strong.)

An Example Might Help

Figure 81 outlines a possible situation you might encounter at work. You find a 10 percent level of tardiness unacceptable. You have set a realistic goal of 2

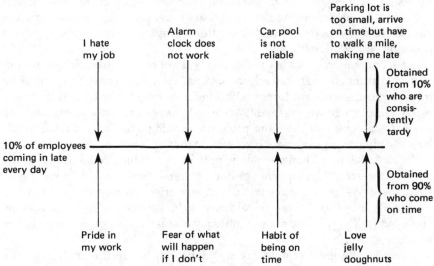

FIGURE 81. Lewin's force field analysis applied

percent tardiness. You have identified both sets of forces, as shown. Here are the options that can be employed to change this situation:

OPTION ONE. Increase the driving forces. One possibility would be to send each employee a memo that says, "Just one reminder of our new time incentive program: One more tardy and you're fired."

OPTION TWO. Remove a restraining force. Give all tardy employees a clock radio as a Christmas (Hanukkah) gift. (An option two approach to the small parking lot would be to spend $100,000 building a bigger one. Look at how much fun, and less expensive, option three is.)

OPTION THREE. Reinterpret the situation. You could talk to each person who is chronically tardy and say something like, "You know, when I first started working here, I was often late also. Then one morning I accidentally hit all green lights and got here fifteen minutes early. I was amazed: That little parking lot was nearly deserted. When I got inside, I discovered jelly dough-nuts (bet you didn't know that) instead of those stale glazed ones that are left at five after eight. But here's the best part, especially if you're not thrilled about being here: By parking close to the door, I found I could be out the door, home, and on the golf course by the time you walk the mile to where you park." (Conclusion: If you don't like your job, but you love jelly doughnuts, and if the lot's too small, come early.")

There are some principles you need to consider in using this approach to organizational change. First, while this technique can be used in any change situation, it works best with groups and organizations. The reason it is not recommended for use in changing individuals is that the driving and restraining forces would be psychological and emotional. Unless you are a psychiatrist or the person is very insightful and open, the forces are very hard to identify and work with.

Second, the magnitude of all forces will not be the same. Forces are not balanced so much quantitatively as qualitatively. This can be indicated by drawing more significant forces with longer or broader arrows. If there are twelve reasons why an organization should change and only one reason not to—that someone will blow the place up—adding additional driving forces will only put people under such stress that they will break.

Third, the three change-strategy options do not have to be used one at a time. All three can be employed at once. Several thrusts could be employed simultaneously—for example, two to increase driving forces, three to remove restraining forces, and three to reinterpret the situation. The more options employed (as long as they are not mutually exclusive), the greater the chance for success.

Finally, the great strength of this approach lies in the analysis of the forces in any situation and the exploration of optional change strategies. These steps are obviously closely tied to the problem-identification step and alternative-solutions step in the problem-solving model presented in Leadership Technique Section #8. The two approaches to creating change and solving problems can be used effectively together.

Leadership Technique #14
THE WORLD'S WORST-KEPT SECRET:
HOW TO CHANGE
EVERY SINGLE PERSON YOU KNOW

All of us go through life sending out subtle and not-so-subtle messages to others: Why don't you change to accommodate me so that I can be happy and comfortable? And if everyone would respond to our message, we could lead a very relaxed, if boring, life. The catch is that everyone is sending us the same message: You change to meet my needs.

Now, at last, you will be let in on the world's worst-kept secret: how you can change every single person you know. The reason for the odd title goes back to my original use of this idea in training programs over the last decade. I used to call this Bothwell's Rule, but after every program people would say "You got the idea from Christ ... Buddha ... Mohammed ... Aristotle ... Confucius ..." And I would say "Yes, they all said it in one form or another." That's why it's the world's worst-kept secret, because these ideas have been around for several thousand years.

Then why call it a secret? If so few people use these principles they know to be true, they must be a secret. You'll see what I mean in a minute; you know the rule, but do you follow it?

First, let's take a look at you. The first thing you notice about yourself is that you are a very well-rounded individual. Now you will learn to change everyone you know. (Why would you want to change strangers?) What does it mean to know someone? It means to have a relationship with someone. What does it mean to have a relationship with someone? It means that your life and his or her life overlap. Figure 82 portrays you and the people you know. The shaded area indicates the current form and extent of your relationship.

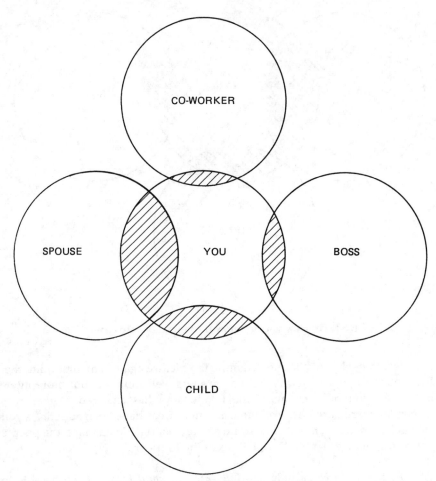

FIGURE 82. You and selected relationships

Now to the rule. You know the secret so well that you can complete the sentence yourself.

Rule: *The way that you change every single person that you know is to . . . change yourself.*

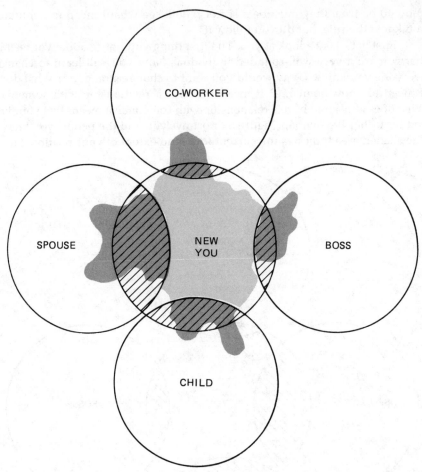

FIGURE 83. The new you and how those relationships have changed

Now let's see why this is true. Examine the picture again. The first thing that you notice about yourself is that you are less well-rounded, but more interesting. As you have changed, the relationship has changed. Some areas formerly covered are now excluded, and new areas have been added. As you change, the relationship changes; and as the relationship changes, the people you know change. To see how, let's examine four corollaries.

C1 *Change is based on influence. Influence is a mutual process.* To be able to change people is to be able to influence them. In an interpersonal sense there is no such thing as unilateral influence. If we send out the change message mentioned earlier that says, "I'm okay, you're a jerk!" people will turn you off. To the extent that people feel you are open to *their* influence they will open themselves up to *your* influence. To the extent that they feel you are closed to them, they will feel closed to you.

This is a most common failure in raising children and training subordinates: sending a message that says, "I'm perfect; you're messed up. I'm going to straighten you out." The child will tune you out and go out in the alley and learn from Jimmy through a process of mutual influence. The secret of greatness, in terms of personal growth and the influence you can have on others, is the realization that you have something to learn from others—all others.

C2   *To change others you must begin by accepting them as they are.* To the extent that people feel accepted, they feel free to learn, adapt, grow, change. To the extent that people do not feel accepted, they feel the need to retrench, to defend, to counterattack. You can assume that if your change effort begins with an "I'm going to straighten you out" message, little listening or changing will follow. What is required is that you send that terribly difficult message that says, "I appreciate you and accept you as a person, and because I appreciate you, I cannot accept this (specific) irresponsible act."

Corollaries 3 and 4 sound very similar. They are making related, but quite different points.

C3   *To get something you must give it away, and if you try to take it and keep it, you'll lose it.*

C4   *You will get what you give.*

How do you get respect from those who follow you? By demanding it, right? Wrong! You get respect by giving respect. If you try to "take" their respect and hang onto it, you'll lose it. How do you get others to listen to you? By listening to them. How do you get others to care for you? By caring for them.

What did Lao-tzu mean when he said, "To lead the people you must walk behind them?" Perhaps you get others to follow (serve) you, by following (serving) them.

Whatever message you send out to others will come back in kind. You give love; you get love. You give hate; you get hate. You give indifference; you get indifference. It must happen. This "law" of human relations is as inexorable as the law of gravity.

However, so that you don't say "Bothwell tricked me," you must read the fine print. Otherwise you will say, "I gave Frank love and respect, and he spit in my face." The law says if you send out love, you will receive love . . . from somewhere. It does not necessarily work one on one. The other person always has the free agency to respond in a nonreciprocal way. (You will find, however, that it usually works even one on one.) What's the alternative?

There is another piece of fine print. It's possible that the law has a multiplier effect. You send out a pint of love, you get a quart back. You are never "ahead of the game." That is something to ponder.

What do every one of these four principles have in common? They are all *irrational*:

- To change others you change yourself?
- You influence others by letting them influence you?

- To change a person you must accept them as they are?
- You get what you give away?

Your head will tell you no. Your heart will tell you yes. I'm not afraid to state these principles, because they really work. You can find out the truth either way. If you don't like the approaches outlined here, try influencing others unilaterally; try changing others without accepting them; try demanding and keeping respect, attention, love. The history of the race is replete with the documented failures of these other approaches.

If you would change the world, first change the one part of that world you have most control over—yourself. You will start a revolution with eternal repercussions.

6

Leadership and the Future

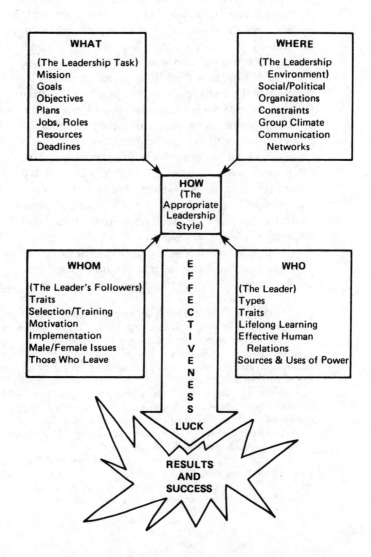

WHAT

(The Leadership Task)
Mission
Goals
Objectives
Plans
Jobs, Roles
Resources
Deadlines

WHERE

(The Leadership
    Environment)
Social/Political
Organizations
Constraints
Group Climate
Communication
    Networks

HOW
(The
Appropriate
Leadership
Style)

WHOM

(The Leader's Followers)
Traits
Selection/Training
Motivation
Implementation
Male/Female Issues
Those Who Leave

**E
F
F
E
C
T
I
V
E
N
E
S
S**

WHO

(The Leader)
Types
Traits
Lifelong Learning
Effective Human
    Relations
Sources & Uses of Power

LUCK

**RESULTS
AND
SUCCESS**

The first five chapters of this book have presented the history of leadership and the world of work, and have looked at how you, the leader, apply techniques of effective leadership in the here and now. The final leadership view is of the future. Let's move back now to the mountain peak and seek to gain the broader view of the tremendous challenges ahead and the part you might play in meeting them. These challenges come just at a time when there seems to be a dearth of good leaders.

WHERE HAVE ALL
THE LEADERS GONE?

"What has happened to our leaders? Why aren't we producing leaders like we used to?" asks Robert Townsend. Is he alone in this view of the dearth of leadership available to guide us through the multitude of modern maladies? Apparently not. In the late 1970s Eric Severeid on CBS and Howard K. Smith on ABC, within about two weeks of each other, both mused publicly about the scarcity of quality leaders. They expressed concern for the lack of leadership in government, business, education, and religion.

During the past decade, in several hundred leadership programs I have conducted, the participants have been asked to brainstorm a list of twenty of the world's greatest leaders. One striking similarity among 99 percent of the thousands of names given is that they were all deceased. In analyzing this phenomenon with the participants, two justifications are repeatedly given. One is that it takes time to identify great leaders, so only historical perspective can provide names for the list. That may be true, but it also is probably a cop-out. Surely people like George Washington, Winston Churchill, Napoleon, and Julius Caesar, whose names consistently appear, were seen as great leaders in their own time. The second explanation is that we are not producing leaders the way we used to. Yes . . . again.

If this latter view is true, as Eric Severeid, Howard K. Smith, Robert Townsend, and these leadership trainees suggest, and as I believe, how can this be explained? Let me provide some possible explanations:

1. Perhaps great leaders only appear in times of social, economic, or religious crisis. There seems to be strong evidence for this. Leadership theory is situationally based. An environment or climate has to exist in which people express a desire to be led. Almost without exception the leaders' names I've consistently seen (maybe three dozen individuals repeated several hundred times) have been people who lived and led in time of war, depression, revolution, or religious upheaval. If this analysis is correct, it would suggest that we're also not producing crises like we used to. This can be misleading, however, as the names given are usually separated by several hundred years, and few were contemporaries in the same crisis.

2. The nature of society has changed, and with it, perhaps there has been a change in the leadership climate. Three factors dominate developed countries today: rapid social change, large bureaucratic organizations, and legalistic norms. Each of these social phenomena could work against the exercise of true leadership. Change might make it difficult to coalesce a group of followers around stable issues. Bureaucracies might absorb and turn out leaders, and laws and regulations might restrict their ability

236

to do what leaders do. As Peter and Hull observe in their book *The Peter Principle* (New York: Morrow, 1969, p. 53):

> Most hierarchies are nowadays so encumbered with rules and traditions and so bound in by public laws, that even high employees do not have to lead anyone anywhere, in the sense of pointing out the direction and setting the pace. They simply follow precedents, obey regulations, and move at the head of the crowd. Such employees lead only in the sense that the carved wooden figurehead leads the ship.

3. The pluralistic, heterogeneous nature of modern society might magnify conflicts of values and goals, working against follower unity and leader identification.

4. Maybe it is more difficult today to identify the great goals as rallying points. It could be that people feel there are no new frontiers to conquer, no great causes to undertake. Whether or not this is true (cancer, world hunger, space), if it is perceived to be true for the masses, it dampens the ability of any leader to rally the troops.

5. The mass media has influenced leadership in several ways. Probing exposés have created suspicion and mistrust of all leaders by focusing on the misdeeds of a few. There is a broad cynicism as to leaders' motives and the purity of their acts. Leadership has become a series of media events, and it may be that the cost of producing and maintaining the leader's image has become exorbitant. The media may make it difficult to separate fantasy from reality. The news, docudramas, and plots that reverse heroes and villains all serve to make it difficult to know whom to believe and whom to follow.

6. Potential leaders today might not experience the sense of calling and destiny that some felt in the past. The ear is often turned to outer voices rather than to inner voices and seeks group approval over visionary risk.

7. Many today are simply unwilling to take a stand. Being "for" something creates instant enemies; better to speak out of both sides of your mouth than to take a position at all. A Lou Harris poll in the mid-1970s showed Americans identifying moral leadership as the nation's number-one need.

These seven explanations of possible barriers to current leadership can be placed on the book's leadership model and shown to cover every one of the four areas of concern.

WHAT (The Leadership Task)
3. Goals and values are in conflict.
4. People don't perceive any great goals to rally around.

WHERE (The Leadership Environment)
1. There is currently no great social crisis to rally people around.
2. Change, bureaucracy, and legalistic norms, the current environment, do not lend themselves to leadership.

WHOM (The Leader's Followers)
5. Followers have become suspicious of leaders because media exposure reveals them to be less than perfect.

WHO (The Leader)
6. Potential leaders are distracted by outer voices and cannot perceive an inner sense of call.
7. Leaders today are unwilling to stand up and be counted.

The breadth of these leadership barriers might explain why more good leaders cannot be currently identified.

DON'T PUT YOUR MONEY
ON THE DINOSAUR IN THE SIXTH:
THE AILING SYSTEM
WE CALL BUREAUCRACY

Not only do we lack quality leadership, we face the challenges of this quarter century with the very bureaucratic structure that is supposed to hold things together seeming to come unglued. The industrial revolution and the bureaucratic revolution, discussed in detail in Chapter 2, were both supposed to create Utopia. It now seems clear that the very functions and purposes that bureaucracy was designed to fulfill have become dysfunctional and counterproductive.

By the early 1980s, in most places, large bureaucratic organizations are in trouble. The symptoms are everywhere apparent. Organizations have become so large that no one is sure who's doing what to whom, let alone how to diagram the organization. Bureaucratic rigidity results in hardening of the categories, which blocks communication and cooperation. The modern bureaucracy takes a reactive rather than proactive approach to the social ills that rush upon us. Unions strike other unions, and everyone wants more pieces of the existing pie, rather than working to create a bigger pie. Line fights with staff, everyone has multiple bosses, and the struggle is for status and title, not for increased production and service. The computerization of our decision making has provided a dangerous detachment of decision makers from accountability. Workers in many mega-corporations face days of frustration, boredom, and alienation.

This does not sound like Utopia. The cumulative result of the interaction of these negative forces is the indisputable fact that the dinosaurs in which most of us live and work are suffering from a terminal illness. This would signal the advent of a new revolution and the birth of a new approach to Utopia. What form this new approach will take and whether productive changes can occur before our massive social problems overtake us remains to be seen.

LOOK WHAT'S COMING TO DINNER:
LEADERSHIP CHALLENGES AHEAD

Whether or not it is true that there is no one great crisis to rally leaders today, it seems clear that we are facing a macrocrisis that is an accumulation of the many ills of our day. Among the challenges we currently face might be included:

1. Natural disasters over which we still have relatively little control.
2. Disease that ravages millions despite (and often because of) advances in modern medicine and sanitation.
3. Decaying inner cities.
4. Pollution of water and air and the problems of toxic and nuclear waste.
5. Crime and conflict among people and groups.
6. Hunger brought on by drought, diminishing numbers of farmers, uncontrolled pests, poor distribution, hoarding, and ever-increasing population.
7. The dissolution of the family.
8. Things (schools, corporations, government, cities, countries) getting too big.
9. International war, cold and hot.
10. Economic distresses, including inflation, depression, unemployment, excessive taxes, soaring interest rates, and debt.
11. The content of the media, with an emphasis on sex, violence and immediate gratification, and a process that changes patterns of sexual relations, child rearing, social class, authority, politics, government, and leisure.
12. Technology run amok, leading to eventual overdependence and breakdown or "us working for them" (the robots).
13. Drugs and other addictions.
14. Mental illness, depression, withdrawal, loneliness, alienation, and suicide.
15. Dwindling sources and the misuse of energy.
16. Multinational corporations that owe allegiance to no single country or principle.
17. Products and services that are shoddy and unsafe.
18. The tremendous imbalance of wealth and poverty.
19. The tremendous imbalance of education and ignorance.
20. The all-pervasive threat of nuclear holocaust.

In his brilliant book, *A Choice of Catastrophes,* Isaac Asimov divides his list of catastrophes into the following categories:

1. Those that are statistically unlikely.
2. Those that are probable but not likely to come for aeons.
3. Those that loom in the immediate future that:
   A. Can be avoided.
   B. Cannot be avoided.

About this last category Asimov states:

> There are no catastrophes that loom before us which cannot be avoided. If we behave rationally and humanely; if we concentrate coolly on the problems that face humanity; if we recognize that it is not one's neighbors who are the enemy, but misery, ignorance and the cold indifference of natural law—then we can solve all the problems that face us. We can deliberately choose to have no catastrophes at all.

While this is a comforting conclusion to a disturbing book, the conclusion really begs the point on both levels. Statistics only state the relative possibility of some event occurring. While any event may not occur for millions of years, it could happen tomorrow. History is filled with disasters that statistically were improbable: a large meteor hitting the earth, a volcano erupting, a flood, a dam breaking, a *Titanic* sinking, a nuclear power plant malfunction, and on and on. Each event was highly improbable and yet it occurred. And in today's complex world, any one of these could trigger a catastrophe with international consequences.

Secondly, Asimov's catastrophe-free world ignores the demonstrated reality of the nature of people. The history of the human race and the headlines of today are replete with people behaving irrationally and inhumanely, of not concentrating "coolly on the problems that face humanity," of seeing one's neighbors *as* the enemy. It must be kept in mind that in any situation—war, plague, famine, depression, riot, natural disaster—someone is benefiting. Those people who benefit usually act to maintain a status quo that is to their advantage.

We face not a choice between having catastrophes or having *no* catastrophes, but a choice *of* catastrophes. (And we may not even have that choice.)

WHICH WAY AMERICA?
(AND THE WORLD)

Where are the leaders who will lead us away from the brink? Are they just now being born? Are they functioning quietly in the background, waiting to step forward? Are they speaking even now to an uninterested world? Do they have to be a few great ones, or could they be tens of thousands of common ones all in the right place at the right time?

I believe they are there. I believe they must step forward, take a stand, and lead . . . now. *I believe you could be one of them.* What do you believe? What will you do? Right now?

A WORLD OF GREAT LEADERS:
THE HIERARCHY OF REWARDS

What did you just ask yourself? "What's in it for me?" A fair question from one about to save the world . . . or at least your part of the vineyard. There are many rewards—in fact, a hierarchy of rewards. This hierarchy is patterned after Abraham Maslow's hierarchy of needs. (See Figure 84.)

This hierarchy covers most of the things a person could really want in life. But there may be even more to be gained from your efforts as a leader. John Covey has pointed out that a person who is self-actualized, by devoting himself or herself to a principle, a group of people, or a cause, can actually turn the hierarchy upside down. (See Figure 85, page 242.)

You don't have to be in a great position to be a great leader. Great leadership is based on an understanding of great principles and the ability to apply them consistently and courageously for the benefit of yourself and others. Thousands like you, doing the same, could rebuild our bureaucratic house of cards, this time on rock instead of sand.

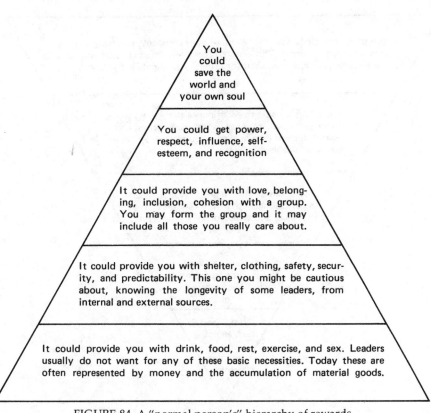

FIGURE 84. A "normal person's" hierarchy of rewards

GOING FISHING

Give a man a fish and you feed him for a day. Teach a man to fish and you feed him for a lifetime.

Lao-tzu

There you have it: a world beset with problems, a world that really needs your leadership. But where do you start? Obviously, from where you are right now. As mentioned earlier, it often takes historical perspective to determine who the truly great leaders are. Most great leaders started out as common men and women in ordinary situations performing their duty. That, of course, is what you have to do. But you are destined for greatness, if you can understand and continue to grow.

So far, this book has given you many fish (in some cases you could tell by the smell). Now let's talk about fishing. Once you have learned how to learn you are launched on your journey to success. To aid you in your personal and professional development you have several key resources that can assist you.

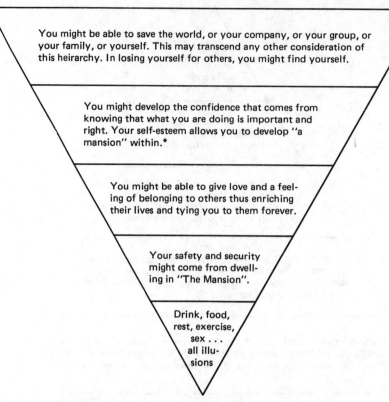

FIGURE 85. An "actualized person's" hierarchy of rewards*

First, there are other people. Life is not a playground, it is a schoolroom. Every person you encounter has something to teach you. Great or small, superior or subordinate, each has something to contribute to your growth. Watch, listen, and learn.

Secondly, there are marvelous opportunities available today in adult education. Classes, forums, home study programs, training classes, videotapes, and all forms of news media provide opportunities for gaining knowledge and perfecting techniques.

Finally, and most importantly, is a vast source of knowledge that is very accessible and can be obtained at low cost or no cost. I refer to books. There are so many good ones. You can become familiar with them at a free public library. But once you have found the books that you really want to be a part of your life—buy them. If you check them out of the library, they'll sit on a

*Reed Bradford in his book *A Teacher's Quest* (Provo, Utah: Brigham Young University Press, 1971) presents his idea of "The Mansion." The concept is that each person has the ability to realize that he or she has a divine soul, that there are certain principles that lead to personal fulfillment, and if life is lived in harmony with those principles the individual can develop an internal mansion that can give him or her dignity and joy each day throughout life regardless of external experiences.

shelf while you worry about whether or not they're overdue. If you exchange your dollars for them, a little voice will keep saying, "Read it, you dummy," and you will. Also, when the book is yours, you can mark it up, dog-ear it, cross-reference it, and work to get the information fixed in your gray matter.

To assist you in the quest there is an extensive Bibliography at the conclusion of this book. These are some of my favorite books. I would love to have included many more quotes from them, but space limitations dictated otherwise. That's not all bad, because you should cast your nets into the depths of their pages and harvest the pearls they contain. Read my favorite books, then read the books in *their* bibliographies, then read . . .

My final question is, What will you do with all the pearls of wisdom placed among the pages of this book? There comes a point where you have to stop talking and start . . . I'll conclude with one more fishing story. You'll get the point.

The story is told of the old man who was known throughout his neighborhood as being an outstanding fisherman. He always brought home a record catch of fish. One of his neighbors was a forest ranger who considered himself a pretty good fisherman, but he was never able to bring back a catch like the old man. One day he said to him, "If you don't mind sharing some of your secrets, I'd like to go with you and find out how you really catch that many fish." The old man said, "Sure, come along." So they loaded the boat on the car. In the morning they started out at the crack of dawn.

As the sun was rising above the mountain peaks they found themselves rowing out into a beautiful little lake. The ranger looked with great interest at the man's rod and reel and other equipment. "Well," he said, "time to start. Let's see how you get those record fish." The old man smiled, reached down inside his fishing keel, and pulled out a stick of dynamite. He lit the fuse and threw it out over the surface of the lake. With a tremendous KAAABBOOOOOMMM the dynamite went off, sending shock waves bouncing down through the lake. In a couple of minutes, dozens of glassy-eyed fish were floating up to the surface of the lake. The old man began rowing around in the boat, picking up the largest ones to drop into his keel to take back as his record catch. The ranger sat in the boat with his mouth hanging open, unable to believe what he had just seen. "I can't believe you did that," he said, "you're not allowed to dynamite fish. That's against federal law. I'm a federal law enforcement officer; anybody who's caught dynamiting fish is going to end up getting put in jail. I'm really sorry that you did that in front of me, but I'm going to have no choice but to place you under arrest." The old man looked at the ranger very gloomily, then suddenly a light came to his eyes. As his smile curled up again he reached down inside the keel, picked up a second stick of dynamite, lit it, and handed it to the ranger. Then he said, "Here, ranger, you want to talk or you want to fish?"

An Annotated Bibliography

(ON LEADERSHIP AND
OTHER VERY READABLE BOOKS)

Indexed to Chapters and
Leadership Technique Sections

ALLEN, JAMES. *The Gift of Inner Peace.*   Kansas City: Hallmark Editions, 1971. /Chapter 4/
  This is a small jewel of a book that provides basic ideas for developing inner harmony and coping with tensions and stress. These are skills that are very important to leaders who work daily in "pressure cooker" situations.

ALLISON, GRAHAM T. *The Essence of Decision.*   Boston: Little, Brown, 1971. /Leadership Technique #9/
  A classic book on decision making. Takes a historically significant event (the Cuban missile crisis) and illuminates several different perspectives for viewing how decisions are actually made and implemented in a bureaucracy.

ARGYRIS, CHRIS. *Personality and Organization: The Conflict Between the System and the Individual.* New York: Harper, 1957. /Chapter 2/
  This was the book that originally established Argyris's illustrious writing career. It set the theme for much of his work: the dysfunctional relationship between a mature human being and a bureaucratic organization. It also displayed the Argyris style of thorough research presented in clear, interesting prose.

ARGYRIS, CHRIS. *Interpersonal Competence and Organizational Effectiveness.*   London: Tavistock Publications, 1962. Homewood, Ill.: Dorsey Press, 1962. /Leadership Technique #3/
  In this book Argyris concentrates on the process of organizational diagnosis and the process and nature of laboratory education that was especially popular in the fifties and sixties. An important book for group-oriented leaders and OD consultants to be familiar with.

ARGYRIS, CHRIS. *Integrating the Individual and the Organization.*   New York: John Wiley and Sons, 1964. /Chapters 2 & 3, Leadership Technique #3/
  In this wide-ranging book, Argyris explores the process of integrating individuals into the organization. The book contains both organizational theory and process information on areas such as hiring, evaluating, and terminating employees.

ARGYRIS, CHRIS. "Interpersonal Barriers to Decision Making," *Harvard Business Review* (Mar–Apr 1966), pp. 84–97. /Leadership Technique #9/
  In this article, Argyris shows the critical connection between the group climate and interpersonal relations and the group's ability to make effective, high-quality decisions. Every leader who feels his or her group is booked in quality decision making should read and consider this article.

ARGYRIS, CHRIS. *Intervention Theory and Method: A Behavioral Science View.*   Reading, Mass.: Addison-Wesley, 1970. /Leadership Technique #3/

244

An important book for any leader or consultant who is going to use the organizational development techniques outlined in Leadership Technique Section #3, "Organizational Development." Shows both the steps to be taken and the cautions and concerns that should accompany these processes.

ARGYRIS, CHRIS. *Management and Organizational Development: The Path from XA to YB.* New York: McGraw-Hill, 1971. /Chapter 5/

This is the book that took the ideas of Doug McGregor and expanded and developed them for leaders of the 1970s. The book should be of interest not only to practicing leaders, but also to organizational development professionals.

ARGYRIS, CHRIS and DONALD A. SCHÖN. *Theory in Practice: Increasing Professional Effectiveness.* San Francisco: Jossey-Bass Publishers, 1974. /Chapters 4 and 5/

This book, written with coauthor Don Schön, took McGregor's premise from the 1960s into a new and interesting context. It showed the shocking gap between what we say and what we do, and created the need for the books that would follow.

ARGYRIS, CHRIS. *Increasing Leadership Effectiveness.* New York: John Wiley and Sons, 1976. /Chapter 5 and Leadership Technique #12/

Builds on the theory of the 1974 book and examines ways that individual leaders can begin to close the gap between the beliefs that they espouse to their followers and their actual leadership practices.

ARGYRIS, CHRIS and DONALD A SCHÖN. *Organizational Learning: A Theory of Action Perspective.* Reading, Mass.: Addison-Wesley, 1978. /Chapters 2 and 5/

This fascinating work explores what must go on within organizations if they are to close the gap between their pronouncements and their practices. An exciting concept that takes the McGregor theory from 1960 to Argyris's 1971 book, the expanded conceptualization of the problem in 1974, to the individual solution in 1976, and the organizational application in 1978.

ASIMOV, ISAAC. *A Choice of Catastrophes.* New York: Simon and Schuster, 1979. /Chapter 6/

A sweeping menu of the options available for ending this great experiment we call Earth. Most sobering are the final set of catastrophes directly of our own making and still under our control.

BACH, RICHARD. *Jonathan Livingston Seagull.* New York: MacMillan, 1970. /Chapter 4/

The book that inspired a generation to expand their quest for actualization. A story warm, profound, and humorous. A best seller as *nonfiction*.

BACH, RICHARD. *Illusions.* New York: Dell, 1979. /Chapter 4/

If anything, an even better sequel to *Jonathan Livingston Seagull.* The same general theme of the quest for actualization, but this time with people rather than seagulls. Profound insights and some stimulating thoughts on what is illusion and what is reality.

BALDRIDGE, V.J. et al. *Policy Making and Effective Leadership.* San Francisco: Jossey-Bass, 1978. /General/

A discussion of leadership in the academic systems of higher education; college and university administrations. Reviews institutional bureaucracy, autonomy, and faculty morale.

BASS, BERNARD M. *Leadership, Psychology and Organizational Behavior.* Westport, Conn.: Greenwood Press, 1973. New York: Harper & Row, 1960. /General/

A very thorough social psychology text, primarily theoretical in nature. An expansive but dated bibliography of 1,115 sources.

BEAL, G.M.; J.M. BOHLEN; J.N. RAUDABAUGH. *Leadership and Dynamic Group Action.* Iowa: Iowa State University Press, 1962. /General/

Explores individual behavior within a democratic group, techniques for the leader to achieve group goals more effectively. Skills in human relations are analyzed. Good book with illustrative pictures to complement reading. An in-depth look at aspects of the group with minor attention given to style or approach.

BECKHARD, RICHARD. *Organization Development: Strategies and Models.* Reading, Mass.: Addison-Wesley, 1969. /Leadership Technique #3/

A most comprehensive guide to the practice of organization development from one of the premier practitioners. This book should be read carefully by any leader interested in developing a self-renewing organization.

BENNIS, WARREN G. *Changing Organizations.* New York: McGraw-Hill, 1966. /Leadership Techniques #4 and #13/

A scholarly analysis of organizational change strategies and techniques. To be read by the consultant or leader about to implement organizational changes and wishing to avoid many of the pitfalls that await the uninformed.

BENNIS, WARREN G. *The Leaning Ivory Tower.* San Francisco: Jossey-Bass, 1973. /Leadership Technique #13/

Vintage Bennis, with some very funny stories and some very sobering reflections on how even the experts have a lot to learn. Helps the rest of us put where we are as change agents into perspective.

BENNIS, WARREN G. *Organizational Development: Its Nature, Origins and Prospects.*   Reading, Mass.: Addison-Wesley, 1969. /Leadership Techniques #3 and #13/

Explores what organizational development is, where the needs for it exist, how it is applied, and some cautions and concerns associated with its use.

BENNIS, WARREN G. *The Unconscious Conspiracy: Why Leaders Can't Lead.*   New York: AMACOM, 1976. /General/

This collection of essays outline Bennis's analysis of the challenges faced by the leaders of modern organizations. It parallels and supports many of the general themes of this book, including the problems faced by leaders in bureaucracies and why there is such a shortage of good leaders. It is excellent.

BLAKE, ROBERT and JANE S. MOUTON. *The Managerial Grid.*   Houston: Gulf Publishing Company, 1964. /Chapter 5/

This book presents the theory of the managerial grid that has been widely quoted and is now used as a basis for training programs and organizational development efforts.

BOGARDUS, EMORY S. *Leaders and Leadership.*   New York: Appleton-Century-Crofts, 1934. /General/

Significant primarily for its historical role in leadership thought. It takes a sociological perspective and focuses primarily on the trait approach. Ends with lists of famous leaders; forerunner to the more recent *The 100.*

BOLLES, RICHARD NELSON.*What Color is Your Parachute?*   Revised edition. Berkeley: Ten Speed Press, 1972. /Leadership Technique #11/

Everything you always wanted to know about career planning and development, job hunting, resumé writing, and vocational success.

BOLT, ROBERT. *A Man For All Seasons.*   London: S. French, 1960. /Chapter 4/

A premier play and movie, filled with significant insights on leadership, loyalty, and integrity.

BOULDING, KENNETH. "General Systems Theory: The Skeleton of Science." *Management Science* (April 1956), pp. 197–208. /Chapter 2/

The work that launched systems theory and thinking, which is a basic thrust of much modern social science.

BRADFORD, REED H. *A Teacher's Quest.*   Provo, Utah: Brigham Young University Press, 1971. /Chapter 3, Chapter 4/

A small jewel of a book filled with inspired wisdom on motivation and goals, principles of effective teaching, and a basis for lasting human relationships. Some key leadership insights sprinkled throughout.

BROWNE, C.G. and T.S. COHN. *The Study of Leadership.*   Danville, Ill.: Interstate, 1958. /General/

A book of readings and research presenting the thinkings of psychologists and sociologists on leadership, what it is, and how it works.

BURNS, JAMES MacGREGOR. *Leadership.*   New York: Harper and Row, 1973. /General/

The focus is primarily on political leadership. The book is comprehensive, theoretical, and in places, anecdotal. Insights not easily generalizable to other fields.

COHEN, MICHAEL D. and JAMES G. MARCH. *Leadership and Ambiguity.*   New York: McGraw-Hill, 1974. /General/

An interesting study of how things actually get accomplished by leaders in bureaucracies. Some of the techniques analyzed here are quite Machiavellian, but probably reflect how leaders function and survive given human nature.

DOWNTON, JAMES V., Jr. *Rebel Leadership.*   New York: Free Press, 1973. /General/

Focuses on "the leadership of those who initiate attacks against the political system." Charisma is explored in detail. The book has an extensive annotated bibliography. Insights not easily generalizable.

DRUCKER, PETER F. *Managing for Results.*   New York: Harper and Row, 1964. /Chapters 1 and 4 and Leadership Technique #1/

If George Ordiorne is the "father of MBO," then Peter Drucker is the grandfather. This excellent book began the movement of focusing leadership and controls on results, not personalities or busywork.

DRUCKER, PETER F. *The Effective Executive.*   New York: Harper and Row, 1967. /Chapter 4 and Leadership Technique #9/

A fine book for exploring personal keys to effectiveness. Do not be put off by the title; it applies to many more than just executives. Must reading for every manager and leader.

246

DRUMMOND, HENRY. *The Greatest Thing in the World.*   New York: Grosset and Dunlap, Inc., 1959. /Chapter 4/
A powerful look on one of the most important factors in human relationships.

DYER, WILLIAM G. *The Sensitive Manipulator.*   Provo, Utah: Brigham Young University Press, 1972. /Leadership Techniques #3, #4, #13, and #14/
This book catches your attention with its title, then delivers practical ideas in its pages. Bill Dyer is one of the clearest, applied social science writers around and should be read by leaders wishing to succeed.

DYER, WILLIAM G. *Team Building: Issues and Alternatives.*   Reading, Mass.: Addison-Wesley, 1977. /Leadership Technique #3/
This is the complete book on team-building approaches and techniques. It should be read by anyone concerned with group unity and productivity.

FRENCH, JOHN R.P., Jr. and BERTRAM RAVEN. "The Basis of Social Power." *Studies in Social Power.*   Dorwin Cartwright, ed. Ann Arbor, Michigan: Institute of Social Research, 1959, pp. 150–168. /Chapter 4/
The pioneer article on sources of interpersonal power. Still widely quoted two decades later.

FRENCH, WENDELL L. and CECIL H. BELL, Jr. *Organization Development.*   2nd ed., Englewood Cliffs, N.J.: Prentice-Hall, 1978. /Leadership Techniques #3, #13/
A complete work on the techniques of organizational development. Short, clearly written, and useful. A guide for practitioners.

FIEDLER, FRED E. *A Theory of Leadership Effectiveness.*   New York: McGraw-Hill, 1967. /General/
Based on years of research on the subject of leadership. Filled with charts, diagrams, and statistics, the book has great appeal to scholars and graduate students.

GALL, JOHN. *Systemantics: How Systems Work and Especially How They Fail.*   New York: Quadrangle/New York Times Book Co., 1975. /Chapter 2/
The book is humorous, but the quality varies from the superficially obvious to the profound. It is the "Murphy's Laws" of bureaucracy.

GIBB, C.A. *Leadership: Selected Readings.*   Baltimore, Maryland: Penguin Books, 1970. /General/
Selected readings on leadership personality, interaction theory, and emergence of leaders.

GLASSER, WILLIAM. *Reality Therapy.*   New York: Harper and Row, 1965. /Chapters 3 and 4, Leadership Technique #14/
The theory in this book, though brief, is thought-provoking and useful for leaders, counselors, teachers, and parents. A radical and needed departure from classical psychoanalytic theory.

GOBLE, FRANK. *Excellence in Leadership.*   Ottawa, Ill.: Caroline House, 1978. /General/
This book is designed for the leader who is concerned with organizational excellence and the techniques that inspire followers to accomplish goals.

GORDON, T. *Group Centered Leadership—A Way of Releasing The Creative Power of Groups.*   Boston: Houghton Mifflin, 1955. /General/
Provides definition and analysis of leadership group settings. Provides the result of research into various forms of leadership as they affect the group's effectiveness.

GOULDNER, ALVIN W., ed. *Studies in Leadership.*   New York: Harper, 1950. /General/
A scholarly treatise on leadership, important in its time but now very dated.

GORDON, WILLIAM J. *Synectics.*   New York: Harper, 1961. /Leadership Technique #8/
The introduction of some exciting new approaches to problem recognition and problem solving.

GREENLEAF, ROBERT K. *Servant Leadership.*   New York: Paulist Press, 1977. /General/
An interesting, down-to-earth leadership book with many applied concepts. Looks at business, education, and the church.

HARDIN, GARRETT. *Exploring New Ethics for Survival: The Voyage of the Spaceship Beagle.*   New York: Viking Press, 1972. /Chapter 6/
A book with an ecological bent, it has some profound insights on the view of life on this planet and constituting a threatened and inescapably closed system.

HARRIS, THOMAS ANTHONY. *I'm O.K., You're O.K.*   New York: Harper and Row, 1969. /Chapters 2 and 4, Leadership Technique #4/
The book that launched transactional analysis. Some ideas helpful to relationships, but the pop psychology can be misapplied.

HELLER, JOSEPH. *Catch-22.*   New York: Simon and Schuster, Inc., 1961. /General/
A fictional view of bureaucracy in its most hilarious and dangerous forms.

HERZBERG, FREDRICK, et al. *Motivation to Work,*   2nd ed. New York: John Wiley & Sons, Inc., 1959. /Chapter 3, Leadership Technique #2/
Early theoretical concepts of motivation by pioneer Herzberg. A foundation for the research

and theory that followed in subsequent Herzberg articles and books on his two-factor theory.

HERZBERG, FREDRICK. *Work and the Nature of Man.* New York: T.Y. Crowell, Co., 1966. /Chapter 3, Leadership Technique #2/
Launched the two-factor theory as a major force in motivational thought.

HODGETTS, RICHARD M. *Management: Theory, Process and Practice,* 2nd ed. Philadelphia: W. B. Saunders, 1979. /General/
A recent, comprehensive text on basic principles of management leadership and systems theory. Appeals most to college undergraduates.

HOFSTADTER, DOUGLAS R. *Godel, Escher, Bach: An Eternal Golden Braid.* New York: Basic Books, 1979. /Chapter 2, Leadership Technique #4/
A sweeping book. At times very profound, at times very complex and difficult to follow, at times both at once. Some excellent insights into the challenge of communication, the human-technology interface and the possibilities of artificial intelligence. The dialogues are superb. I challenge you to stretch your brain and read it all . . . I did!

HOLLANDER, E. P. *Leaders, Groups and Influence.* New York: Oxford University Press, 1964. /General/
A social psychology book that takes a scholarly, research-oriented approach to leadership and group behavior.

HORNEY, KAREN. *Our Inner Conflicts.* New York: W. W. Norton and Company, Inc., 1945. /Chapter 4/
Presents a number of personality concepts that have influenced subsequent trait approaches to leadership.

IRISH, RICHARD K. *Go Hire Yourself an Employer.* Garden City, New York: Doubleday Anchor Books, 1973. /Leadership Technique #11/
A funny and comprehensive guide to mounting a job-hunting campaign. You must read the sections on interviewing and salary negotiation.

JONGEWARD, DOROTHY, DRU SCOTT, and contributors. *Affirmative Action Guide for Women.* Reading, Mass.: Addison-Wesley Publishers, 1973. /Chapter 3/
Despite a title that tends to put people off, this is a very good book that should be read by both sexes, about men and women in the world of work.

KANTER, ROSABETH MOSS and BARRY A. STEIN, eds. *Life in Organizations.* New York: Basic Books, 1979. /Chapters 2 and 4 and several Leadership Techniques/
This book is a collection of essays, articles, excerpts, and first-person chapters by Kanter and Stein. There is theory to tie this all together, but the effort is to provide practical advice for the organizational person.

KANTER, ROSABETH MOSS. *Men and Women of the Corporation.* New York: Basic Books, 1977. /Chapter 3/
This book is an important examination of the relationships of men and women in the world of work. It examines how power, communication, authority, accountability, and leadership are supposed to work and often how they fail.

KANTER, ROSABETH MOSS. "Power Failure in Management Circuits." *Harvard Business Review* (July/Aug 1979), pp. 65–75.
A fresh and refreshing expansion of sources and uses of interpersonal power in organizations. Kanter has emerged as a leader of scholarly thought on organizational life.

KATZ, DANIEL and ROBERT L. KAHN. *The Social Psychology of Organizations.* New York: John Wiley, 1966. /Chapter 2/
An excellent book for understanding systems theory as applied to organizations. Theoretical, appealing more to college students.

KEPNER, CHARLES H. and BENJAMIN B. TREGOE. *The Rational Manager.* New York: McGraw-Hill, 1965. /Leadership Technique #8/
A classic approach to managerial problem solving. Very comprehensive, if somewhat dry and straightforward.

KOLB, DAVID A., IRWIN M. RUBIN, and JAMES M. McINTYRE. *Organizational Psychology,* 2nd ed. Englewood Cliffs, N.J.: Prentice-Hall, Inc., 1974. /Chapters 3 and 4, Leadership Technique #12/
This source is mentioned specifically for Kolb's learning-styles theory, which is most important and has so many implications for leaders, teachers, and anyone involved with relationships.

KORDA, MICHAEL. *Power: How to Get It and How to Use It.* New York: Random House, 1975. /Chapter 4/
One of the most quoted works on power. Can be very Machiavellian in spots.

LAKEIN, ALAN. *How To Get Control of Your Time and Your Life.* New York: McKay, 1973. /Leadership Technique #10/

Nobody does it better with time management. A must-read book.

LASSEY, WILLIAM R. *Leadership and Social Change.* 2nd revised and enlarged edition. Iowa City: University Associates, 1976. /General/
A compilation of essays designed for courses in the sociology of leadership. A very impressive list of contributors. The content varies from research to applied concepts.

LAWRENCE, JEROME and ROBERT E. LEE. *Inherit the Wind.* New York: Bantam, 1969. /Chapter 4/
A moving portrayal of two leaders who were giants. Particularly significant is the final scene between Darrow and the reporter.

LEWIS, C. S. *The Weight of Glory and Other Addresses.* Grand Rapids, Mich.: W. B. Eerdmans Publishing Co., 1965. /General/
A great book for exploring human potential and destiny and considering the awesome responsibility of human relationships.

LIKERT, RENSIS. *The Human Organization.* New York: McGraw-Hill, 1967. /Chapters 2, 4, and 5/
A most important book by a man whose research and thought translates into ideas that are useful and important. The originator of several key management concepts.

LINDGREN, H.C. *Effective Leadership in Human Relations.* New York: Hermitage House, 1954. /General/
Self-examination and understanding translated into practice for the leader in a position of power and authority. Examines patterns of leadership, relates leadership to effective communication, and discusses delegation and power.

LIPPITT, GORDON L. *Organization Renewal.* New York: Appleton-Century-Crofts, 1969. /Chapter 2, Leadership Technique #3/
Introduces and expands the concept of what self-renewing organizations are and presents approaches to creating them.

LORING, ROSALIND and THEODORA WELLS. *Breakthrough: Women Into Management.* New York: Van Nostrand Reinhold Co., 1972. /Chapter 3/
An award-winning book that must be read by every woman and should be read by every man in the world of work. Particularly powerful is the chapter on myths as barriers, entitled, "Won't Women . . ."

LUTHANS, FRED. *Organizational Behavior,* 3rd ed. New York: McGraw-Hill, 1981. /General/
A very good textbook that covers all the important principles in this developing social science field. Contains several ideas very useful to leaders.

MACCOBY, MICHAEL. *The Gamesman.* New York: Simon and Schuster, 1976. /General/
Another important book that clearly translates study and thought into useful insights for corporate leaders and managers.

MACKENZIE, R. ALEX. *The Time Trap.* New York: AMACOM, 1972. /Leadership Technique #10/
Another important book on time wasters and how to make more effective use of your time.

MANDINO, OG. *The Greatest Miracle in the World.* New York: Bantam Books, 1977. /General/
A marvelous little book that explores the concepts of human potential, service, and life's meanings.

MARGULIES, NEWTON and ANTHONY P. RAIA. *Conceptual Foundations of Organizational Development.* New York: McGraw-Hill Book Co., 1978. /Leadership Technique #3/
Another comprehensive book, with good theory chapters and a number of usable case studies. This book is more academically oriented.

MASLOW, ABRAHAM HAROLD. *Motivation and Personality.* New York: Harper Brothers, 1954. /Chapter 3/
A classic book that presented Maslow's most quoted theory, the hierarchy of needs. Should be read to find out what Maslow was saying, as opposed to what others say Maslow was saying.

McCLELLAND, DAVID. *The Achieving Society.* New York: D. Van Nostrand Company, 1961. /Chapter 3/
This book presents McClelland's research and theory regarding the human need for achievement. Much of the book would be of more interest to scholars than to practitioners. However, there are sections that could be read and applied to increase the motivation of employees, team members, and children.

McCLELLAND, DAVID. *Power: The Inner Experience.* New York: Halstead Press, 1975. /Chapters 3 and 4/
The focus of this book is power, ranging from the interpersonal aspects to its manifestation in social forces such as war. Interesting correlation with McClelland's theory of the human need for achievement.

McGREGOR, DOUGLAS. *The Human Side of Enterprise.* New York: McGraw-Hill, 1960. /General/

In my opinion, the best management book written in the past quarter century. Many profound ideas that go beyond "Theory X to Theory Y." A must-read book.

MOLLOY, JOHN T. *Dress for Success.*   New York: Warner Books, 1976. /Chapter 4/
A book to look at for the leaders concerned with form rather than substance. Appearance should work for you, but will not replace performance.

MORRISEY, GEORGE L. *Management By Objectives and Results.*   Reading, Mass.: Addison-Wesley Publishing Company, 1970. /Chapter 1, Leadership Technique #1/
A book that followed the pioneer MBO books of the 1960s and was able to offer new insights and more developed concepts.

MYERS, M. SCOTT. "One More Time—How Do You Motivate Employees?" *Harvard Business Review*   (Jan/Feb, 1968), pp. 53–62. /Chapter 3, Leadership Technique #2/
An article with some key ideas on motivation. This article has been a mainstay of the job enrichment thrust.

ODIORNE, GEORGE S. *Management By Objectives.*   New York: Pitman Publishers, 1965. /Chapter 1, Leadership Technique #1/
The book that popularized the management-by-objectives process. Should be read by anyone planning to use MBO.

OLSEN, MARVIN ELLIOTT. *The Process of Social Organization.*   New York: Holt, Reinhart & Winston, 1968. /Chapter 2/
A clearly written, expansive treatment of the very basic ideas of organizations and organizational life. A solid foundation for anyone interested in organizational behavior.

OSBORN, ALEXANDER F. *Applied Imagination.*   New York: Scribners, 1953. /Leadership Technique #8/
You can see the date, so you may question its inclusion here, but it is one of the classics from the man who introduced brainstorming to problem solving.

PETER, LAURENCE J. *The Peter Prescription.*   New York: William Morrow, 1972. /General/
The sequel, *PP-II.* What can be done to resolve a number of the problems introduced in the 1969 book (below). Read them in chronological order.

PETER, LAURENCE J. and RAYMOND HULL. *The Peter Principle.*   New York: W. Morrow, 1969. /General/
Key insights on how and why things go wrong as people move up the organization.

PETRILLO, L. and B. BASS. *Leadership and Interpersonal Behavior.* New York: Holt, Rinehart and Winston, 1961. /General/
A collection of essays on the basic assumptions dealing with leadership, democracy, organization, authority, the follower, and major experimental trends. Has a section dealing with patterns of communications that influence power, and explains organizational leadership with reference to the formal and informal approach.

PRINCE, GEORGE M. *The Practice of Creativity.*   New York: Harper and Row, 1970. /Leadership Technique #8/
Another of the interesting books in the area of creative problem solving and decision making.

REDDIN, WILLIAM J. *Effective Management by Objectives: The 3-D Method of MBO.*   New York: McGraw-Hill, 1971. /Chapter 5, Leadership Technique #1/
Combines principles from the management-by-objectives movement with Reddin's theory of eight leadership styles.

SAGAN, CARL. *The Dragons of Eden.*   New York: Random, 1977. /General/
Of particular interest are the chapters on the brain, the link of our mental powers with the technology of computers, and the challenge to expand human potential.

SARASON, SEYMOUR. *The Creation of Settings and the Future Societies.*   San Francisco: Jossey-Bass, 1972. /Chapters 1, 3, and 4/
Despite the awful title, this is a must-read book for anyone who is going to start an organization or enterprise. It contains some of the finest chapters ever written containing insights into leaders and their core groups.

SAYLES, LEONARD R. *Leadership: What Effective Managers Really Do . . . and How They Do It.* New York: McGraw-Hill, 1979. /General/
The subtitle tells the tale. This is not a book on leadership; it is a practical guide about and for managers.

SCOTT, WILLIAM C. and DAVID K. HART. *Organizational America.*   Boston: Houghton Mifflin Company, 1979. /Chapters 2 and 6/
A very interesting and scholarly book that weaves organizational theories and flaws into the fabric of our society. A good expansion of some of the ideas presented in this book's final chapter.

SIMON, HERBERT A. *Administrative Behavior,*   2nd ed. New York: Macmillan, 1957. /General/

This book won Simon the Nobel Prize for economics in 1978. The book talks about decision making in bureaucratic organizations and provides valuable insights as a forerunner to later decision books such as Allison's.

STEELE, FRITZ. *Consulting For Organizational Change.* Amherst: University of Mass. Press, 1975. /Leadership Techniques #3 and #13/
One of the few good books available on the whys and hows of consulting. This book must be read by any person who aspires to be a consultant or any leader who plans on using a consultant.

STEINMETZ, LAWRENCE L. *Human Relations: People and Work.* New York: Harper and Row, 1979. /Chapter 4/
Covers the basic principles of human relations in a work environment. Most useful to supervisors, but written in a textbook fashion; of much interest to college students.

STEINMETZ, LAWRENCE L. *Managing the Marginal and Unsatisfactory Employee.* Reading, Mass.: Addison-Wesley, 1969. /Chapter 3/
This book takes a needed look at an important concern for leaders and practicing managers that has not been treated nearly enough in the literature.

STOGDILL, RALPH M. *Handbook of Leadership: A Survey of Theory and Research.* New York: Free Press, 1974. /General/
The content of this book is suggested by the subtitle "A survey of theory and research" on leadership. More appealing to the scholar than to the practitioner.

TANNENBAUM, ROBERT and WARREN H. SCHMIDT. "How to Choose a Leadership Pattern." *Harvard Business Review* (Mar/Apr 1958), pp. 95–101. /Chapter 5/
An *HBR* classic that expanded the view of leadership styles and presented them in a way easy to understand and helpful to leaders in assessing the reasons for their successes and failures.

TANNENBAUM, ROBERT, IRVING R. WESCHLER, and FRED MASSARIK. *Leadership and Organization.* New York: McGraw-Hill, 1961. /General/
A dated look at the leadership theory of the 1950s. The book is more theoretical than applied. It has a nice annotated bibliography.

TEAD, ORDWAY. *The Art of Leadership.* New York: Whittlesey House, 1935. /General/
Primarily of value as a historical view of the trait approach to leadership popular in this period. The ideas on women as leaders and how to treat subordinates would be unacceptable in today's social context.

TOFFLER, ALVIN. *Future Shock.* New York: Random House, 1970. /Chapter 6/
An important book in exploring the impact of technology and rapid change on people as individuals and the fabric of society.

TOFFLER, ALVIN. *The Third Wave.* New York: Bantam, 1981. /Chapter 6/
A look at the future, exploring the interesting possibilities of "Where do we go from here?" While Toffler's visions may not always be right, they are always thought-provoking.

TOWNSEND, ROBERT C. *Up the Organization.* New York: Knopf, 1970. /General/
A book I have recommended over the last decade to more people in more places, than any other. Profound, funny, readable! Turns many of your organizational stereotypes out to pasture . . . and good riddance.

VROOM, VICTOR H. and PHILIP W. YETTON. *Leadership and Decision Making.* Pittsburgh: University of Pittsburgh Press, 1976. /Leadership Technique #9/
Based on some solid research and thinking about the key leadership process of decision making in groups.

WEATHERSBY, GEORGE B. "Postsecondary Education." *Society* (Jan/Feb 1976), pp. 60, 62, 63. /Chapter 4/
If you still believe that higher education has passed you by, read this and consider the alternatives as they apply to you.

WEICK, KARL E. *The Social Psychology of Organizing,* 2nd ed. Reading, Mass.: Addison-Wesley, 1979. /Chapter 2/
Another important book for shaking the cobwebs out of your brain. A creative approach to how organizations should work and often don't.

YUKL, GARY A. *Leadership in Organizations.* Englewood Cliffs, N.J.: Prentice-Hall, 1981. /General/
A good, scholarly book on managerial leadership. Combines theory and practice nicely. Designed for use as a textbook. Contains a comprehensive and up-to-date bibliography.

Index

253